DATE DUE

GAYLORD   PRINTED IN U.S.A.

Black Portraiture in

AMERICAN FICTION

Black Portraiture

I N

AMERICAN
FICTION

Stock Characters, Archetypes,
and Individuals

CATHERINE JUANITA STARKE

Basic Books, Inc., Publishers

NEW YORK   LONDON

For Bill
as always

To all black men and women in America who—
throughout the centuries, despite pejorative
cultural attitudes—maintained strong senses of
personal identity and integrity and who lived out
their lives with firm self-knowledge, self respect
and dignity, this book is gratefully dedicated.

Contents

Black Portraiture in
AMERICAN FICTION

CHAPTER

1

CONTEXTS

An investigation into the nature of black portraiture in American fiction must take into consideration the special cultural factors influencing the lives of black people, such as the attitude of the white majority to the black minority, resulting in the assignment of special roles to and affecting personality formation of blacks and whites. These specific factors constitute the formation of one of America's great cultural conflicts: black versus white.

Cultural Attitudes: Northern and Southern

As early as 1700, the black-white conflict, probably the most divisive of all, was defined, along with now familiar rationale and the prediction of social polarization, by Samuel Sewall in the polemical pamphlet, "The Selling of Joseph."

> Few [whites] can endure to hear of a Negro's being made free; and indeed they [blacks] can seldom use their freedom well; yet their continual aspiring after their forbidden Liberty, renders them Unwilling Servants. And there is such a disparity in their Conditions, Colour & Hair, that they can never embody with us, and grow up into Orderly Families to the Peopling of the Land: but still

remain in our Body Politick as a kind of extravasat Blood.[1]

Nearly a century and a half later, James Fenimore Cooper described a Pinkster, or Whitsuntide celebration, among blacks in the novel *Satanstoe* (1845), in which he reemphasized differences separating blacks from whites, Northern style.

> By this time nine-tenths of the blacks of the city . . . were collected in thousands in those fields, beating banjos, singing African songs, drinking, and worst of all, laughing in a way that seemed to set their very hearts rattling within their ribs. Everything wore the aspect of good-humor, though it was good-humor in its broadest and coarsest forms. Every sort of common game was in requisition, while drinking was far from neglected. Still not a man was drunk. A drunken negro, indeed is by no means a common thing. The features that distinguish a Pinkster frolic from the usual scenes at fairs, and other merry-makings, however, were of African origin. It is true, there were not now . . . many blacks among us of African birth; but the traditions and usages of their original country were so far preserved as to produce a marked difference between this festival and one of European origin.[2]

Thirty-five years later, after the Civil War, George Washington Cable, in *The Grandissimes* (1880), wrote lines for a white Creole reaffirming the general attitude, Southern style.

> H— my young friend, when we say, "we people," we *always* mean we white people. The non-mention of color always implies pure white; and whatever is not pure white is to all intents and purposes pure black. When I say the "whole community," I mean the whole white portion; when I speak of the "undivided public sentiment," I mean the sentiment of the white population. What else could I mean? Could you suppose, sir, the expression which you may have heard me use—"my down-trodden country" includes blacks and mulattoes? . . . Not that

there is a prejudice against the negro. By no means. Wherever he can be of any service in a strictly menial capacity we kindly and generously tolerate his presence.[3]

Nearly a century later, the virulence of Cable's Creole and the condescending superiority of Cooper can still be found covertly, even though unexpressed overtly, in certain segments of the society. Nearly two hundred years after Sewall argued against slavery, his rationale, based on the disparity between blacks and whites, still has a familiar ring. Blacks remain, for the most part, an "extravasat blood" in the body politic. Furthermore, blacks and whites are still in conflict, with blacks struggling to release themselves from the restraints of caste and with whites struggling to prevent removal of all such constrictions. The struggle still prevents social unity.

Role of Blacks in Society

Unlike other groups, some of whom came to America long after blacks and whose members may have moved from immigrant status to full membership in society within a few generations despite persistent religious and ethnic prejudices, blacks with few exceptions have remained in social "limbo," neither completely inside nor completely outside the society. Sewall, Cooper, and Cable pinpoint two of the three major reasons for their ambiguous social position—physical characteristics of skin color and hair, presumed inferiority, and inherited rituals of race relations.

Possibly the most persistent deterrent to social integration and unity has been skin color symbolism which separates human beings into polar categories representing, at one end, the common acceptance of black as a symbol of evil and, at the other, white as a symbol of virtue. More precisely, black people have been categorized in terms of what white people call the "darker vision": that which is impure, the farthest from excellence, that which causes malaise and ought to be avoided, that which is mysterious and somehow oddly attractive and repellent simultaneously. In an obverse way, the value system now functions disadvantageously for whites who are often categorized by blacks as insincere, hypocritical, wicked, the essence of evil. Neither categorization considers the person.

The second deterrent to unity has been the popularly held belief that blacks are members of an inferior race and that whites are members of a superior one. Symbolic values of black and white, function here also. In part, this belief was a consequence of the former enslavement of blacks. Slaveowners, using observable skin color differences along with Old Testament pronouncements about the children of Ham as symbolic referents, insisted on the concept of black inferiority to justify, in defiance of Christian ethic, the economically profitable use of slave labor and the emotional gratification of presumed superiority. In part also, the belief was supported by observable technological advancements among whites, which ironically today are viewed with alarm because of their contribution to ecological imbalance throughout the world. Finally, there was the idealistic appeal to ancient Greek democracy, with blacks subservient and giving leisure to whites, and the latter responsible for the welfare of the former.

These two deterrents, the symbolic color-value system and the myth of white superiority, sanctioned the establishment, growth, and perpetuation of the third deterrent, the ritual of non-reciprocal social interaction, instituted during slavery and maintained tenaciously since emancipation. The ritual required blacks and whites to behave toward each other in certain prescribed ways. Forms of address give some indication of the nature of the ritual. It was customary for blacks to address white slaveowners as *master* (massa), *mistress* (mistis), *miss* (missy), *boss* or *buckra* either with or without given name. Owners addressed their slaves as *aunt, uncle, mammy,* sometimes *daddy, boy.* Even when kinship existed between participants in the ritual, none was ever mentioned or implied by whites using these terms of address. Their use does reflect, however, the familistic-feudal pattern of life in the Old South. *Nigger* as a term of address appears to have been used by both groups of participants only as a designator of skin color and without intention of offense;

but symbolic values of blackness and whiteness being what they were, the term soon acquired derogatory connotations. When used by whites, it was particularly offensive; yet blacks used it among themselves without comparable emotional sensitivity. Some other blacks preferred the more dignified name, *Negro*. Still some others found it offensive and preferred the more ambiguous *colored*. Both of these have become "snarl" words and are vigorously rejected by young, contemporary blacks who have discovered beauty and value in blackness and insist on being so designated. Even *nigger*, once the ultimate obscenity, seems to have lost most of its offensiveness for all blacks, except when it is prefaced by white, as in "white nigger," the popular name for black bourgeoisie.

Another aspect of the complex ritual, the required behavior of the slave when spoken to by whites, helps also to explain the nature of the third deterrent. In these situations the slave was expected to stand attentively, respond politely, bow servilely to the extent, at times, of extreme evasion and deceit. The purpose of the ritual was to channel the attention and behavior of the participants, black and white, in line with the doctrine of white supremacy, thereby freeing them as individuals from the responsibility of thinking about its validity or of questioning existing interpersonal relations. After emancipation, legal sanction continued in support of the rituals with the so-called "separate but equal" enactments. As a result, ghosts of all three deterrents, symbols, myth and ritual, persist well into the twentieth century.

The peculiar social position of American blacks may be described from still another viewpoint. Unlike some groups that have maintained proud ties to an ancestral homeland and ethos, most blacks until recently have not felt similar identification with Africa or any of the patterns of African culture. Yet in the 1920's, when the "melting pot" concept was still prominent in American life, Schomburg recognized as vital for black survival the need to reconstruct a group tradition in which black identity and pride could function as "compensation for persecution" and as an "antidote for prejudice."[4] Later, when white immigrant groups were beginning to see values in "old country" ties and when the concept of a "mosaic" social pattern was supplanting the "melting pot," Frazier explained why blacks were different from the white groups, spelling out how blacks had been deliberately stripped of their African customs and systematically forced to adopt the folkways of an alien culture even to the extent of worshipping a deity not reflecting their own image.[5] A few years later, in contrast to Frazier, Herskovits maintained that an African heritage still existed in black life and went on to demonstrate how useful it could be not only as a psychological antidote for prejudice but as an explanation and even justification of the differences setting blacks apart from others.[6] It was not, however, until the rise of African countries from colonial rule to independence that American blacks in large numbers began wanting to identify with Africans and African cultures. Up to that time, their only link with Africa, for reasons explained by Frazier, was skin color, about which, under the existing symbolic value structure, they were ambivalent, if they did not actually hate their own black skins. Moreover, because they knew nothing of the richness of their heritage, they were more than a little ashamed of it, in their ignorance regarding it as a link with savage primitivism. As a consequence, it seemed better to have no past than to be connected with primitive tribalism.[7]

Another important question arises as to whether or not Africa can become a physical as well as a psychological home or "promised" land for masses of American blacks. Possibly but not imminently has to be the answer; for similarity of skin color has not proved adequate to insure acceptance by Africans. Richard Wright, when he visited the country that is now Ghana in 1953, was dismayed by Africans' mistrust of him, bewildered by his inability to break through the wall of differentness separating him from them, and appalled by his ignorance of tribal beliefs and customs. A few minutes after his ship had been docked, he was questioned pointedly about what part of Africa his ancestors had come from, and his interrogator, upon receiving a negative answer, asked why Wright had never exerted himself to obtain this piece of highly important information. For reasons beyond Wright's control, he lacked the most rudimentary knowledge required for admittance into tribal society.[8] Peter Abrahams, a "coloured" South African expatriate, explains that tribal society is

> . . . exclusive and not, like Western society, inclusive.
> . . . Anybody not an insider is an enemy, actually or
> potentially; is someone to fear, someone to keep at bay.
> There is no choice, no volition about this. It is something ordained by the ancestral dead.[9]

Despite Wright's yearning to identify with Africa, despite his blackness and their blackness, he remained an outsider; he did not know his ancestors and consequently, according to tribal belief, his ancestors could not know him. Similarity of skin color was not enough to admit him to fraternity with the indigenes. He felt their rejection keenly, particularly when they called him *massa* or *baas,* terms of address reminiscent of old slave ritual. Obviously, they considered him a "black European," and they had had too many bad experiences with their own "whitewashed" black elite to react favorably toward anyone so indoctrinated by foreign contacts.

Richard Wright visited Africa during the time that Ghanaians were struggling for independence from Britain. Nine years later, after independence, Ed Smith, a Peace Corps volunteer, who had high hopes for personal fulfillment as he began teaching in Ghana, soon discovered, like Wright, that similarity of skin color is not enough to insure full acceptance by Africans. What disturbed him most, however, was what he called their "colonial mentality"—their tendency to denigrate blackness and to exalt whiteness.[10] After some months, he was thoroughly disillusioned, admitting frankly that he was not nor could he ever be African; after two years he eagerly anticipated his departure. Bill Sutherland, who has lived and worked in Africa since 1952, throws some light on Wright's and Smith's disillusionment when he observes that American blacks often expect more than can possibly be attained by their African experiences: solutions to personal identity and reference group problems. Africa ought not to be made the scapegoat for their failures.[11]

Malcolm X visited Africa while Smith was still there and reported frankly, after discussions with African leaders, that

only those Afro-Americans with skills or other definite contributions to make toward the development of Africa would
be welcomed as immigrants.[12] His experiences, however, were
different from those of Wright and Smith. Everywhere he
went, he was warmly received as a popular hero. At Ibadan
University, he was made an honorary member of the Muslim
Students' Society and given the Yoruba name, *Omowale,*
which means "the son who has come home."[13] One final
comment casting doubt on African acceptance of American
blacks en masse, with even greater candor than that of
Malcolm X, comes from Ousmane Sembene, Senegalese play-
wright and novelist:

> Black Americans have difficulty understanding Africa
> because they themselves are so busy searching for a cul-
> tural base. What they must come to realize is that they
> are *Americans* and we are *Africans,* and that our prob-
> lems are not necessarily the same.[14]

It seems, then, that the chances for African assimilation of
large numbers of American blacks, after centuries of separation, are about as likely as assimilation of any other ethnic
group by the land from which it originally came. What seems
needed is a strengthening of ethnic bonds through increased
knowledge of African traditions and customs and understanding of African struggles, since independence, for economic and political stability.

Adaptation of blacks to a submissive role and whites to a
dominant one has resulted in undesirable concomitants that
hinder development of healthy individuals in a unified society. Early research shows a pattern of self-hatred, hostility,
and aggression[15] among blacks, with documented evidence
that self-rejection began as early as age three,[16] that it persisted into adult life,[17] and that it adversely affected relationships not only with whites but also with other blacks.
The pattern among mulattoes was shown to be equally complex and paradoxical.[18] More recently Grier and Cobbs have
given much needed insight, from the vantage point of blackness, into what they call the "norm" for survival among
blacks:

. . . it is necessary for a black man in America to develop a profound distrust of his white fellow citizens and of the nation. He must be on guard to protect himself against physical hurt. He must cushion himself against cheating, slander, humiliation, and outright mistreatment by the official representatives of society. If he does not protect himself, he will live a life of such pain and shock as to find life itself unbearable. For his own survival . . . he must develop a *cultural paranoia* in which every white man is a potential enemy unless proved otherwise and every social system is set against him unless he personally finds out differently.[19]

The psychiatrists go on to show that never being able to take any aspect of their lives for granted has led to culturally induced depression, masochism, and antisocialism among blacks.[20] Especially disturbing is one final statistic from Hendin concerning the suicide rate among blacks: twice that among whites of comparable sex and age. He pinpoints frustration, self-hatred, depression, and murderous rage as contributive causes.[21]

Adaptation of whites to a dominant role has resulted in similar undesirable concomitants. Overvaluation of self and corollary undervaluation of others have led to what Kardiner and Ovesey have called "extreme manifestation of the ego-perversion of dominance," permitting the "subjection of another human being to a pure utilitarian use" for selfish, materialistic advantages. In order to justify the procedure, "the sense of guilt makes it imperative to degrade the object further."[22] The resulting behavioral pattern is avoidance and/or hatred of the demeaned object. Personal narratives of white Southerners reveal unwholesome effects of the myth in terms of its leading to dishonesty and hubris,[23] personality conflicts,[24] and distortions.[25] For a long time Northern whites were able to delude themselves with the belief that they were less prejudiced than those in the South, forgetting, if they ever knew, their own history of anti-black violence, such as the lynching and killing of blacks in 1863, in New York City, and in 1917, in East St. Louis, Illinois. Podhoretz reveals the existence and nature of white hatred for blacks in the

North, writing honestly of the rage that consumes him, at times, in relationships with blacks and of the "disgusting prurience" that wells in him when he sees an interracial couple. In response to the crucial question of whether or not he would like it if his daughter were to marry a black man, he searches his conscience and writes,

> No, I wouldn't like it at all. I would rail and rave and rant and tear my hair. And then I hope I would have the courage to curse myself for raving and ranting, and to give her my blessing.[26]

These personal narratives disclose some of the unwholesome effects of caste on whites. Their statements have been confirmed by social psychologists and psychoanalysts as a complex pattern of attitude formation and conditioning, including embarrassment, anxiety, moral uneasiness, and hostility, sometimes evoking projective techniques used defensively to evade guilt.[27]

Relations between whites and blacks suffer in still another way because of self-fulfilling prophecy: an individual's perception of the outcome of a given situation can influence the outcome; or, stated differently, anyone can find evidence to support a preconceived notion if he looks hard and long enough for confirmation. When whites and blacks meet, therefore, the response of each to the other is, more often than not, in line with concepts held by his particular group and by which he has been "programmed" to reject the other.[28]

Since World War II, attacks have been made on all of the deterrents, the most significant being an attack on the myth of white supremacy. UNESCO struck the first blow by separating the fact from the myth of race and affirming the following principles: that all men are members of the same species, *homo sapiens;* that cultural differences cannot be justified on grounds of inherited genetic differences; that in every culture can be found "a rich variety of personality and character types" possessing a wide range of intelligence and temperament; and that all normal people can learn "to share a common life, to understand the nature of mutual service and reciprocity, and to respect social obligations and contracts."[29]

Attacks on caste ritual by blacks and whites together have been evidenced in such enactments as fair employment practices, open housing, and other civil rights legislation, in such decisions as the 1954 Supreme Court pronouncement on school desegregation, and in such challenges to segregation laws and discriminatory practices as freedom marches and rides, "sit-ins," "wade-ins," "kneel-ins"—all designed to integrate blacks and whites. Foremost among these challenges were the ones led by NAACP, the Urban League, CORE, and SCLC, led by Martin Luther King, Jr., whose gentle but determined revolution lent inspiration to all of the others with its idealism of "I have a dream," and "We shall overcome," of being liberal, moderate, eager to turn the other cheek in Christian charity, and of the redemptive effects on whites of undeserved black suffering. Its long-range purpose was idealistic, nothing less than the reconstruction of American society through attacks on the consciences and appeals to the better natures of whites. This was a period of hope for social unification, hope doomed to remain unfulfilled because of steady and determined erosion by the majority of whites who had no intention of obeying either enactments or decisions and saw no personal advantage in being influenced by challenges of either blacks or other whites to alter their self-aggrandizing belief in white supremacy.

Understandably the most potent and far-reaching attacks on the deterrents have had to come from black people themselves, and these can be attributed to the spirit of rebellion that has periodically flared up among blacks ever since the first slave asserted his manhood, knowing well that, in all probability, he would die in the assertion of it. Since slavery, many blacks have striven to keep alive that same pride in black identity. These have been the ones who rejected, as invalid, the myth of black inferiority and white superiority and have worked determinedly to overthrow rituals prescribed to maintain it. Just after the turn of the century, Du Bois, while stating the American black's dilemma, unequivocally affirmed black identity:

One ever feels his two-ness—an American, a Negro; two souls, two thoughts, two unreconciled strivings; two warring ideals in one dark body, whose dogged strength alone keeps it from being torn asunder.

The history of the American Negro is the history of this strife,--this longing to attain self-conscious manhood, to merge his double self into a better and truer self. In this merging, he wishes neither of the older selves to be lost. He would not Africanize America, for America has much to teach the world and Africa. He would not bleach his Negro soul in a flood of white Americanism, for he knows that Negro blood has a message for the world. He simply wishes to make it possible for a man to be both a Negro and an American, without being cursed upon by his fellows, without having the doors of Opportunity closed roughly in his face.[30]

Early in the 1920's, the Marcus Garvey movement, officially the Negro Improvement Association, with its emphasis on racial purity, and since the 1930's, the Nation of Islam, popularly called the Black Muslims, with its emphasis on black supremacy provided symbolic reasons for self-pride. Such chauvinism was soothing balm for egos that had taken a beating for hundreds of years. Prior to his pilgrimage to Mecca in 1964, Malcolm X was vehemently anti-white, preaching a doctrine of black excellence and white depravity and exhorting blacks to cease begging whites for social integration. His message was so vibrantly black-assertive that even blacks who could not entirely agree with him were excited by it. Whatever the reaction, however, none could deny respect to him as a man; for none could ever doubt that he was his own man. While at Mecca, he underwent what was for him a soul-searching experience when he witnessed black and white Muslims worshipping, as he puts it, in the "spirit of unity and brotherhood," or "color-blindness." It was a unity that he had never before thought possible between blacks and non-blacks.[31] For the first time in his life, evidently, he participated as one among equals in a diverse group not polarized by symbolic color values. From reading his candid confessions of how he felt at the time, it seems clear that what mankind needs to recognize, in order to prevent a pendulum swing from one pole to another of the color value system, is that there are no superior and inferior human groups, but that there are superior and inferior individuals within all human groups which must learn, somehow, to live amicably together.

The celebration of blackness and black manhood has been articulated with poetic imagery by Eldridge Cleaver who, spurning the culturally assigned role of "Black Eunuch" and rising like the phoenix, proclaims the black's recovery of his birthright, as a man, in his love letter to all black women from all black men, speaking to them over the centuries

> . . . not in the obsequious whine of a cringing Slave, . . . neither do I greet you in the new voice, the unctuous supplications of the sleek Black Bourgeoise, nor the bullying bellow of the rude Free Slave—but in my own voice do I greet you, the voice of the Black Man. . . . I have returned from the dead.[32]

The contributions of these men to the formation of a group sense of identity have taken vigorous hold on the lives and fired the imaginations of black people throughout the country, even the unseen, silent ones who do not participate in more visible activities. This sense of group identity has been called, among other things, Negritude, a designation that encompasses, in addition to color, all of the experiences of black people, as participants and recipients, in society. This means shared joys, sorrows, insults, violence—resulting in a group mentality and unique concepts for ordering existence, despite observable differences among members. It means, further, the power to make decisions about their own existence. It means, symbolically, no longer standing at the back door, with hat in hand, patiently waiting for cultural handouts.

Some whites are unwilling to accept the changes in black attitudes and behaviors and tend to overreact in as paranoid a manner as some blacks tend to overreact to real or imagined wrongs done them. Some blacks also are critical of the new identity, belittling its outward manifestations, such as hair style and garments. Cause for concern, if not alarm, arises when one realizes that violence is endemic to American society. Desire to alleviate tension increases when one learns that blacks and whites living outside the United States are often able to enjoy mutually rewarding relationships that are usually impossible at home. For example, a white American who has lived in black Africa writes that as guests at a wedding of a black American and an African, he and his wife suddenly realized that they were spending more time with the Africans than with the black Americans because "Black and White Americans (unless they *really* know each other) display an excessive . . . politeness that gets to be a strain—as if all of us are tacitly aware of the generations and generations of mutually embarrasing memories."[33] It would be ironic if the more obscene forms of racial antagonisms were, because of their violence, more easily dispelled than the shared guilt, just described, which seems a kind of *folie à deux*, with blacks and whites playing some sort of macabre game with each other.

Aesthetic Symbols of Culture and Personality

When one tries to recall some fictional images of blacks encountered in novels, plays, or short stories, one probably remembers a few, if not all, of the following: A kindly old slave, an unhappy white-looking girl, a vicious brute, an exotic primitive, a comic show-off, a butt of prejudice, or a violently angry youth. All of these familiar types have been created in national letters to implement authors' purposes; and none can be judged satisfactory or unsatisfactory, from the standpoint of literary characterization, solely because one happens to like or dislike a particular image. Such depictions do become cause for concern, however, when one is concerned about youthful self-concepts and intergroup relations, especially when images are perceived emotionally and uncritically; for perceptions without concepts still remain blind; and personal reaction is controlled, too often, by preconceptions and positive or negative halos that have little, if any, relation to the thing perceived. Cause for concern increases when one realizes that an image one holds is often more powerful than reality in shaping attitudes,[34] and that neither desirable self-concepts nor wholesome attitudes can emerge so long as individuals are perceived in terms of static group traits.

A system of examining these images that permits dispassionate interpretation, that controls their personal impact with the use of knowledge and reason—without encouraging embarrassment, self-pity, hostile defensiveness, guilt, or prejudicial reinforcement—can provide alternate attitudes and alternatives for action in interpersonal relationships and bring greater depth of meaning to literature. Several excellent investigations have been made into the use of black characters in novels and plays written by white authors.[35] Numerous other studies of a more general nature have been made which analyze the contributions of black authors to national letters,[36] but none has taken an intensive and comprehensive look at black characters in the whole range of American literature.

To promote an understanding of black images in fiction, three important questions ought to be asked: What kinds of images have authors created since 1800? How have cultural myths and attitudes influenced their portraiture? Can a trend showing shifts in portraits and cultural beliefs be documented? The time span indicated in the first question is important insofar as black portraiture is concerned. Literature of the seventeenth and eighteenth centuries offers little problem. Early writings—consisting mainly of diaries, chronicles, didactic and political tracts—are concerned primarily with the colonists' struggles for physical, spiritual, and political survival; and much of it, in a strict sense, cannot be considered creative fiction. The few blacks appearing in late eighteenth-century fiction are, for the most part, shadowy figures usually lacking rudimentary aspects of character development. Furthermore, it was in the early nineteenth century that black characters began to appear with greater frequency in our literature.[37] Toward the middle part of the century, the question of slavery dominated American life and letters. After emancipation and continuing into the twentieth century, the main issue with regard to blacks was caste. The reflection and influence of both of these on fictional personality are the major concern of this investigation.

When new questions are asked, new methods appropriate

to cope with them must be found. Needed here is the newer approach offered by the anthropological-psychological concept of aesthetic experience, which sees the artist as responsible participant in the evolution of culture and his work of art as symbol of some phase of his culture. Shoemaker's analysis provides a pattern for this approach.

> The several schools of psychology are dealing with the various modes of expression and development of self. Modern anthropology is concerned with language as the reservoir of human experience and with the arts generally as symbols of culture effecting the integration of self in the community through a patterned presentation of human values. From these sources have grown the expanding ideas of aesthetic experience in the arts as the creative-critical process originating in the artist's interaction with his environment and ending in the observer's reflective commitment upon the presentation of values in the work of art.[38]

The creative-critical process, seen as an artist's compulsion to assess his culture and its values, results in an end product, his work of art, that not only symbolizes cultural values but also creates and shapes them.[39] The basic concept of this critical method is the relationship between literature and culture and the function of both in the formation and development of human personality; for it has been shown that culture, society, and personality form a unit so inextricably interrelated that no single component can be examined in isolation of the other two; moreover, that culture dominates the others in determining the general as well as the status personality types that may be found in all societies; and finally, that literature and other art forms contain evidence which reflects a culture pattern, its social structure and the motives of participants in it.[40]

Similarly, literary scholars accept the view that creative writings convey images of culture, social relationships, and the motivations of human personality within the socio-cultural complex. Scholars tend to regard the history of American literature generally as a series of European and other cultural influences that constitute national letters. Scholars

of black literature or of blacks in literature tend to agree. For
example, Gloster, in *Negro Voices in American Fiction* examines novels as reflections of the interests, thoughts, experiences, and psychology of blacks in relation to "problems arising from their [blacks'] juxtaposition with the white majority
of the country";[41] and Bone, in *The Negro Novel in America,*
explores an hypothesis of cultural dualism among blacks, on
the one hand, toward assimilation and, on the other, toward
nationalism and preservation of identity.[42]

The second important element of critical method used
here is the psychological. So long as imaginative literature
purports to portray the thoughts, speech, and behaviors of
"virtual" but lifelike beings, the psychology of human behavior is relevant to literary criticism. Maud Bodkin's interpretation of Jung's concept of archetypes exemplifies a way
in which psychology and literature may be used to explore
human values and provides a basis for the second category
of this investigation. She demonstrates how the study of
archetypes, as thematic motifs, provides a useful way of
identifying poetic images, of comparing the different forms
the images have taken in literature, and of exploring audience responses to the images.[43] Jung's concept of archetypes
has been variously interpreted as "primordial images," "embodiments of the collective unconscious," or "universal psy-
chic forces." A few years before his death, Jung restated his
theory, emphasizing the relation between archetypes and
instincts and certain "dynamic qualities which . . . are designated as 'autonomy' and 'numinosity.' "[44] Maud Bodkin, many
years earlier, frankly admitted that that part of Jung's concept concerning the instincts was difficult to evaluate for
literary purposes; whereupon she interpreted an archetype
as a thematic pattern "which persists amid variation from
age to age, and which corresponds to a pattern or configuration of emotional tendencies in the minds of those who are
stirred by them."[45] Without entering into a possible controversy, it is important here to stress key ideas common to both
writers: first, ideas, themes, and dominant representations;
second, autonomy and persistence; and third, numinosity and
emotional tendencies.

The association of psychology with literature has not

always led to happy results. Sometimes psychological methods, and particularly those of psychoanalysis, have been used to criticize literature and other forms of art in ways and to extremes that have little to do with aesthetic values inherent in works of art. In some instances the main purpose has not been to use psychological concept and method to appraise a work of art but, rather, to throw light on authors' motives and behaviors. In this investigation, therefore, the analysis of both sociocultural environment and the "personalities" of literary characters is limited to those cultural and psychological clues for which there is specific evidence in the literary work. Also, characters are regarded as word images of human types, not as actual human beings who might have lived and whom authors might have known. Nor are characters to be judged solely by authors' alleged feelings about blacks, nor *solely* on the basis of historically emerging status or class aspirations among blacks; they are judged on the basis of what is stated in the texts. Nor are value judgments made of short stories, novels, or plays using characterization of blacks as the only measuring rod. Literary evaluations are made only after careful analysis of all of the components of a work. Its scene, plot, symbols, its statement, the author's style, among other things, are respected as a unified artistic creation providing aesthetic experience for audiences.

The first clue to sociocultural conditioning of black "personality" in fiction is the name assigned to the character. Naming appears to be closely associated with certain culturally induced taboos in civilized as well as in primitive societies. In most cultures, people and objects cannot remain nameless; and if, for one reason or another, namers avoid using a certain set of names for persons and objects, then other names, designative epithets, or euphemisms must be substituted. This kind of naming often conceals devious motives at work among the namers.[46] In literature, the name assigned can be a pertinent clue to the personality of the character. Charles Dickens reserved his most descriptive names for those characters about whom he writes the least, their names being sufficient to delineate them clearly in a reader's mind and thus to type them.[47] Ideas associated with quaint and imaginary names, such as national origin, known persons with similar names, suggestive auditory-verbal similarities, and length of name—indicative of lack of respect— are also clues to character delineation.[48] Sometimes authors reserve certain names for particular types of characters. For example, it was found that a cluster of unattractive, quaint, peculiar names were most often used to stereotype unmarried women in American novels.[49]

Since namings in both culture and literature adhere to certain documentable patterns, this clue becomes an important one to look for in short stories, novels, and drama, along with a second clue, the physical appearances of black characters. As noted earlier, skin color and bodily configurations of blacks combine to form a unique symbolic value system in American society. It seems sufficient at this point to add only one other aspect, that is, the comic dimension. In her study of American humor, Constance Rourke observes that, to white Americans, black skin and thick lips historically have been considered ludicrous.[50]

Both of these clues are somewhat external to the character itself, although they may serve to type him and may color his "personality" in subtle ways. It is even more important to get inside the character to discover finer and more intricate aspects of the black personality in fiction. To achieve this end, a psychology of fictional personality has to be formulated.

Basic to a psychology of personality is recognition of the concept that personality is never a static quality; it is a process of "becoming," a drive toward self-actualization that continues as long as a person is alive. Personality as process can be observed in literature, for example, in the growth toward self-realization and mature responsibility of Hamlet, Raskolnikov, or Isaac McCaslin. The list can be extended with other examples through the range of literature, not always as examples of healthy and mature personality but as process toward whatever personality development or deterioration is needed to fulfill the author's purposes. Insofar as this investigation is concerned, recognition of the healthful drive toward self-actualization and determination does not imply a belief that all blacks in fiction should be so delineated. An expectation of this kind is as unreasonable in literature as it is in life. We may expect some black characters to exhibit this impetus and that it may be documented in the range of nineteenth- and twentieth-century literature.

When one looks at literature from the coign of "becoming" or self-actualization, he finds three interrelated elements useful in examining fictional characterizations: identity, responsibility, relatedness. The beginning of personality lies in the sense of identity. Gordon Allport writes, "Each person is an idiom unto himself, an apparent violation of the syntax of the species."[51] Such a person is not simply a utilitarian extension of others but is an individual in his own right, possessing self-esteem, self-love, self-identity. The second element in the process is a sense of independent responsibility, which is integral to a sense of identity. The mature, healthy personality not only knows who he is and what he wants to be, but has become master of his own drives. If he has acquired both of these senses, he becomes the initiator of some action rather than always an executor, however clever or imperfect, of the commands and appeals of others. In becoming an initiator of action, he is called upon to make mature decisions, fully recognizing the alternatives involved in any decision he might make and assuming responsibility for consequences.[52] The third basic element is closely related to the first two. It is the sense of relatedness that a person has with other people. The concept of self in relation to others varies according to the perception of what the self is. In a healthy personality it is evidenced by a feeling of comradeship with others, his contemporaries as well as persons of other times and places. In comradeship with others, the mature personality maintains and defends his own dignity and integrity.[53] Conversely, some relationships are determined by a submissive-dominant pattern in which participants enter into perverse unity with each other,[54] a pattern that does not describe the healthy personality in relationships with other people. A proper sense of relatedness with others means that an individual is neither completely dominant nor submissive, that his behavior approaches a balance between these extremes. Although no two individuals are exactly the same in appearance, height, intelligence, aspirations, and so forth, each recognizes in the other essential attributes that

make a human being *homo sapiens* rather than something
less. As human beings, their relationship is equal and transactional, a relationship described by Dewey and Bentley
many years ago as "transdermally transactional," which, if
taken literally and interpreted colloquially, suggests that each
participant in a transactional event "gets inside the skin" of
the other. Each affects and is affected by the other. As in
osmosis, some part of each becomes part of the other; and,
as a result, neither is precisely what he was prior to the
event. It is a double-directed, interdependent process based
on a view of man as determiner of his own existence, never
completely the pawn of other men or of natural and environmental forces.

When characters are sorted according to symbols of culture (names and physical descriptions) and criteria of fictional personality as shaped by culture (identity, independent
responsibility, relatedness to other characters), they fall into
three flexible, overlapping categories: stock characters, archetypes, and individuals. As it is highly doubtful that writers
ever deliberately set out to delineate fictional images in terms
of categories as defined here, these must be approached with
caution. They are not absolute, dogmatic, exclusive entities
but useful devices for identifying dominant aspects of a
literary portrait and for permitting some objectivity in the
discussion of fictional personality—an objectivity that can be
useful at this time of social change and increased intergroup
tension. Further, the categories do not indicate linear or
hierarchical progression, with stock characters as the lowest
order and individuals as the highest. Fictional character,
like human personality, often is a combination of various
traits. Characters analyzed in the next three chapters are
categorized according to dominant traits in their portraits.
This does not mean that portraits in one section are totally
free from characteristics found in one of the other sections.
It does mean, however, that if such traits are present in a
particular portrait, they are recessive and contributory, in
some sense, to the dominant ones.

Those characters, usually minor figures, whose sole function is to create atmosphere, to authenticate scene, or to contrast the virtues and vices of other characters are designated

here as stock characters and are analyzed in the next chapter. Stock blacks, because of skin color values, provide excellent contrast for white characters. Now it sometimes happens that a stock black is brought, so to speak, downstage center, with full spotlight focused upon him as the major figure of a drama or novel. In such cases the stock element of contrast with whites reflecting certain attitudes is merely magnified by this treatment. Archetypes comprise the second category and are examined in the second analytical chapter. These are the more complex figures that have risen in literature, acquiring mythic proportions as embodiments of cultural beliefs, values, and aspirations and fears that are accepted uncritically, that are supported and maintained by prescribed ritual, and that recur in literature with enough regularity to personify, by their persistence, some conscientious feeling or some facet of man's unconscious mind. In their subsequent persistence, they seem to lead lives of their own, attracting meanings and emotional halos not always identical with primal manifestations of their thematic motifs. Examples among white figures in literature include Huck Finn as rebel, Ahab as monomaniacal avenger, and Hamlet as thinker called to violent action. In their portraits may be found, in varying degrees, overtones of still earlier figures, such as overtones of Orestes and Oedipus in Hamlet, of Satan and Faust in Ahab, and perhaps Telemachus and Quixote in Huck. In turn, overtones of all three can be found in contemporary literature. Those black figures examined in chapter three are larger-than-life characters embodying in their portraits dominant cultural ideas and conscientious feelings that have persisted deviously in American literature. Contained in the third category are the more complex word pictures of blacks who can be called mature or maturing individuals. These figures, analyzed in chapter four, possess senses of identity that are separate and distinct from other characters, the ability to make some significant decisions within the plot structure, and the sense of transactional relatedness with other characters.

In order to uncover and assess patterns and trends of black portraiture, it has been necessary to examine characters contained in a wide range of nineteenth- and twentieth-century popular literature. The sample has been drawn, therefore, from the most readily available editions of works and has not been limited to "good" literature. Because the range is wide and no comprehensive list of writers delineating black figures exists, the sample is inclusive rather than exclusive, the purpose being to collect as many portraits as possible and not to eliminate any portrait that is different from some of the better known ones. Only when documentation became excessively repetitious were portraits eliminated from the sample.

Notes

1. Samuel Sewall, "The Selling of Joseph," *Early American Reprints, 1639–1800*, ed. by Clifford K. Shipton, No. 951.
2. James Fenimore Cooper, *Satanstoe; or the Littlepage Manuscripts: A Tale of the Colony* (New York, 1945), pp. 65ff.
3. George Washington Cable, *The Grandissimes* (New York, 1957), p. 59. It should be noted that Cable fought actively against racial injustices during the latter part of his life. See Philip Butcher's excellent study, *George W. Cable* (New York, 1959).
4. Arthur A. Schomburg, "The Negro Digs Up His Past," *The New Negro, An Interpretation*, Alain Locke, ed. (New York, 1925), p. 231.
5. E. Franklin Frazier, *The Negro Family in the United States* (Chicago, 1939), pp. 21–22.
6. Melville J. Herskovits, *The Myth of the Negro Past*, Beacon Paperback Edition (Boston, 1958), p. 298. First published in 1941.
7. See Harold R. Isaacs, "The American Negro and Africa: Some Notes," *Phylon*, XX, 3 (Third Quarter, 1959): 219–233.
8. Richard Wright, *Black Power: A Record of Reactions in a Land of Pathos* (New York, 1954), p. 35.
9. Peter Abrahams, "The Blacks," *Holiday*, XXV (April, 1959): 122.
10. Ed Smith, *Where To, Black Man?* (Chicago, 1967), pp. 105, *passim*.
11. Ernest Dunbar, ed., "Bill Sutherland: Tanzania," *The Black Expatriates: A Study of American Negroes in Exile* (New York, 1968), p. 109.
12. George Breitman, ed., *Malcolm X Speaks: Selected Speeches and Statements* (New York, 1965), p. 210.
13. *The Autobiography of Malcolm X* (New York, 1964), pp. 351, *passim*.

14. Guy Flatley, "Senegal Is Senegal, Not Harlem," *The New York Times,* Section II, November 2, 1969, p. 17. © 1969 by The New York Times Company. Reprinted by permission.
15. Abram Kardiner and Lionel Ovesey, *The Mark of Oppression: A Psychosocial Study of the American Negro* (New York, 1951), pp. 365ff.; Bertram P. Karon, *The Negro Personality: A Rigorous Investigation of the Effects of Culture* (New York, 1958), pp. 171ff.
16. Kenneth B. Clark and Mamie P. Clark, "Racial Identification and Preference in Negro Children," *Readings in Social Psychology,* 3rd ed., Eleanor E. Maccoby *et al.,* eds. (New York, 1958), pp. 602–611.
17. James A. Bayton, "The Racial Stereotypes of Negro College Students," *Journal of Abnormal and Social Psychology,* XXXVI (January, 1941): pp. 97–102; Daniel Katz and Kenneth W. Braly, "Verbal Stereotypes and Racial Prejudice," *Readings in Social Psychology,* 3rd ed., Eleanor E. Maccoby *et al.,* eds. (New York, 1958), pp. 40–46.
18. Walter White, "The Paradox of Color," *The New Negro, An Interpretation,* Alain Locke, ed. (New York, 1925), pp. 361–382.
19. William H. Grier and Price M. Cobbs, *Black Rage* (New York, 1968), pp. 177ff. © 1968 William H. Grier and Price M. Cobbs. Reprinted by permission of Basic Books, Inc.
20. *Loc. cit.*
21. Herbert Hendin, *Black Suicide* (New York, 1969), *passim.*
22. Abram Kardiner and Lionel Ovesey, *op. cit.,* p. 379.
23. William Alexander Percy, *Lanterns on the Levee: Recollections of a Planter's Son* (New York, 1941), p. 298.
24. Lillian Smith, *Killers of the Dream* (New York, 1949), pp. 18ff.
25. *Ibid.,* pp. 30–31.
26. Norman Podhoretz, "My Negro Problem and Ours," *Commentary,* XXXV (February, 1963): 98–101. Published by permission of Farrar, Straus & Giroux, Inc.
27. See T. W. Adorno *et al., The Authoritarian Personality* (New York, 1950), p. 149; Gordon W. Allport, *The Nature of Prejudice* (Garden City, N.Y., 1958), pp. 236–257, 345–348, *passim;* Gunnar Myrdal, *An American Dilemma* (New York, 1944), pp. xiv, xlvii, *passim.*
28. See *The Report of the National Advisory Commission on Civil Disorders* (New York, 1968).
29. Ashley Montagu, *Statement on Race,* 2nd ed. (New York, 1952), pp. 11–17.
30. W. E. Burghardt Du Bois, *The Souls of Black Folk: Essays and Sketches* (New York, 1961), p. 17. Originally published in 1903.
31. George Breitman, ed. *Malcolm X Speaks: Selected Speeches*

and Statements (New York, 1966), p. 59; and *The Autobiography of Malcolm X* (New York, 1964), p. 338.

32. Eldridge Cleaver, "To All Black Women from All Black Men," *Soul on Ice* (New York, 1968), p. 205. Copyright © 1968 by Eldridge Cleaver. Used with permission of McGraw-Hill Book Company.

33. William Attwood, "Malcolm X; A Very Personal Recollection," *Look* (January 7, 1969), n.p.

34. See H. A. Overstreet, "Images and the Negro: Do Our Writers Really Know and Understand This American?" *Saturday Review of Literature,* XXVII (August 24, 1944): 5.

35. An early study is Sterling A. Brown's "Negro Characters As Seen by White Authors," *The Journal of Negro Education,* I (January, 1933): 180–201. Another is Walter L. Daykin's "Negro Types in American White Fiction," *Sociology and Social Research,* XXII (September–October, 1937): 45–52.

36. Two outstanding studies are Hugh Gloster's *Negro Voices in American Fiction* (Chapel Hill, N.C., 1948), and Robert Bone's *The Negro Novel in America* (New Haven, Conn., 1958).

37. See Walter L. Daykin, *op. cit.,* 46.

38. Francis Shoemaker, *Aesthetic Experience and the Humanities: Modern Ideas of Aesthetic Experience in the Reading of World Literature* (New York: Columbia University Press, 1943), p. 7.

39. See Susanne K. Langer, *Feeling and Form: A Theory of Art Developed from "Philosophy in a New Key"* (New York, 1953), p. 263; Robert N. Wilson, "Aesthetic Symbolism," *The American Imago,* II, 3 (Fall, 1955): 276–277; Melvin Rader, ed., *A Modern Book of Aesthetics: An Anthology,* 3rd ed. (New York, 1960), pp. xxxff.

40. See Ralph Linton, *The Cultural Background of Personality* (New York, 1945), pp. xiii, 2, 5, 151, *passim;* A. L. Kroeber, *Configurations of Culture Growth* (Berkeley and Los Angeles, 1944), p. 21; Clyde Kluckhohn, *Mirror for Man: The Relations of Anthropology to Modern Life* (New York, 1949), pp. 298ff.

41. Hugh M. Gloster, *Negro Voices in American Fiction* (Chapel Hill, N.C., 1948), p. vii.

42. Robert A. Bone, *The Negro Novel in America* (New Haven, 1958), pp. 7, 67–68, *passim.*

43. Maud Bodkin, *Archetypal Patterns of Poetry: Psychological Studies of Imagination* (New York, 1958). Originally published 1934.

44. C. G. Jung, Preface, *Psyche and Symbol,* Violet S. de Laszlo, ed. (Garden City, N.Y., 1958), p. xvi.

45. Bodkin, *op. cit.,* pp. 2ff.

46. See Edward Clodd, *Magic in Names and in Other Things* (London, 1920), pp. 36ff., 88, *passim.*

47. Elizabeth H. Gordon, "The Naming of Characters in Charles Dickens," *University of Nebraska Studies in Language, Literature, and Criticism* (1917), p. 4.

48. See E. N. Alspach, "On the Psychological Response to Unknown Proper Names," *American Journal of Psychology, XVIII* (July, 1917): 436.
49. Dorothy Y. Deegan, *The Stereotype of the Single Woman in Novels: A Social Study With Implications for the Education of Women* (New York, 1951), pp. 83–84.
50. Constance Rourke, *American Humor: A Study of the National Character* (New York, 1931), p. 82.
51. Gordon W. Allport, *Becoming* (New Haven, Conn., 1955), p. 19.
52. See Erik H. Erikson, "Identity and the Life Cycle," *Psychological Issues*, I (1959): 89, 93, 98; Erich Fromm, "Values, Psychology, and Human Experience," *New Knowledge in Human Values*, Abraham Maslow, ed. (New York, 1959), p. 153; Abraham Maslow, "Psychological Data and Value Theory," *New Knowledge in Human Values* (New York, 1959), p. 126.
53. See Erik H. Erikson, *op. cit.*, p. 98.
54. See Erich Fromm, *op. cit.*, p. 152.
55. John Dewey and Arthur F. Bentley, *Knowing and the Known* (Boston, 1949), p. 130.

CHAPTER

STOCK CHARACTERS

When one examines novels and drama containing black images, he discovers that the stock characters have not always been identical during the past century and a half, that they may be differentiated generally as accommodative chattels, as counter images to the chattels, and as buffoons that are outgrowths of the chattels. At the same time that differences are noted, there is evidence also of a changing tone in cultural attitudes. In the early part of the nineteenth century, blacks were regarded as slaves by divine edict. When doubt arose concerning the validity of using human beings as salable commodities, shifts in attitude were conveniently made to preserve the concept of white superiority by further demonstrating black inferiority. Blacks were idealized by some Americans as darker-skinned, inferior brothers for whom social justice ought to be insured or as legally free, emotionally enslaved inferiors who preferred the old social order. During the latter decades of the century and continuing well into the twentieth, other shifts became necessary, revealing "egopervision of dominance," noted earlier in the work of Kardiner and Ovesey. As a result, blacks were vilified as brutes by some people or regarded as ludicrously irresponsible inferiors by others.

The basic belief supporting the predominant attitude is found in this observation of John Pendleton Kennedy, written in 1832:

... he [the Negro] is in his moral constitution, a dependent upon the white race, dependent for guidance and direction even to the procurement of his most indispensable necessaries. Apart from this protection he has the helplessness of a child,—without foresight, without thrift of any kind. . . . He grows upward, only as the vine to which nature has supplied the sturdy tree as a support.[1]

Supported by the myth of white superiority and black inferiority, authors could, without compunction, depict blacks as accommodative chattels in our literature.

Accommodative Slaves

To James Fenimore Cooper goes the somewhat dubious honor of delineating the first full-length portrait of the contented slave in our literature,[2] a character named Caesar, who is given a small but sustained role in *The Spy*, first published in 1821. He is one of a group of low-life or common characters that are used as contrasting images to heighten the virtues of the nobler landed gentry: Caesar's owner, Mr. Wharton; his children—Sarah, Henry, and Frances; the mysterious Mr. Harper, later identified as George Washington; and Peyton Dunwoodie, a proud, aristocratic Virginian. *The Spy* glorifies the American struggle for independence and dramatizes the emotional conflicts of transplanted Englishmen who are torn between ancestral ties to Britain and admiration for the rebel cause of individual and political freedom from tyranny. Ironically, that rebellion with its high ideal excluded all people like Caesar who were the personal property of others.

Examining Caesar's name, physical description, and personality, we find that all three reflect cultural attitudes to which the Whartons and other whites and he, as recipient and object, had become well adjusted. Cooper, editorializing in the manner of earlier novelists, writes that the faithful black, ". . . as if in mockery of his degraded state, had been complimented with the name of Caesar."[3] This kind of naming reveals sardonic humor, the obvious purpose being to ridicule and dehumanize the object by reducing it to the status of subhuman creature in a process similar to the naming of a prized horse or pet dog. Because of this association, Caesar is comparable to "man's best friend," and the animal image is reinforced by descriptions of his physical appearance and personality.

Cooper's skill in describing Caesar's crazily constructed body leaves no doubt that a seriocomic subhuman image is being built. He begins slowly, almost reverently.

> The short curly hair of Caesar has acquired from age a coloring of gray, that added greatly to the venerable cast of his appearance. . . . The shining black of his youth had lost its glistening hue.[4]

Then he lets fly his first barbs:

> His eyes, which stood a formidable distance from each other, were small and characterized by an expression of good feeling, occasionally interrupted by the petulance of an indulged servant. . . . His nose possessed, in an eminent manner, all the requisites for smelling, but with the most modest unobtrusiveness; the nostrils being abundantly capacious, without thrusting themselves in the way of their neighbors. His mouth was capacious to a fault, and was only tolerated on account of the double row of pearls it contained.[5]

The perceptive reader knows by now, even as he is amused by Cooper's wit and skill in understatement, that this character, the only well-drawn black character in the novel, is being made ridiculous because his appearance does not begin to approximate that which is considered handsome among whites. From this point on, the description rises in comic intensity and becomes ludicrous caricature.

> In person Caesar was short, and we would say square, had not all the angles and curves of his figure bid defiance to anything like mathematical symmetry. His arms were long and muscular, and terminated by two bony hands, that exhibited on one side a coloring of blackish gray, and on the other a faded pink. But it was in his

legs that nature had indulged her most capricious humor. There was an abundance of material injudiciously used. The calves were neither before nor behind, but rather on the outer side of the limb, inclining forward, and so close to the knee as to render the free use of that joint a subject of doubt. In the foot, considering it as a base on which the body was to rest, Caesar had no cause of complaint, unless, indeed, it might be that the leg was placed so near the center as to make it sometimes a matter of dispute whether he was walking backwards.[6]

Anticlimactically and somewhat sentimentally, the description ends with the tossing of a "bone" to the lovable, faithful old canine-like character.

> But whatever might be the faults a statuary could discover in his person, the heart of Caesar Thompson was in the right place, and, we doubt not of very generous proportions.[7]

Despite this last concession the image of a laughable subhuman has been developed too skillfully and lingers in the reader's consciousness.

His personality strongly supports the Roman name and ludicrous appearance. Three incidents provide clues to his self-rejection. The first occurs at the beginning of the novel when Harvey Birch, the peddler-spy, has a rendezvous with General Washington at Locusts, the Wharton estate in Westchester County. Under the guise of selling merchandise and purveying news events, Harvey laconically mentions that a defeated American officer lives "somewhere among the niggers to the south." In a show of equality, Caesar repudiates the epithet, nigger, and adds: "A black man so good as a white . . . so long as he behave heself."[8] The second incident occurs several chapters later when Locusts has been captured by rebels. Caesar's young master, a British officer on furlough, has been imprisoned in the Wharton house. Caesar watches the rebel guard night and day for the right moment when Henry might safely get away. When the moment comes, Henry rides off, calling back gratefully to the old man, "God bless you, Caesar, salute the girls."[9] Caesar mulls over Henry's parting words and comes to this conclusion: ". . . salute a young lady—Miss Fanny wouldn't let old colored man kiss a red cheek."[10] The verb *salute,* in one of its now obsolete meanings, was synonymous with *kiss.* Henry's precise meaning is obscure; but whatever the meaning and without questioning the propriety of a servant's kissing his mistress, Caesar did not consider himself worthy to carry out the request, primarily because he is black and therefore inferior.

The third incident comes near the end of the novel during a conversation between Betty Flanagan, a stereotyped alcoholic camp follower, and Sergeant Hollister, a foot soldier of the rebel forces. In his presence they discuss the color of Caesar's soul, both agreeing that they do not agree with those whites who say that blacks have no souls. The night being cold, Betty invites Caesar to have a drink of whiskey; ". . . 'twill warm the black sowle within your crazy body, and be giving you spirits as you are going homeward."[11] The sergeant pompously explains that the souls of blacks are as white as the soul of Major Dunwoodie, who is the handsome young man of the novel. This topic, though specious at best, reveals how deeply assigned merits of blackness and whiteness had sunk into human consciousness and influenced attitudes. At the end of the conversation, Caesar agrees with the sergeant so hastily that he unmasks his inner feelings, "Be sure he [my soul] be. . . ,"[12] thereby revealing, for the third time, rejection of his black skin and preference for that which is white. Only death can release him from the black body that he hates and the tyranny of culturally manipulated black-white symbolism that brands him inferior from the moment of his birth.

Regarded by others as inferior, Caesar can be given no important decision-making role within the context of the novel. His assistance in Henry's escape, noted earlier, is part of his function as watchdog for his owners. At the novel's climax, he helps Henry escape from the rebels a second time, on this occasion from a prison. It is not he but Henry who conceives and executes the plan of escape: to disguise Henry to look like Caesar and Caesar to look like Henry so that the slave can exchange places with his young master in prison.

Caesar's black skin and "crazily-constructed" body merely perform a useful function; he is not the active agent. Considering himself inferior, he cannot be expected to enter into anything resembling a reciprocal or transactional relationship with most lower-class whites much less upper-class ones. It is only with Katy Haynes, another low-life character, that he enjoys social reciprocity. She is the goodhearted, mercenary housekeeper of lower-class Harvey Birch and his father, Johnny. In this role she is on a similar but not identical social level with Caesar, who is a servant of the upper-class Whartons. The difference is that she is free and white.

His primary function in the novel is to serve others and do what he is told to do. This function he performs in several ways. Ceremoniously he greets guests, welcomes acceptable but unfamiliar visitors, and ushers all into the master's presence. With reverence and ritualistic dignity, he glides unobtrusively in and out of rooms, waiting tables, fetching and carrying for guests and family. Psychologically, he serves as abetter and comforter to his owners and their friends. Because he is a faithful watchdog who can speak, he is able to allay Mr. Wharton's fears about his son's safety and to assist in Henry's escapes from the rebels. Finally as a device in the novel's overall structure, Caesar's function is to lighten tensions. His appearance, sensitive outbursts, naïveté, and petulance supply touches of comic relief throughout, as does his stock response in moments of stress. At a half-joking threat of physical harm, at the prospect of witnessing emergency surgery during a skirmish, at the mere contemplation of anything supernatural—such as passing a cemetery or seeing Johnny Birch's rise from his deathbed to save his son from injury—Caesar is reduced by terror to a quivering, cringing creature, his teeth chattering in his mouth.

Nothing is said in the novel about Caesar's personal life. The reader learns that he is married to Dinah, the cook. His only concern for her occurs when he influences Sarah to buy a length of dress goods as a present for her. Later, when Locusts is set afire and Caesar just manages to escape with the Whartons, no reference is made to her whereabouts or safety; nor can the reader be sure that Caesar is concerned about her welfare. We see him looking back at the house with "a heavy heart"; but we are not told exactly what it is that caused his grief. All of his life had been spent in that house, vicariously experiencing the lives that the Whartons led. In that attachment, he is a pathetic, comical, inferior extension of the people he adores and might have been mourning the destruction of the Wharton house and the sentimental memories he has about it. Variant forms of this slave image remain constant in our literature, even though tensions of plantation life, manumission, emancipation, and segregation alter situations in which the stock characters are presented.

Before examining some of the others, consider briefly Cooper's black female. Although he does not give her full treatment, what he does is enough to suggest the basis for Aunt Jemima of pancake fame. In Dinah, the reader sees a stout, black-faced woman who smiles toothsomely, bows servilely, clothes her stout body in brightly colored, gaudily patterned calico—in sum, an ungainly type whose only function is to cook for the Whartons and to provoke mirth. A younger, more sparkling female appears briefly but vibrantly in another of Cooper's novels, *Satanstoe* (1845). This is what the reader sees: ". . . Mari was a buxom, glistening, smooth-faced, laughing, red-lipped, pearl-toothed, black-eyed hussy, that seemed born for fun."[13] Her description contains a primitive quality that is repeated and magnified by other authors.

Hector in William Gilmore Simms's *The Yemassee* (1835) and Jupiter, affectionately called Jup, in Edgar Allan Poe's short story, "The Gold Bug" (1843), although similar to Caesar, add a dimension to the contented slave image that does not appear in *The Spy* but could have been anticipated, that is, the slave's reaction to being given his freedom. Physically, both are animal-like menials: Jup grins from ear to ear like the Cheshire cat, and Hector's mouth shows a "full array of big teeth, stretching away like those of a shark, from ear to ear."

Both are manumitted by benevolent and grateful masters. Although legally free, Jup "could be induced, neither by threats nor promises, to abandon what he considered his right of attendance upon the foot-steps of his young 'Massa Will'."[14]

He prefers to remain a faithful, protective custodian of his master's physical welfare, rather than become master of his own destiny as a free man. He gives devoted service even though that service proves to be more of a hindrance than a help on one important occasion. In the expansiveness of the novel form, Simms develops the servile dependency of his character to a greater extent. During one of the pre-revolutionary brushfire skirmishes among Colonials, British, and Yemassee Indians in South Carolina, Hector's master, Lord Palatinate of the territory, is in danger. Hector, armed with a knife and a gun, rescues him. Out of gratitude, the master frees him, saying, "I cannot call you my slave when I would call you my friend. . . . You fought for me like a friend, and I am now your friend."[15] This is Hector's opportunity to enter into reciprocal relationship with a politically powerful white who sought his friendship. This is the slave's vehement reaction:

> I d—n to h—ll, Maussa ef I guine be free! I can't loss you company. . . . 'tis onpossible, Maussa, and dere's no use for talk 'bout it. De ting ain't right; and enty I know wha' kind of ting freedom is wid black man? Ha! you make Hector free, he turn wuss more nor poor buckrah— he tief out de shop—he git drunk and lie in de ditch— den, if sick comes, he roll, he toss in de wet grass of de stable. You come in de morning, Hector dead. . . . No Maussa—you and Dugdale [the master's dog] berry good company for Hector. I tank God he so good—I no want any better.[16]

The decisions of the two characters reflect cultural belief that Negroes, being inferior to and dependent upon whites, are fortunate in their servitude to those whites who assume responsibility for their welfare.

Other slightly variant manifestations of the contented slave image are characters who have not been "complimented" with Greek and Roman names. In their relationships with whites, some are like cute and playful puppies, others like primitives, and some others like tired old mastiffs. Carey in *Swallow Barn* (1832) by John Pendleton Kennedy, Tom and

Jack in *The Partisan Leader* (1836) by Nathaniel Beverly Tucker, Abram in *The Forayers* (1855) by Simms, and Pete in *The Octoroon* (1859) by Dion Boucicault all fall within this grouping.

Hoary-headed, banjo-playing Carey is a seriocomic, vainglorious menial who is permitted a great deal of freedom with whites. With other slaves, he behaves in a surly, bullying fashion and regards himself their superior. Like Caesar Thompson, he is major-domo of his master's mansion and an "instinctive" rider of horses. He breeds and trains horses, gives chaste advice to young white lovers, and persuades all whites to do the things that they want to do. Added to the portrait is the ignorant slave's penchant for malapropism. Speaking of a spirited horse, he says, "It was a marcy she wa'nt foundered outright . . . anyway which she deserved for being so obstropolous."

The Partisan Leader, a novel which the title page claims was secretly printed in 1836 but afterwards suppressed, contains an interesting slave type that shows more clearly than some of the others the close attachment of whites for their blacks. Suppression of the novel was probably due to the role ascribed by Tucker to President Martin Van Buren (1837–1841). The black character is Tom, a house-slave of Bernard Trevor. The plot is set in Roanoke before Secession. Trevor's nephew, Douglas, comes to visit after a long absence. The uncle sits petting his dog, Carlo, who has just gleefully greeted Douglas. Mr. Trevor muses:

> Give me a rough coat, or a black skin, for a true friend; one that will not grudge any superior advantages that I may possess.

Then speaking benevolently to Tom in a passage that points up Tucker's polemic against Abolition and justification of Secession:

> "Tom," added he in a tone of marked gentleness, "the fire is low. No, not yourself, old man," he continued as the Negro whom he addressed moved toward the door; "not you, my good old friend. Just ring the bell, and let one of those lazy dogs in the kitchen bring in some wood.

But why don't you speak to your young master Douglas?
I am sure you remember what cronies you were when
you were teaching him to ride."

"I'm mighty proud to see you, sir," said the old man,
taking the offered hand of Douglas, with an air of affectionate humility. "But it was not my place, sir," added
he, answering his master's words, "to speak first. I made
sure [was certain] Master Douglas would remember me
after a while."[17]

Completely self-effacing, Tom is different from the more
ebullient Hector, Jupiter, and Carey. Just to see Douglas
makes the patient, worn-out mastiff proud. Tucker sentimentally shows the close but non-reciprocal relationship between Tom and the whites:

"I do remember you, Tom," said Douglas cordially,
"and many a time, on parade, have I been thankful to you
for teaching me to hold my reins and manage my horse."

"You will find it hard," said Mr. Trevor, gravely, "to
convince Tom that you remember him, if you call him by
that name. Tom is Delia's daddy, and Lucia's and Arthur's, and Virginia's daddy, [all are cousins] and so will
be to the day of his death. If he ever ceases to be your
daddy, too, Douglas, I shall move to reconsider the vote
[to secede] we just now passed unanimously."[18]

His half-joking threat shows how really serious he, a staunch
Secessionist, considers this relationship to be. Douglas apologizes:

"It is a vice the northern air has blown upon me,"
said Douglas, blushing. "I felt the truth of what you said
just now, and am not more sure of being affectionately
remembered by any that I used to know, than by my good
old daddy."[19]

At this point Mr. Trevor asks Tom to see that the travelers'
horses have been properly stabled. Obsequiously, Tom leaves
the room.

"What a graceful and gentlemanly old man!" said
Douglas, looking after him.

"His manners," said Mr. Trevor, "are exactly suited to his situation. Their characteristic is proud humility. The opposite is servile sulkiness, of which, I suspect, Douglas, you have seen no little."

"I have seen nothing else," said Douglas, "among the servants of the North. If the tempers of our Negroes were as ferocious, and their feelings as hostile, we should have to cut their throats in self-defense in six months."[20]

Tucker's idealization of the contented slave is a deviation from the basic pattern for propagandistic purposes: to glorify plantation life and to support the beliefs of Southerners that they were the only ones who knew the true nature of the black inferiors and recognized the just validity of their enslavement. In contrast to contented slaves like Daddy Tom, free blacks became hostile and dangerous because of their inability to cope with stresses imposed by freedom. Tucker does not delineate his character in some of the ways used by Cooper, Poe, and Simms. Moreover, he explicitly rejects Cooper's caricature of Caesar. In a footnote to Daddy Tom's last response to Douglas, he writes:

I crave the forbearance of all critics, who have taken their ideas of a Virginia house servant from Caesar Thompson, or any such caricature, for giving Tom's own words, and his own pronunciation of them. It is not my fault if there is but little peculiarity in his phraseology. His language was never elegant, and frequently ungrammatical. But he spoke better than the peasantry of many countries, though he said some things a white man would not say; perhaps because he had some feelings to which the white man is a stranger.[21]

Despite Tucker's footnote, he succeeds in making his stock black as inferior to whites as does Cooper, by virtue of the fact that Tom's relationship with the Trevors is non-reciprocal. Though he is devoted to them and they to him, in their minds he is in the same category as the dog Carlo. Notice Bernard Trevor's first speech. Further, though Tom has had a part in training Douglas to be the upstanding man that he is, Tom is never in any sense a father image. Instead he is a black daddy and of lesser significance.

Another character in *The Partisan Leader* deserves mention in this category. He is Jack, the ringleader of the Black Watch, a group of slaves trained and armed to protect their master and his interests against those who would set them free. The Trevor estate is temporarily in the possession of a small troop of Northern soldiers. The officer in charge of the troop is inside the house threatening Mr. Trevor while outside a soldier stands guard. Jack, who according to Tucker is an intelligent boy, feigns "typical" slave ignorance and behavior as a means of infiltrating the enemy troop and effecting the capture of its members. As he shuffles toward the sentinel, he is challenged and ordered to give the proper countersign. Pretending stupidity, he yells, "Law-Gorramighty, what dis?" Then he proceeds to make disparaging remarks about his master and to complain about his hard life on the plantation, ending with, "No, Massa, I love soldier, 'cause I hear 'em say soldier come after white, set poor nigur free." Thus winning the sentinel's confidence, Jack gives him and his companion some drugged wine; and with the aid of the other Negroes of the Black Watch, he jails them in a storehouse and helps the Trevors to escape. According to Tucker, despite his intelligence and cleverness, Jack was not smart enough to have conceived the plan himself.

Abram Johnson in Simms's *The Forayers* is built physically like a "noble savage," with a "broad massive trunk, like that of Hercules" and "noble features."[22] Almost immediately after Simms's description, any illusion that might have been built is shattered. Willie Sinclair, his young master, comes unexpectedly to 'Bram's cabin, after having been absent for some time. Finding 'Bram asleep, he hits him, somewhat playfully, with a hickory branch. 'Bram, startled, roars, "Wha' da debbil dat! Who dat, I say, da hit maussa nigger wid hick'ry?" Recognizing Willie, he yells, "Ki! Mass Willie, da you?" This dialogue follows rapidly:

"And this is the way, you rascal, that you watch camp when I am gone?"

"Psho, maussa, I bin see you all de time. I know he bin you from de fuss."

"Then you must have a famous passion for hickory,

you rascal, to receive three cuts of it before letting me
know that you were awake."

"Psho! de hick'ry ain't hutt."

"Ah, will you try a little more of it?" but the black re-
treated, rubbing his shoulders afresh.

"Thank you, Mass Willie; but 'scuse me, ef you please;
no more dis time. Nex' time, maybe, I will tank you for
anoder tas'e."[23]

All fun and games and high good humor, but the noble
primitive is quickly reduced to an ungainly mastiff.

The last of the contented slaves in this sampling of those
with ordinary names is Pete, "an old uncle," in *The Octoroon*,
by Dion Boucicault. Old Pete has significance here only insofar as he reveals the utter selflessness of this type and his
shrewdness in convincing other slaves to become as selfless
as he. Everything at Terrebonne, the Peyton plantation in
Louisiana, including the slaves, must be sold. Pete, thinking
only of his old mistress's feelings and the dignity of the
Peyton name, prepares them for the sale.

> PETE: Now den, if Grace dere wid her chilr'n were all
> sold, she'll be screetchin' like a cat. She didn' mind how
> kind old Judge was to her; and Solon, too, he'll holler,
> and break de old lady's heart.
>
> GRACE: No, Pete; no, I won't. I'll bear it.
>
> PETE: I don't tink you will any more, but dis here will,
> cause de family spile Dido, de has. She nebber woth
> much, dat 'a nigger.
>
> DIDO: How dar you say dat? You black nigger, you. I
> fetch as much as any odder cook in Louisiana.
>
> PETE: What's de use of your takin' it kind, and comfortin'
> de Missus' heart, if Minnie dere, and Louise, and Marie,
> and Julia is to spile it?
>
> MINNIE: We won't Pete; we won't.
>
> PETE: (to the men) Dar, do ye hear dat, ye mis'able
> darkeys; dem gals is woth a boat load of kinder men, dem
> is. Cum, for de pride of de family, let every darkey look

his best for de Judge's sake—dat ole man so good to us, and dat ole woman—so dem strangers from New Orleans shall say, dem's happy darkeys, dem's a fine set of niggers; everyone say when he's sold, "Lor' bless dis yer family I'm gwine out of and send me as good a home."[24]

Some other slave characters, appearing before the Civil War, have names that are more descriptive and delineations that are slightly different from the basic stock character pattern.

In *The Cavaliers of Virginia* (1834), by William Alexander Caruthers, there is a stately, gray-haired man named Congo, familiarly shortened to Ol' Cong, who serves as hunt overseer for the landed gentry. As he performs the slave ritual required of him, his gleaming eyes and instinctive handling of animals suggest something of the primitive quality implied in his name.[25]

Fleece and Old Ebony are descriptive names assigned to the *Pequod*'s cook in *Moby Dick* (1851). They conjure up the image of an ancient black face surmounted by wooly white hair. He is first seen shambling along to comply with "Massa Stubb's" command to preach to the sharks that are noisily devouring a whale's carcass tied to the *Pequod*. His task is to improve their eating habits.

The ground was laid for this episode earlier in the novel, when Ishmael stumbled into a dimly lighted church in New Bedford:

It seemed the great Black Parliament sitting in Tophet. A hundred black faces turned round in their rows to peer; and beyond, a black Angel of Doom was beating a book in a pulpit. It was a Negro church; and the preacher's text was about the blackness of darkness and the weeping and wailing and teeth-gnashing there. Ha, Ishmael, muttered I, backing out, Wretched entertainment at the sign of "The Trap!"[26]

As noted in Constance Rourke's analysis, black skin is one of the components of American humor. If this is true, the Negro preacher's sermon to a black audience, on the "blackness of darkness," compounds that component and extends the image to a ludicrous degree. Fleece's "preaching" echoes the earlier episode. With straight face, he does as he is bidden, identifying himself with the animals:

> Fellow-critters: I'se ordered here to say dat you must stop dat dam noise dare. You hear? Stop dat dam smackin' ob de lips! Massa Stubb say dat you can fill your dam bellies up to de hatchings, but by Gor! you must stop dat dam racket![27]

Stubb, gluttonously devouring a whale steak at the capstan, keeps the joke in motion as he sanctimoniously admonishes Fleece about cursing. Fleece balks for a moment, then calls the sharks "Belubbed fellow-critters," and exhorts them to control their voracious nature so that their angelic qualities can emerge and be seen. The natural duality that Melville gives to the animals resembles that which has been ascribed to man. Finally Stubb admits that it is impossible to change sharks' (men's) behavior and orders him to pronounce the benediction. Raising his arms as if he were a preacher, but not using the words of one, he becomes a macabre replica of the "black Angel of Doom" in the church scene.

> Cussed fellow-critters! Kick up de damndest row as ever you can; fill your dam bellies 'till dey bust—and den die.[28]

Prior to Fleece's appearance in the novel, Melville had created no black character who could function as butt of a farcical joke. Daggoo was obviously unsuitable if he were to continue as irrepressible and instinctive "squire" along with Tashtego and Queequeg. Little Pip, reserved for a more universal and tragic role in Melville's manipulation of black-white symbols, was also unsuitable. Only a gullible, obedient slave stereotype could function adequately.

Fleece's portrait contains most of the outer trappings of this slave type: the name, appearance, shuffled-gait, accommodativeness—automatically to obey—and, as we have observed, the gullibility to comply with Stubb's orders. In each instance, Fleece acquiesces, saying, "All 'dention [attention]." Yet the portrait does not precisely coincide with the stereotype. As Fleece leaves the scene, we see his ability to evaluate the situation and the swinish Stubb; "I'm bressed if he ain't more of shark dan Massa Shark himself."[29]

Like Fleece and Congo, Benny Bowlegs in Simms's *The Forayers* (1855) is not typical of the contented slaves. Despite minor variances from the type, his physical appearance and selfless attachment to young "Mass Will" place him among the stock characters. His name suggests the physical defect that brands him with inferiority in this romantic novel of idealized whites who are all symmetrically proportioned. Former cavalryman and wartime henchman of the colonel, Ben in his old age is the competent manager of The Barony, his master's estate, and forceful "driver" of other people. The relationship between him and his master is almost reciprocal.

> "Push!" was the whole sum of Ben's policy. Push at the beginning, push at the middle, push at the end; be always pushing! And Ben's pushing made crops! He never slept on performances *done,* as Negroes and common people are very apt to do. He passes to new ones. He was a moral steam-engine, working himself, and driving everyone ahead. He pushed his master as well as his brother-slaves; and assigned him his tasks with the pertinacity of one who resolved to be something more than a counselor.
>
> His reverence for his master was never such as simply to endeavor to *please* him. Ben Bowlegs delivered the truth in spite of consequences. Was Colonel Sinclair about to blunder? Ben interposed abruptly enough, with "Look yer, Maussa, ef you wants to play h–ll wid de crap, da's jist de way for do um. Better now, you go see arter dem blood haus in de pastur' . . . Da's what you to see arter! Leff de crap to you driber. You kin truss him!"[30]

With his young master, Ben's brusqueness is submerged in adoration. This is shown most clearly when Willie Sinclair returns from a dangerous mission and admits that he had often been hungry while he was away.

> . . . ebery time I sets down to my dinner—I says, Lawd,
> ef I could only gee Mass Willie a bit ob dis bacon or
> a plate ob dis rice, or a wing ob dis chicken, or a dozen
> ob dese eggs, or a bowl ob dis coffee, or somet'ing or
> udder, such as I has a-hissing and a-smoking before
> me; wha's evver I hab for my own eating dat day.[31]

Ben's attachment recalls the black daddy image we saw
earlier in *The Partisan Leader*. Figuratively, in Negro character delineation, Simms is speaking from the same rostrum
as Tucker. Both are trying to justify slavery. It is only in
this way, however, that Ben resembles Daddy Tom. Ben is
lustier than Tom, ready to combat the "marauding rap-
scallions" who threaten the plantation and any of its inhabitants; for The Barony is his home, and its inhabitants
are his family.

Counter Images

Appearing concurrently with the contented slave image
and its variant forms is a counter stereotype that goes
farther than either Tucker or Simms in idealizing Negro
characters. Obviously propaganda, Mrs. Sophia Little's novel
Thrice Through the Furnace (1852) contains examples of
such idealization. She admits that the 1850 Fugitive Slave
Law aroused her to fight against the social evils of slavery
that destroyed "all the purity of attachment between the
sexes."[32]

The names of Mrs. Little's countertypes are romantically
florid and tend to type the characters as effectively as the
names assigned to most accommodative slave types. Two
mulatto youths are named Gilbert and Jasmyn; the principal females are named Marian, Cornelia, and Sybil. Mrs.
Little's descriptions of her characters are as "purple" as
their names. Jasmyn is tall, slender, unusually handsome,
and somewhat effete. According to Mrs. Little, his name is
well suited to his "poetical soul and sweet nature."[33] Marian
has "rose-tinted olive" skin, "large, soft, gazelle-like eyes,"
"pearly teeth and roseate lips," "raven curls."[34] Cornelia is

"a noble specimen of the Americanized African," and her figure is "replete with natural strength and dignity."[35] In contrast, an accommodative slave named Pete, who spies on other slaves and reports to the master, is black, "short, thick and grotesque."[36]

A sampling of their speech is all that is needed to complete this counterimage. On her deathbed, the mother of Gilbert and Marian confesses, "Thou and thy sister . . . are the children of our Master. God has forgiven me, for thou knowest the sin was not mine."[37] When Marian learns of the mother's death, she cries, "Gibby, dear Gibby. . . . Oh! is mother dead? Ah! What shall we poor children do?"[38]

Pomp (Pompey) in John T. Trowbridge's once famous anti-slavery novel, *Cudjo's Cave* (1863), is another idealized black portrait. In no sense is he ironically complimented with the name of a famous ancient. If anything, he is more perfect than any mortal ever was or could be.

> A form of imposing stature appeared. It was that of a Negro upwards of six feet in height, magnificently proportioned, straight as a pillar, and black as ebony. . . .[39]
>
> The Negro's demeanor was well calculated to inspire calmness and trust. There was something truly grand and majestic, not only in his person, but in his character also. He was a superman.[40]

This is what Penn Hapgood, a Quaker abolitionist, thinks of Pomp:

> He thought him the most perfect specimen of a gentleman he had ever seen; always cheerful, always courteous, always comporting himself with the ease of an equal in the presence of a guest. His strength was enormous. . . . But his grace was no less than his vigor. He was, in short, a lion of a man.[41]

Pomp and another runaway slave, Cudjo, hide out in a mountain cave not far from the town in which their owners live. The townsfolk are divided over the slavery question, and bands of Secessionists and Unionists fight periodically near the fugitives' cave. Pomp's relationship with Cudjo and all others is non-reciprocal because he is

always in total command of himself and of any situation
in which he finds himself. In one episode the Unionists
take refuge in the forest that surrounds the cave. A fire
breaks out. In their frantic haste to escape a ring of fire
encircling them, the men forget everything else. Pomp, having observed their panic, calmly and rationally admonishes,

> Gentlemen, . . . keep cool. I understand this ground
> perhaps better than you do. Don't abandon your game;
> you have lost your meal and potatoes and you will have
> need of the bear.[42]

In a skirmish, when everyone else is excited, if not terrified, his

> . . . eyes blazed, but he was perfectly cool. On one
> knee, his left foot advanced,—holding his rifle with
> one hand, and parting the bushes with the other, he
> smiled as he observed the situation.[43]

He is as coolly assured in verbal combat, having been
educated, along with his former master, in Europe. Deslow,
another character, defends the rights of slaveholders, even
though he is against seceding from the Union.

> "Not that I had anything against you Pomp . . . but
> you know as well as we do that we can't countenance
> a Nigger's running away, under any circumstances."
> "No!" said Pomp, with sparkling sarcasm. . . . "Your
> secessionist neighbors revolt against the mildest govern-
> ment in the world, and resort to bloodshed on account
> of some fancied wrongs. . . . But a Negro must not re-
> volt, he must not even attempt to run away, although
> he feels the relentless heel of oppression grinding into
> dust all his rights, all that is dear to him. . . . A white
> man may take up arms to defend a bit of property; but
> a black man has no right to rise up and defend either
> his wife, or his child or his liberty, or even his own life
> against his master!"[44]

Deslow tries to convince Pomp that the relationship between master and slave is that of property to its owner.
Pomp's logic is irrefutable:

. . . a man's natural, original owner is—himself. Now,
I never sold myself. My father never sold himself. My
father was stolen. . . . The man who bought him bought
what had been stolen. By your own laws you cannot
hold stolen property.[45]

The character's decisions bear further testimony to his
idealization. As a runaway slave who might reasonably be
worried about being captured, he chooses to remain in danger and to work along with Barber Jim, a free black, and
with the Unionists, despite his disapproval of some Unionists who either own slaves or defend slavery. His decision
is prompted by humanitarian and patriotic ideals. In another instance, he has an opportunity to avenge the wrongs
done him. He captures his evil owner, judges him, sentences
him to death, and is ready to kill him when the daughter
of a pacifist intercedes, not so much to save the owner's
life as to prevent Pomp from committing an ignoble act.
He spares the man, in a speech that is reminiscent of Pros-
pero's renunciation:

. . . our little accounts are now closed for the present,
and my business with you ends. I trust you will pardon
the inconvenience I have found necessary to subject you
to . . . I no longer have any ill will towards . . . you.
Go in peace, I emancipate you. . . . You are free.[46]

Comprising a tightly knit, contrasting unit of characterization along with Pomp, we find Cudjo, who reverts to
primitive behavior and will be analyzed later within that
context, and Toby, who represents another extension of the
accommodative slave and throws light on our next category
—the legally free but still enslaved stock character. But
first we might profitably examine Barber Jim, who was
mentioned earlier.

Barber Jim represents a character type that is unusual
in fiction published before the end of the Civil War. He
is different from the Caesars, Daddy Toms, and idealized
Pomps. With him, personal interests come first in importance, and humanitarian concerns for others second. Formerly a slave, he bought his freedom and that of his family

by working hard, shrewdly assessing situations, and taking
advantage of his opportunities. With freedom for himself
and his family accomplished, he established himself in a
barber shop that became headquarters for Unionists in the
community. There is a strong suggestion that the shop may
have been a way station in the Underground Railroad. An
interesting sidelight to his other activities is that he sold
bootleg liquor. Unfortunately, Trowbridge does not give him
as much space and attention in the novel as he does Pomp,
Cudjo, and Toby.

Free Slaves

Although Toby is free at the time the story takes place,
he prefers to remain in the service of his former master
and seeks no other reward than to serve him, his family,
and their friends. In his mind, he owns all of them, except
his master's elder daughter who is married to a worthless
Secessionist. On the day of her marriage, he vows, "I washes
my hands of her! She ain't no more chile ob mine!"[47] He
firmly believes that his white "family" cannot survive without his devoted care. When the Secessionists force the
master to take refuge in Cudjo's cave, the old servant, left
alone, insists simplemindedly, "Massa can't lib widout ol'
Toby, dat's a fac'."[48]
Later when he and his young mistress are separated
while searching for the cave, he accidentally meets a friend
of the master and cries sorrowfully, "Don't say you hain't
seen her, Massa Penn! Ye kill ol' Toby if ye do! I done
lost her." When Penn tells him that both master and young
mistress are safe, Toby responds selflessly, "Jes say . . . ye'll
take me to see em, den dis ol' nigger'll bress you and de
Lord and dem, and be willin' fur to die!"[49]
At the end of the novel, Toby's earnings, amassed over
the years since his manumission, assist the family to escape
to Ohio. The only way that they can show their gratitude
is by taking him with them; he will accept nothing else.

If you's gwine to tank anybody, ye better jes' tink
and tank yersef! Who gib ol' Toby his freedom, and

'den 'spose to pay him wages? Reckon if't hadn't been
fur dat, massa, I neber should had de bressed chance
to do dis yer little ting fur de family![50]

Although he is legally free, he is so emotionally attached
to his former owners that he cannot leave them.
Probably the most sentimentally drawn of earlier free
slaves are those created by Joel Chandler Harris. Among
these, the best known are Uncle Remus, Ananias, and Free
Joe. Uncle Remus is a warm, lovable, darky-daddy who
shows his emotional attachment to his white "family" when
he boasts, "All old Miss's chilluns call me daddy."[51] His
own wife and children rank second in his affections. How
Remus came to include Miss Sally's Northern husband in
the circle of those he loves is related by him to the Northerner's sister, Theodosia, when she visits the South after
the war.

During the war, Remus was left to protect Old Miss and
the other women when Mars Jeems rode off to war. Ironically, Remus was as much a rebel as any of the Southern
whites. Like a good watchdog, he observed troop movements and devotedly guarded the women and their possessions. He was particularly careful about watching a
Union soldier who sat perched in a tree, shooting down
stray rebels who happened to ride down a road leading to
his master's plantation. One day he saw Mars Jeems coming past the tree in which the soldier was stationed. Without hesitation, he shot the soldier and saved his master's
life. At this point, Miss Theodosia interrupts the narrative
to berate the old man for shooting a soldier who was risk-
ing his life to liberate slaves. What she did not realize was
that devotion to his "white folks" was stronger than the
lure of freedom: ". . . we'en I see dat man take aim, en
Mars Jeems gwine home to Ole Miss en Miss Sally, I des
disremembered all 'bout freedom en lammed aloose."[52] The
wounded soldier lost an arm but was nursed back to health
by Ole Miss, Remus, and Miss Sally; later he became the
young woman's husband. Again Miss Theodosia interrupted,
"But you cost him an arm." With simple dignity, Remus
pointed to Miss Sally and said, "I gin 'em dem," and then

he pointed to his own strong arms and added, "en I gin 'em deze— . . . En ef dem ain't nuff for anny man den I done los' de way."[53]

Ananias is compelled, by some urging within himself, to return to his master after three years of freedom following the Civil War. The Georgia scene depicted by Harris is one of utter desolation and Ananias is "the forlornest spectacle of all" when he returns, dressed in a ragged blue army outfit, having just returned from following Sherman's army on its march to the sea.

Harris skillfully manipulates name and appearance to build a pathetically ludicrous image:

> "I'm name' Ananias, suh," he replied.
>
> The name seemed to fit him exactly, a meaner looking negro Lawyer Terrell had never seen. There was not the shadow of a smile on his face, and seriousness ill became him. He had what is called a hang-dog look. . . . With a good deal of experience with negroes, Lawyer Terrell had never seen one whose countenance and manner were more repulsive.
>
> "Well," said the lawyer, . . . "Ananias is a good name."
>
> "Yessir," he replied; "dat w'at mammy say. Mammy done dead now, but she say dat dey wuz two Ananiases.
>
> Dey wuz ole Ananias en Young Ananias. One on um wuz de Liar, en de udder wuz de Poffit."
>
> Lawyer Terrell laughed. . . .[54]

His name and face coupled with his cast-off Union uniform make him understandably suspect in postwar Georgia. How could anyone trust him or believe that he still loves his old master? Everything about him gives the lie to his true motives and feelings that are made known later in the story. When asked why he has returned, he replies, "Dat my home, suh. . . . I wuz des 'bleege ter come back."[55]

Bit by bit, the events contributing to this situation are gradually revealed. Ananias had never been liked or trusted by his master; and when Sherman's army marched into the area, Ananias was accused of treachery, on circumstantial evidence. Actually the guilty ones were the poor-white overseer and another slave, the carriage driver, both of whom the master trusted. Ananias was unable to vindicate himself; for his culture called him inferior, and he had been too well conditioned to doubt or question:

> I know'd dey didn't like me . . . en I wuz mos' out'n my head, kaze I ain't know w'at ter do. 'Tain't wid niggers like it is wid white folks, suh. White folks know w'at ter do, kaze dey in de habits er doin' like dey wanter, but niggers, suh—niggers, dey is diffunt. Dey dunner w'at ter do[56]

and this:

> . . . I dunner w'at de name er God come 'cros me. I wuz dat full up dat I can't talk. I tried ter tell Marster dez 'zackly how it wuz, but look like I wuz all choke up. White folks kin talk right straight 'long, but niggers is diffunt.[57]

Acting upon instinct, he joined Sherman's forces, supposing they would pay him, and vowed to return later to vindicate himself somehow and to let his master know that he was not a deserter in times of distress.

His story, related to Lawyer Terrell, won the white man's confidence despite his name, appearance, and behavior which helped form derogatory opinions about him. But he still was unable to speak out. Only by his behavior could he show his young master and young mistress that he loved them. By this time, the poor-white overseer had become affluent by using underhand methods to transfer land and holdings from his former employer to himself, thus reducing the employer to poverty. Ananias equalized the disadvantages somewhat by stealing food from the overseer for the master and young mistress. His thievery was discovered; he was arrested and arraigned. Colonel Fluellen, the master, was sorry to see Ananias in such trouble but would not promise to pay his bail, even though he had survived on the food his former slave had stolen. The colonel still believed that this Negro could not be trusted. Nor did anyone else in the community trust him. It happened that Lawyer Terrell, at this time the greatest lawyer practicing in the circuit, was in court when Ananias's case was called. Somehow believing in Ananias,

Lawyer Terrell agreed to defend "the boy." Under his skillful questioning, Ananias was able not only to vindicate his thefts but to exonerate himself in the eyes of his master and the community. The master approached him afterwards,

> "Come, boy, let's go home."
> "Me, Marster?" said the Negro, looking up with a dazed expression. It was the tone, and not the words, that Ananias heard.
> "Yes, old fellow, your Miss Nelly will be waiting for us."
> "Name er God!" exclaimed Ananias, and then he arose and followed his old master out of the court-room.[58]

Ananias never questions his master's failure to understand him. Nor does he censure the master in any way for being so obtuse. Just being allowed to serve the master is enough.

Harris's main character in "Free Joe and the Rest of the World" (1884), unlike Remus and Ananias, is not emotionally attached to a white master. He is that anomaly of antebellum days in the South, a free Negro enslaved by the system. Harris, a Southern apologist for slavery, describes some of the difficulties Joe encountered.

> He was a black atom, drifting hither, and thither without an owner, blown about by all the winds of circumstances and given over to shiftlessness.[59]

The free Negro was regarded fearfully by whites because

> . . . he was the embodiment of that vague and mysterious danger that seemed to be forever lurking on the outskirts of slavery, ready to sound a shrill and ghostly signal in the impenetrable swamps, and steal forth under the midnight stars to murder, rapine and pillage,—a danger always threatening, and yet never assuming shape; intangible, and yet real, impossible and yet not improbable.[60]

In addition to the white man's fear of him, Joe was exiled from the support and comfort that other Negroes could give him.

If the slaves secretly envied him his freedom (which is to be doubted, considering his miserable condition), they openly despised him, and lost no opportunity to treat him with contumely.[61]

We can appreciate Harris's skill in building a case for slavery. Joe was in a worse position as a free man than he had been in when he was enslaved. Challenged by every white he met, he became not the slave of one man but of all. The only people with whom he might associate freely were poor whites, called "trash" by the aristocratic landed gentry and their slaves. Had Joe still been a slave he would have behaved as scornfully toward them. In addition, as a free man, his slave marriage to his wife Lucindy was all but nullified. Her master refused him permission to visit her. In stealth, they used to meet near the house of Becky Staley, a poor white, who had a reputation as a seeress in the neighborhood. When Lucindy's master discovered that they were meeting secretly, he sent her away. Joe became worried, consulted Becky, whose cards indicated that Lucindy had gone on a journey, a revelation that meant only one thing to Joe: his wife had been sold. Becky's brother was not helpful when he reminded Joe of the old saying, "new master, new nigger." Joe repudiated both of them and continued waiting, certain that as soon as she could, Lucindy would return to him. One morning Becky and her brother found him dead. He had been as bound by the slave system as those who had not been freed.

The free slave image was used by many authors after Harris and Trowbridge. Among these are Frank Stockton's Uncle Elijah in "The Cloverfields Carriage" (1886), Thomas Nelson Page's assortment of quaint uncles in *In Ole Virginia* (1887) and in *Red Rock* (1898), Charles Waddell Chesnutt's Uncle Julius in "The Goophered Grapevine" (1887), Sarah Orne Jewett's Peter in "The Mistress of Sydenham Plantation" (1890), Thomas Dixon's Nelse in *The Leopard's Spots* (1902), and O. Henry's Uncle Caesar in "A Municipal Report" (1910).

In "The Cloverfields Carriage" by Stockton, Uncle Elijah, dignified coachman for the Cloverfields during slavery, felt

compelled after emancipation to assert his independence by
seeking employment elsewhere. He found it hard to relinquish his former respected position in the community and
disliked his "yaller" replacement, Montague Braxton, intensely. Much more, he missed the close association he had
with his white "family." One night he saw their carriage
being driven recklessly down a road toward the railroad station. Thinking that his Miss Jane might be in danger, he
jumped into the vehicle, subdued the horses, only to discover
that Montague was alone. By that time, the carriage had
reached the station. Elijah decided to rest there a while before returning it to Miss Jane. It just happened that a train,
carrying his mistress's estranged son, stopped at the station.
The young man, seeing Elijah, as if he were waiting for him,
could travel no farther from his home and the people he
loved. Elijah, realizing that he had been instrumental in re-
uniting his mistress and her son, was emptied of his pride
and returned home also.

> He forgot he had a vote, he forgot he could serve on
> a jury. He simply took off his hat, and coming forward
> said: "Yaas, Miss Jane, dis is me."[62]

Among the free slaves created by Thomas Nelson Page,
probably the best known are Uncle Sam and Unc' Edinburg
in his collection of tales, *In Ole Virginia*. Both are nostalgic
raconteurs of idyllic plantation life, "befo' de wah." Uncle
Sam and his master's white-pelted dog were the only sur-
vivors living on what had been his Marse Chan's plantation.
To Sam the dog had become a symbol of his owner's sacred
memory, and Sam had transferred all of his devotion for the
white man to the animal. In the manner of a fractious but
loving slave, he fussed petulantly with the dog:

> "Yo so sp'ilt yo'kyahn hardly walk." . . . "Jes' like
> white folks—think 'cuz you's white and I's black, I got to
> wait on yo' all de time. Ne'm mine, I ain' gwine do it!"[63]

This onesided conversation was overheard by a stranger.
When Sam realized that an outsider had witnessed a personal
and private matter, he felt obliged to explain the situation:

"He know I don' mean nothin' by what I sez. . . . He know I'se jes projickin wid 'im." With characteristic loquacity, Sam began to reminisce about the beauty of the plantation before an unjust war disrupted a way of life that he thought perfect. Unc' Edinburg, another character in Page's collection of short stories, could have been Sam's twin brother in appearance and sentiment. Proudly, Unc' told a Northern white how wonderful Christmas celebrations had been before the war, and how benevolent owners had cared for and protected their slaves. The old man pitied free-issue Negroes who knew nothing of the joys of slavery.

Peter, in "The Mistress of Sydenham Plantation," follows much the same pattern. His only concern in life is to keep his mistress, a victim of amnesia, from discovering that her husband and sons had been killed during the war and that she is no longer mistress of their once beautiful and extensive plantation.

Thomas Dixon's Nelse, in *The Leopard's Spots*, is shown to be as devoted as the others in this sub-category of accommodative chattels; but the author adds to the portrait a comic relationship between the stock character and his wife Eve. In so doing, he makes them conform to the "Butterbeans and Susie" image that emerged from minstrel shows and later became popular in vaudeville. Nelse, learning that slave marriages are not legally binding, plans to remarry his wife but pretends that he will not because Eve is so shrewish and bossy. By this device, he hopes to frighten her into treating him with more respect. Eve, of course, stays one step ahead of him. Like "Bill Bailey's" wife, she puts him out of their house. Penitent, he capitulates, shows her a marriage license, and begs to be allowed to return. She reinforces her position, making him woo her with flowers and other gifts until she brings him to his knees and consents to remarry him.

Uncle Julius, in the late nineteenth-century stories of Charles Waddell Chesnutt, a mulatto, is different from the other characters in this category despite his Roman name, dialect, loquaciousness, and deference to whites. When we first see him in "The Goophered Grapevine," which was published in *The Atlantic Monthly* in 1887, he is sitting near a neglected vineyard on one end of a pine log, that is under a shade tree, enjoying a hatful of luscious scuppernong grapes. When the narrator, a Northern vintner, and his wife approach, he rises respectfully and moves away in the customary manner expected of a venerable accommodationist who must either stand in the presence of whites or find a seat elsewhere. When invited to remain with them, he sits but appears embarrassed.

The Northerner plans to take up residence in a warm climate because of his wife's recent illness and is looking for a suitable vineyard that he might purchase. He asks Uncle Julius if he knows anything about the one adjacent to them; and the old man responds, "Lawd bless yer, suh, I knows all about it. Dey ain' na'er a man in dis settlement w'at won' tell yer old Julius McAdoo 'uz bawn an' raise' on dis yer same plantation." The ice broken, he continues in a way that suggests something approaching a reciprocal relationship: "Well, suh, you is a stranger ter me, en I is a stranger ter you, en we is bofe stranger ter one anudder, but 'f I 'uz in yo' place, I wouldn' buy dis vimya'd." The reason for this advice is not, as it is for other accommodative free slaves, because the old plantation is held sacred by him to the memory of his former owner, Dugul' McAdoo, whom Uncle Julius, in contrast to other free slaves, remembers as lazy and stingy. It is because the vineyard is goophered or conjured. When asked how he knows it is goophered, he cannily goes to work on them: " 'I wouldn' spec' fer you ter b'lieve me 'less you know all 'bout de fac's. But ef you en young miss dere doan' min' lis'n'in' ter ole nigger run on a minute er two w'ile you er restin', I kin 'splain to yer how it all happen'.' "

In rhythmic dialect, he tells how the vineyard was bewitched by the local conjure woman, Aunt Peggy, at the request of old Duguld McAdoo to keep his slaves and those from neighboring plantations, as well as the free blacks and poor whites in the vicinity, from reducing his profits by stealing his scuppernongs. The spell brought about the desired results with only minor accompanying difficulties. One incident, however, proved advantageous to the slaveowner but fatal to one of his slaves, Henry, who ate some of the grapes and had to be taken to Aunt Peggy for removal of the spell. She gave him a drink of her conjure medicine, which tasted

"like whiskey wid sump'n bitter in it," and advised him, as
next step in the cure, to take some sap from the grapevines
and carefully rub it on his bald head. Uncle Julius's humorous narrative of what happened to Henry's hair reveals one
aspect of self-rejection common among Negroes who have
uncritically accepted the idea that straight hair, such as
whites have, is "good" hair, that their own kinky hair is "bad"
hair, and that the closer they approximate the white "norm,"
the better as people they consider themselves to be.

> Up to dat time he wuz es ball es a sweeten' 'tater, but
> des es soon ez de young leaves begun ter come out on de
> grapevines de ha'r begun ter grow out on Henry's head,
> en by de middle er de summer he had de bigges' head er
> ha'r on de plantation. Befo' dat, Henry had *tol'able good*
> ha'r 'roun' de aidges, but soon ez de young grapes be-
> gun ter come Henry's ha'r begun ter quirl all up in little
> balls, des like dis yer reg'lar grape ha'r, en by de time de
> grapes got ripe his head look des like a bunch er grapes.
> Combin' it didn' do no good; he wuk at it ha'f de night wid
> er Jim Crow [currycomb], en think he git it straighten'
> out, but in de mawnin' de grapes 'ud be dere des de
> same. So he gin it up, en tried ter keep de grapes down by
> havin' his ha'r cut sho't. (Italics are not in the original.)[64]

The vines flourished; the harvest increased. Henry became
strong and youthfully hirsute every spring but regressed,
becoming old and bald, every fall, until a Northern vintner
was called in, inadvisedly in Uncle Julius's opinion, to further
increase the crop. He was allowed to tamper with the
vines and did so much damage that both the vines and
Henry withered and died. As proof that the vines had been
goophered, Uncle Julius offers to show the white man the
site of Henry's grave. He continues the tale. New vines were
planted, but some of the old ones survived. It is, therefore,
dangerous for anyone but Julius to eat the grapes from the
vineyard because only he can distinguish the new from the
goophered vines. Anyone else might be afflicted as Henry
was.

In spite of Julius's advice, the Northerner buys the vineyard and brings it back to its former state of perfection. He

later discovers that Uncle Julius, who has always lived on the plantation, has "derived a respectable revenue from the product of the neglected grapevines." Both men are satisfied with the new arrangement, however. According to the narrator, "the wages I pay him for his services [as coachman] are more than the equivalent for anything he lost by the sale of the vineyard."

An early twentieth-century depiction of the free slave is Uncle Caesar in "A Municipal Report" (1910) by O. Henry. In the surprise ending of the story, he, as agent and judge, makes an important decision. He is a coach driver in Nashville, Tennessee, and protector of Azalea Adair, an impoverished gentlewoman. She is married to the town reprobate, "Major" Wentworth Caswell, but is forced to support him by writing literary articles. Inevitably, the money she earns finds its way into Caswell's pockets for his liquor and gambling expenses.

The narrator of the story, a transplanted Southerner, facetiously looks down his nose at the South and especially at the sentimental devotion of blacks for their special white folk. In this vein, he describes the city's atmosphere as thirty parts London fog, ten parts malaria, twenty parts gas leaks, twenty-five parts dewdrops—"gathered in a brickyard at sunrise," and fifteen parts odor of honeysuckle. The description ends: "It is not so fragrant as a moth-ball nor as thick as pea soup; but 'tis enough—'twill serve." Continuing, O. Henry builds the portrait of Uncle Caesar. From the station, the narrator is carried to his hotel in a "tumbril," driven by "something dark and emancipated." He hastily gives "it" the fare, not wanting "to hear it prate about its old 'marster' or anything that happened 'befo' de wah.'" Later "it" was identified.

> He was a stalwart Negro older than the pyramids, with gray wool and a face that reminded me of Brutus, and a second afterwards of the late King Cetewayo.[65]

Describing Uncle Caesar as "older than the pyramids" is part of the surface tone of supercilious humor. Underneath lie respect and admiration for the old man's loyalty as it unfolds in the story. His reference to Brutus suggests not the old ironical pattern of slave-naming so much as the former slave's integrity. Reference to Cetewayo—a fierce, indomitable Zulu chief—implies ascription of these characteristics to Caesar. This magnificent image is believable in spite of his appearance. A tatterdemalion, he wears an ancient Confederate uniform that is held together with a yellow horn button.

The narrator, who comes to Nashville to negotiate a contract with Azalea, hires Caesar's carriage, gives her address, and tries to enter the vehicle.

> . . . the thick, gorilla-like arm of the old Negro barred me. On his massive and saturnine face a look of sudden suspicion and enmity flashed for a moment. Then with quickly returning conviction, he asked blandishingly: "What are you gwine there for boss?"
>
> "What is that to you?" I asked a little sharply.
>
> "Nothin', suh, jus' nothin'. Only it's a lonesome kind of part of town and few folks ever has business there. Step right in."[66]

At the decayed mansion, the narrator gives Caesar the customary fee plus a fifty percent tip.

> "It's two dollars, suh," he said.
>
> "How's that?" I asked. "I plainly heard you call out at the hotel: 'fifty cents to any part of town.' "
>
> "It's a long ways from the hotel."[67]

The narrator who, with nose in air earlier, disclaimed his Southern background, now retorts,

> Don't think you've picked up a greenhorn Yankee. Do you see those hills over there? . . . well, I was born and raised on their other side. You old fool nigger, can't you tell people from other people when you see 'em?[68]

At these words, Caesar shifts tactics, and their relationship continues on a new footing.

> The grim face of King Cetewayo softened. "Is you from the South, suh? . . ."
>
> "Then the charge is fifty cents, I suppose?" said I inexorably.
>
> His former expression, a mingling of cupidity and hostility, returned, remained ten seconds, and vanished.

"Boss," he said, "fifty cents is right; but I *needs* two dollars, suh, I'm obleeged to have two dollars. I ain't *de-mandin'* it now, suh, after I knows whar you's from; I'm jus' sayin' that I *has* to have two dollars tonight, and business is mighty po'."

Peace and confidence settled upon his heavy features. He had been luckier than he had hoped. Instead of having picked up a greenhorn, he had come upon an inheritance.

"You confounded old rascal," I said, reaching down to my pocket, "You ought to be turned over to the police."

For the first time I saw him smile. He knew; *he knew;* HE KNEW.[69]

The money finds its way into Caswell's possession. The next night, he is found dead. His body is carried to a drug-store where, unnoticed by any of the assembled crowd except the narrator, Caesar's yellow horn button falls from the dead man's fist. The narrator pockets it, and later tosses it out of the train window as he travels north.

Faulkner's Tobe, in "A Rose for Emily" (1931), is a more recent depiction of this stock character. Although very little is told about him in the story, much can be inferred; and there can be little doubt that he performed devoted service for his employer. Daily, over a number of years, he was observed by the townsfolk doing the routine things that were necessary to keep his Miss Emily physically alive. What is more, he performed these services in silence, not gossiping about her and the macabre secret locked in the second-floor bedroom of her decaying mansion. The reader can only guess about his revulsion during those years. Freed by her death, he waited just long enough to admit the outsiders who could do the final necessary things, and then "he walked right through the house and out the back door and was not seen again."[70]

Brutes

Toward the latter part of the nineteenth century a second current, running counter to the free-slave pattern, made its appearance. Like all of the other stock blacks, this counter-type reflected cultural attitudes, specifically the self-righteous indignation of whites against those blacks who had the effrontery to challenge the doctrine of white superiority and to promote the doctrine of black equality. Such blacks had to be vilified. Thomas Dixon, foremost exponent of this attitude, wrote,

> . . . and over all the earth hung the shadow of the freed Negro, transformed by the exigency of war from a Chattel to be bought and sold into a possible Beast to be feared and guarded.[71]

Some examples of this counter image are Moses in Thomas Nelson Page's *Red Rock* (1898), Abram in Sarah Barnwell Elliott's "An Incident" (1899), Dick in Thomas Dixon's *The Leopard's Spots* (1902), and Gus in *The Clansman* (1905).

Page's character is called Moses the Trick-Doctor, an association of given name and epithet which identifies him as a false prophet and evil leader of other free but equally ignorant black men. In physical appearance he is grotesque: "a yaller nigger" whose protruding lower jaw, deformed teeth, blue gums, villainously low forehead, and furtive, rolling eyes that "looked in quite different directions" immediately brand him the brute that his behavior proves him to be. He wears large brass earrings and a fetishistic necklace of blue and white beads. Dr. Moses was adept at swaying Negro audiences by appealing to their emotions. The purpose of his carefully contrived appeals was not to help his people but to further his own selfish ends and to promote the punitive schemes of scalawags and carpetbaggers, seeking to manipulate culture symbols in a way that would humiliate Southern whites. One of their schemes was to disfranchise whites and raise the former slaves to positions of political and social importance over whites. Deliberately calculated to offend and infuriate whites was this idea that, according to Page, the disreputable whites had instilled in Moses:

> I'm jest as good as any white man, and I'm goin' to show 'em so. I'm going' to marry a white 'ooman and meck white folks wait on me.[72]

He carried out his plan by attempting to rape an altruistic Northern white woman who had come South to start a school for Negroes, thus proving the idea held by whites in the community that it was foolish to try to educate Negroes. In the end, the free Negroes who remained loyal to their former owners ran him out of the neighborhood.

Sarah Barnwell Elliott gave the name Abram Washington to the "strange Negro" in her short story titled simply "An Incident." His employer's wife disappeared mysteriously; a bloodstained garment was found; and Abram attracted suspicion to himself by running away and hiding in the woods where he was captured by an angry mob of whites. The sheriff tried to protect him even though he disliked helping a Negro. Just as the mob was ready to lynch him, the employer received a telegram from his wife telling him that she was safe and would be home shortly. Abram was released, but in a bitter anticlimax the reader learns that he was possibly a rapist and definitely a psychopathic killer. The wife reported: "I saw him . . . stealing up behind me—with the hatchet in his hand, and a look . . . such an awful, awful look!" Later, in a prison camp, Abram admitted: "I ent do much, . . . I des scare a white lady . . . De hatchet des cut 'e fool little bit; . . . I ent tech um; . . ."[73]

Unlike Abram Washington's, Dick's guilt in *The Leopard's Spots* by Thomas Dixon is never proved. His mischievousness as a child and later as an adolescent cast doubt not only on his innocence, if he was innocent, but more significantly on the wisdom of having abolished slavery and its control over the savage instincts and immoral behavior of blacks. Dick's parents became alcoholics after emancipation, and it was only because of former slaveowners that their son was rescued from an unsavory environment. But according to Dixon, bad blood cannot be purified. Nothing could protect Dick from his inheritance. He was a thief. He influenced his benefactors' son to assist in the disruption of a Negro church meeting, behavior that was excused as a boyish prank.

But when suspicion pointed to him as the raper-murderer of a poor-white child, altruistic whites realized finally that there was nothing good in him. His friends tried to get a fair trial for him, but the jungle beast in Dick had so enraged the decent and civilized townsfolk that they were forced into mob violence.

> . . . the crowd seemed to melt into a great crawling, swaying creature, half reptile, half beast, half dragon, half man, with a thousand legs, and a thousand eyes, and ten thousand gleaming teeth, and with no ear to hear and no heart to pity![74]

Without positive proof of his guilt, Dick was burned to death.

Concerning the guilt of Gus in *The Clansman,* there can be no doubt, if one can believe the evidence on which he was convicted. In any case, it seems that three years after Dixon wrote *The Leopard's Spots* he felt compelled to justify a lynching. After emancipation, Gus ran away, joined the Union army, and returned South after the war as a member of black occupation forces. There is no thinly veiled reference to the primitive in Dixon's description. Gus was all animal.

> He had the short, heavy-set neck of the lower order of animals. He skin was coal black, his lips so thick they curled both ways, up and down with crooked blood marks across them. His nose was flat and its enormous nostrils seemed in perpetual dilation. The sinister bead eyes, with brown splotches in their whites, were set wide apart and gleamed apelike under his scant brows. His enormous cheek bones and jaws seemed to protrude beyond the ears and almost hide them.[75]

Like other stock brutes he was predestined to harass, insult, and ravish. "A single tiger spring, and the black claws of the beast sank into the soft white throat and she was still."[76] He did not kill the girl, but she committed suicide in shame. That shame was extended to the mother, who jumped off a cliff with the daughter. Law officers could find no definite evidence proving Gus the rapist. A doctor, using a powerful French microscope, supplied the proof. He found Gus's animal face and form clearly etched on the retinas of the dead girl's eyes. The Knights of the Ku Klux Klan lynched him.

As no white female was safe from the brutish instincts of men like Gus and Dick, no white male was safe from their female counterpart, Lydia Brown, also in *The Clansman.*

A mulatto "of extra-ordinary animal beauty" and the pos-
sessor of "the fiery temper of a leopardess," her eyes rolled
from side to side, and her haughty dignity was merely a
veneer overlaying the "she-devil" inside.[77] Lydia was mistress
of the "Old Commoner," a Northern senator, whose insistence
on equality for Negroes and whose hatred for Southern
whites made him a formidable adversary in Congress. As the
senator became the most important man in the nation after
Lincoln's assassination, his consort became "first lady" in
the land, using her predatory charms to destroy him and the
nation. Worse yet, she took diabolical glee in humiliating
decent white men, who recoiled at the thought of touching
her, by putting them in the position of not being able to re-
fuse to shake hands with her when the senator forced them
to come to his house on business. As if that were not enough,
it was impossible for her type to remain faithful to any man:
she had an additional lover, a preacher named Silas Lynch,
who was as immoral, unethical, and ungrateful as she. He
had been educated by the senator, at Lydia's insistence, and
later made lieutenant governor of a Southern military prov-
ince by his benefactor. Dixon's description, showing the dual
nature of and cultural attitudes toward the mulatto, is one of
the clearest in literature.

> A man of charming features for a mulatto, who had
> evidently inherited the full characteristics of the Aryan
> race, while his dark yellowish eyes . . . glowed with the
> brightness of the African jungle.[78]

Buffoons

Another powerful stock character, the roots of which
extend back to Topsy (*Uncle Tom's Cabin*, 1852), and possibly farther, is the ludicrously comic Negro whose only literary purpose is to amuse. As we have noted, the Negro has
long been a comic literary figure. Even when he is a despicable character, he is portrayed as a grotesque—a combination
of the laughably ridiculous and the terrifying. The popularity
of the strictly comic image is due in large part to its contin-

ued use in minstrel shows by Negroes and by whites in black-face. Its popularity can be seen also in the frequency of its appearance, over a thirty-year period, in *Saturday Evening Post* stories written by Irvin S. Cobb, Octavus Roy Cohen, and Glenn Allan. If people had not wanted to read stories in which this stock character appeared, it is doubtful that a periodical such as this one, profitably catering as it did to popular demands, would have published them. The influence of popular periodicals in perpetuating literary stereotypes that reflect particular social attitudes is considerable.

One of the earliest writers delineating comic Negroes was E. K. Means, who was so well identified with this image that he boastfully described himself, in 1918, as "a writer of Negro stories who has made himself so completely *the* writer of Negro stories that this book needs no title."[79] His second collection of stories was identified simply as *More E. K. Means.*

Three of the characters he created appear in a number of his stories. They are Figger Bush, Skeeter Butts, and Vinegar Atts, characters whose names serve as humorous accompaniments to their comic descriptions. Figger is

> . . . a scarecrow sort of a Negro, with ragged flapping clothes. His coal black face formed a background for a little stubby, shoe brush mustache, and Figger thought that mustache justified his existence in the world. He had not much use for his coconut head except to support a battered wool hat and grow a luxuriant crop of kinky hair. He had an insuperable aversion to all sorts of work.[80]

Figger's cronies are equally ludicrous. Skeeter Butts is the small, yellow-skinned barkeeper of the Hen Scratch Saloon; Vinegar Atts is the fat, moon-faced preacher of the Shoofly Church, who looks "like a pot-bellied buzzard trying to fly upside-down and backwards."[81]

In "The Late Figger Bush," the main character seeks advice from these companions when he receives a letter from his grandfather in "Yalerbam," stating that the old man is returning home to spend the remainder of his life with Figger, his only relative. Figger is dismayed about the old man's return for two reasons. Twenty years earlier the two parted company abruptly after Figger stole money from the grandfather. Second, Grandfather's coming will necessitate Figger's getting and holding a regular job. The three cronies put their heads together and decide to ask Scootie Tandy, the local belle, to meet the old man at the railroad station pretending to be Figger's bereaved widow. They believe this hoax will influence the grandfather to return to Alabama on the next train. With easy consciences, the rascally preacher and barman promise to help her.

> "Me an' Vinegar will back her up in dat tale." Skeeter assures him. "De revun elder won't mind stretchin' de blanket a little for de sake of savin' a friend."
> "Dat's so!" Vinegar declared. "My life and my job is savin' niggers!"[82]

This is Means's description of Scootie:

> . . . a fat, good-natured young woman who wore red head-rags, wrapped up her kinky hair with strings to give it a better kink . . .[83]

She is no better than the three men, content to cadge clothing and food from the kitchen doors of whites. Having nothing better to do, she agrees to carry out her part in the hoax. For some time, she and Figger have been casting affectionate glances in each other's direction. People were beginning to wonder whether or not the two would marry; but in Skeeter's estimation (in the words of the author), they were "merely watching each other to see which one could live longest without work and without landing in jail for vagrancy."[84]

When Scootie meets Grandfather, she discovers that he has become a wealthy man by local standards. Recognizing fair game when he sees it, she double-crosses Figger and convinces the old man that he should remain in town with her as his housekeeper. For a while it looks as if Figger has outsmarted himself, but he soon hits on another plan. He marries Scootie; whereupon they both live a life of ease with Grandfather.

The most noteworthy example of comic menials is a

character named Jeff, created by Irvin S. Cobb, in the Judge Priest series. Cobb made Jeff the central character of his novel, *J. Poindexter, Colored*, published serially in *The Saturday Evening Post* in 1922. Events are presented in the first person with Jeff as narrator. His name, Jefferson Exodus Poindexter, provides the first clue to his comic portrait.

> The Jefferson part is for a white family which my folks worked for one time before I was born, and the Exodus is because my Mammy craved I should be named after somebody out of the Bible.[85]

After his departure from Kentucky to New York, where he achieves economic but not emotional independence, he changes his name to Col. J. Exeter Poindexter, Esq. This is how he decides on the *Col.* part of his name: " 'Col.' is short for 'cullid'; ain't it? So I jest shortens up 'cullid' into 'Col.' an' switches it from the caboose end to the front end." *Exodus* is changed to *Exeter* because the latter seems "mo' stylish." Tacking *Esq.* at the end makes the name "mo' bindin' like the button on a rattlesnake's tail."[86]

Jeff's simple-minded verbosity, misuse of words, and occasional use of effective low puns are other aspects of this stock image. Explaining why he needs the help of his employer in narrating his story, he employs the first two aspects:

> He says to me he will fix up the spelling wherever needed and attend to the punctuation; but all the rest will be my own just like I puts it down. I reads and writes very well, but someway I never learned to punctuate. So the places where it is necessary to be punctual to make good sense and keep everything regular and make the talk sound natural is his doings, and also some of the spelling.[87]

A very good example of the third aspect occurs when Jeff, writing about legal fees, commiserates, "Lawyers are plenty costive persons to hire."[88]

Cobb's treatment of Jeff is sympathetic, almost loving. He makes Jeff the epitome of stability and common sense in contrast to Jeff's employer, who is naïve in relationships with women and impractical in business. In an encounter with two confidence men, Jeff not only avoids falling into their trap but emerges from the encounter five dollars richer. His employer, Dallas Pulliam, is not so lucky. He is duped into investing in a nonexistent oil company and almost tricked into marrying a fortune-hunting woman. It is Jeff who extricates him from both schemers and sends him back to Paducah a wiser man than when he left. Jeff remains in New York, an affluent co-owner of a Negro theatrical agency.

Despite Jeff's apparent ability to make common sense decisions, he is not an individual as defined here. He is a sympathetically delineated representative of the clever darky in literature who "prefers" Southern attitudes toward him because he is not ready, first of all, to accept himself as the equal of whites. A good example of this inability is revealed when his employer invites him to sit in the train coach for whites when the train passes the mythical line separating North from South. Jeff argues,

> I finds myself more comfortable there than I has been riding up front in the colored compartment, but lesser easy in my mind. I enjoys the feel of them soft seats and yet I gets sort of uneasy setting up amongst so many strange white folks.[89]

Second, he is willing to accept himself as the equal of Northern whites but promises his young master not to alter his servile behavior with Southerners whenever he encounters them. His reason is that Northern whites are underprivileged: "They ain't had the 'vantage of bein' raised the way you an' me is, an' wants to pamper me all up."[90] These arguments are used by Cobb, a twentieth-century Southern apologist, not only to show that Negroes "prefer" segregation but, more importantly that they recognize the superiority of Southern whites.

Unlike Jeff, the comical characters created by Octavus Roy Cohen do not often come in contact with any whites except law enforcement officers. These buffoons live isolated in an all-Negro town in Birmingham, Alabama. Located there are Sallie Crouch's Cozy Home for Colored, Yeast and Snead's Tailoring Emporium, Bud Peaglar's Barbecue Lunch Room and Billiard Parlor, The Sons and Daughters of I Will Arise Auditorium, Midnight Pictures Corporation, along with some other pretentiously named places.

Names and appearances are sufficient to identify the types. Here again, cultural attitudes are evident in names assigned to the characters, some reflecting general American patterns, others reminiscent of the sardonic humor of white medical students and interns who delivered black babies in black neighborhoods and influenced ignorant black mothers to give their babies names that were medical terms for such things as genitalia and pathological conditions.[91] In a family magazine like *The Saturday Evening Post,* Cohen could not use such precise terms, but the ones he uses reflect this pattern. Among the more unusual are Orifice Latimer, loud-mouthed president of the Midnight Pictures Corporation; Honeydew, his ample wife with the heaving bosom; Forcep Swain, an author; Dilemma Williams, "a dusky vampire by whom colored gentlemen wished to be lured to destruction, or worse"; Anopheles Ricketts, a social gadfly, Chlorine Gannit and Sis' Callie Flukers, gossips. All are like playful puppies, complacently leading fun-filled lives.

Cohen's main character is called Florian Slappey, a name that describes him perfectly. He is the frivolous, vain, nattily dressed Beau Brummel of the town. In dress, he favors striped silk shirts and pearl-gray suits with balloon-shaped trousers. He spends his time getting in and out of farcical scrapes, avoiding marriage, imitating whites, and engaging in several varieties of horseplay. Housed in a man-sized body is the happy-go-lucky mind of an irresponsible child. One story will serve to establish Cohen's comical type. Throughout the years that the stories appeared in *The Saturday Evening Post,* the only variables connected with them were artists' illustrations.

In "Horse-and-Buggy Daze" we find Florian struggling with the World War II shortage of gasoline. Ostensibly to help the war effort, but mainly to line his own pockets, Florian decides to start a "cullid folks livery stable." His main difficulties are finding money to back his venture and influencing townsfolk to use horse-drawn vehicles instead of automobiles. Semore Mashby, the local loan-maker, agrees to underwrite the venture and draws up a contract favoring himself instead of Florian. With regard to the second problem, Florian decides to use the prestige of a Negro motion picture star, believing that if she uses his equipment, other people will imitate her; or in his own words, "I'll git Geraldine Watson to come to Bummin'ham fo' two-th'ee weeks to shill for us."[92] Throughout the improbable events that follow, Florian's luck stays with him, as it usually does in all of the stories, and he is victorious at the end of the story.

Glenn Allan's stories, published during the 1940's in *The Saturday Evening Post*, are built around another clever darky type whose name is Herbert Washington but who is called Boysi by all except his employer's wife, a somewhat pretentious character, who reservedly calls him Herbert. His nickname reminds one of the Southern practice of calling all Negro males "boy" no matter how old or venerable they might be. Following the practice of modern writers, Glenn Allan does not give precise descriptions of Boysi's appearance. Artists' sketches, accompanying the stories, visualize him as a dark mulatto.

As cook, butler, gardener, baby-sitter, and, on one occasion, substitute father to his employers' children, Boysi has ample opportunity to make decisions, but all in the nature of services to his "whitefolks." This is not to say that he overvaluates them and neglects himself. As a humorous and clever darky, he is depicted as having the ability to do what must be done, but doing it in devious and enigmatic ways. In one of the first stories published, Boysi decides that his boss needs a new car. Not only does it embarrass him to be seen driving Mr. Oates's dilapidated automobile, but it humiliates him to work for a man who claims he cannot afford a new one. Boysi decides further that an oak-paneled station wagon, that he calls a "yaller cha'iot," is the proper kind of vehicle for the family. A new automobile is the last thing Mr. Oates wants to think about at this time because, first, the family owns two cars and, second, he is having trouble negotiating a loan to expand his business. The bank president hesitates to approve the loan, believing that Mr. Oates is too stodgily unimaginative to succeed in an expanded business.

Boysi, without weighing consequences, hoodwinks the

manager of an automobile agency into letting him negotiate a contract for the new station wagon using an old car as down payment. Mr. Oates, furious at first but encouraged by Boysi's daring, convinces the bank president that his application should be approved. Elated by his good fortune, Mr. Oates jokingly hints that perhaps the family could find use for a third car. Boysi's reaction reveals the "cuteness" that is typical of the humorous menial.

> Then a pall of utter horror overspread his joy, his eyes puckered and he let out a howl of dismay. "Boss, you know what 'at means? It means I'll have th'ee cyars to tend. Well it stric'ly ain't possible. Already, I works from can-see in the morning to can't-see at night without ha'dly settin' down. Boss, if you took a pry bar you couldn't squeeze another minute into my workin' clock. My clock stric'ly don't hold the time to tend th'ee cyars." He paused delicately. "Not at m' present wages."[93]

Contemporary Figures

Contemporary fictional descendants of stock Negroes are delineated by James Gould Cozzens, Chester Himes, and Ossie Davis, showing a trend toward non-stereotyped depictions of these figures.

In James Gould Cozzens's novel *By Love Possessed* (1957), a descendant of the stock Negro servant is named Alfred Revere. He is the grandson of a slave who escaped to relative freedom in the North. There, the former slave took the name Paul Revere, became the sexton of Christ Church, steward of the church's private club, and patriarch of a large family. His descendants for three generations thereafter have followed him in both jobs. Cozzens describes Paul's grandson Alfred as the latter stands talking to Arthur Winner, a lawyer and the novel's main character.

> He stood quiet, his spare frame held straight. He was bareheaded; and the tight dense frizzles of light gray hair clung like wool to his narrow skull. His bony intelli-

gent black face, in which, too, Arthur Winner saw a cast of gray, was grave.[94]

Concerning his sense of identity, we are told that Alfred "held himself high" and that, like his grandfather, "knew the difference between involuntary servitude's shame, and the freeman's dignity of choosing to serve. . . ."[95] As a result, he commands the respect and concern of Arthur Winner, who sees signs of illness on Alfred's face.

Alfred tells Winner that he has been advised by his doctor to retire from work because of a heart ailment, that he has delayed making a decision because he dreads living the life of a semi-invalid. His hesitance is due not so much to concern for other people as for himself and how he wants to spend the remainder of his life. As a precaution, he asks Winner to draw up a will so that his family and his affairs may be taken care of in a decent and orderly manner. Alfred's only regret is that he cannot hand down his responsibilities as steward and sexton to one of his grandnephews, Rodney or Morgan, both of whom are capable of handling the jobs with dignity and authority, as his father had handed them down to him. Neither wants to become a servant, even an authoritative, respected one like Alfred. Each is preparing to become his own boss either in a profession or in business.

When we compare these aspects of Alfred's fictional personality with those assigned by Cooper to Caesar in *The Spy,* a century and a half earlier, one clearly sees changes in cultural attitudes. Alfred is dignified, intelligent, and self-seeking; he takes pride in his family and has the ability to make responsible decisions, fully recognizing, in this case, the personal alternatives involved. As Cozzens adroitly intimates, however, Alfred is like his literary antecedents, the accommodationists. As sexton of Christ Church, it was considered proper that he should attend and participate in religious services;

> . . . but at celebrations of Holy Communion, Paul then and Alfred now, with the delicacy, the politeness of self-respect required of them, came last to the altar rail. The good, the just, man had consideration for others. By delaying, he took care that the members of the congre-

gation need never hesitate to receive the blood of Our Lord Jesus Christ because a cup from which a Negro had drunk contained it.[96]

Ossie Davis, in his comedy *Purlie Victorious* (1961), perceptively manipulates stock images in ways that tend to reduce the impatience and annoyance usually evoked by these figures. Contained within their portraits are elements of buffoons and accommodationists, but each character is shown eventually to be an individual as defined earlier. Each is included here to document changes occurring in Negro portraiture.

Purlie Judson, the name assigned to the main character, at first glance, appears to be just another example of the quaintly humorous naming practice. When first seen in the play, he is a self-made preacher in his middle thirties, and has adopted the shoestring tie and claw hammer coat of every caricatured backwoods preacher in literature. The reader learns that he has just returned to his home community in Georgia for an admirable purpose: to buy back Big Bethel, now a barn but formerly his grandfather's pastorate, where he hopes to preach the "new freedom" and instill black pride in the people of the cotton patch.

This worthy image is diminished almost immediately when he reveals his plan for obtaining money to buy Big Bethel. Some years earlier, Purlie's aunt was left a legacy of money by a white woman, but both she and her only child, a daughter, are now dead. Ol' Cap'n Cotchipee, a stereotyped white landowner, unaware of the daughter's death, still holds the legacy in trust for her. Purlie finds a simple backwoods girl named Lutiebelle Gussie Mae Jenkins, who, in his opinion, can be palmed off as the rightful heiress. This is the typically fraudulent scheme of the stock buffoon. We learn also that Purlie was involved in a similarly foolish scheme during the time of the bus boycott in Alabama. In sympathy with the civil rights movement, he advised cotton patch workers to boycott mules because that was the mode of transportation used to get to the cotton fields.

A third incident shows clearly Davis's manipulation of comic traits. When Purlie learns that Ol' Cap'n has squeezed and kissed Lutiebelle's cheek, he goes forth like a knight in shining armor, to do battle for his lady's honor, threatening to treat Ol' Cap'n the same way that white men would treat him if he pinched and kissed a white woman's cheek. When Purlie returns from his "confrontation," he starts to tell the truth, which was that, aided by Ol' Cap'n's son, he has obtained the legacy without violence. But finding himself the center of Lutiebelle's and Missy's adoring attention, seeing the pride and love in their eyes, and sensitive to their need for ego gratification, he cannot disappoint them or, for that matter, deny himself the pleasure of showing off before them. Like the loquacious preacher that he is, he embellishes his lie with all the details that he thinks they want to hear. Even his brother Gitlow falls under the spell of his oratory. As fantasy becomes reality for him and his audience, Purlie relates in great detail how he confronted the white with every grievance blacks have endured for centuries. When his lie is finally uncovered, he extricates himself: saying that he was preaching prophetic, not literal, truth and that he has never told a lie in his life that he "didn't mean to make come true some day!" Here is combined the "cuteness" of Boysi and the optimism of a visionary who points a realist in the direction both would like to go.

Purlie is different from earlier buffoons. He is shown to have an appreciative sense of black identity, reveling in the personified blackness of the "fat, black, and sassy" church bell that rings forth the new freedom from Big Bethel and lovingly describing Lutiebelle as a "dark and holy vessel," soon to become a joyous symbol of black womanhood. Probably the clearest statement occurs in his sermon at the end of the play when he calls blackness

> a thing of beauty: a joy; a strength; a secret cup of gladness; a native land in neither time nor place—a native land in every Negro face!

Then he concludes with this exhortation:

> Be loyal to yourselves: your skin; your hair; your lips, your Southern speech, your laughing kindness—are Negro kingdoms, vast as any other![97]

Discovering the beauty of blackness, or the acceptance and love of self, is the essential first step toward recovery of black identity. It cannot be superimposed or endowed by even compassionate outsiders; it has to be self-created. Purlie's celebration of the joys of being black as well as his warning against self-denial, rejection, or imitation of non-blacks have become a major thesis of the contemporary black theater.

Purlie never advocates black separatism. When this play was first produced, social integration still seemed an acceptable goal to blacks who had not begun to fear integration as loss of newly recovered black identity. Big Bethel is, therefore, not only integrated racially but ecumenically. It is partly Baptist, Methodist, and Catholic, enjoying "the merriness of Christmas and the happiness of Hannukah." As suitable ritual, Purlie intones a new Trinity: the Declaration of Independence, the Constitution of the United States, and the State Commission Against Discrimination, on which foundation he preaches the New Baptism of Freedom.

Incorporated within the portrait of Gitlow, Purlie's brother, are traits of the free slave and comic menial, characteristics also manipulated by Davis. Gitlow seems despicable at first, willing to go along with any plan, no matter how personally demeaning, that Ol' Cap'n proposes, causing his wife Missy to ask, with an obvious play on words, "How low can you git?" On occasion, however, Davis gives Gitlow lines indicating his real feelings. For instance, after Ol' Cap'n and Gitlow finish harmonizing a spiritual, the white sentimentally calls the black his friend, comments on the other-worldly quality of the song, and says that he looks forward to the day when Gitlow will sing the spiritual over his grave. Gitlow hastily agrees, "Me too, Ol' Cap'n," in a manner reminiscent of the slave who sang gleefully about his owner's death in "The Blue-Tail Fly."

Several female characters—Lutiebelle, Idella, and Missy—are perceptively depicted in the play. With a name like Lutiebelle Gussie Mae Jenkins, the reader instantly identifies the character as Southern and probably black. Purlie calls the name an insult, denoting "a badge of inferiority," and demands that she change it. The servant of whites when Purlie discovers her, she dotes on the words of her "Miz Emmylou" until Purlie's impatient dynamism takes control of her. Idella, Ol' Cap'n's cook and substitute mother for his son Charlie, is unlike her predecessors in literature. Although old and tiny, she is tough enough to handle Ol' Cap'n. When he accuses her of "putting integrationary ideas" into Charlie's mind, she refuses to give him a decent answer, whereupon he decides to punish her by making her stand erectly in front of him until she tells him what he wants to know. In a manner foreshadowing the characters Vi and Ellie in Douglas Turner Ward's *Happy Ending* (1966), and the black servants' handling of whites in Ward's *Day of Absence* (1966), Idella quietly reminds him that his favorite dessert is in the oven. He rescinds the order. Missy is another sharp-tongued wife in literature, the sort who frequently berates and beats her husband. Gitlow and she resemble Butterbeans and Susie of vaudeville fame, except that Missy's portrait is more individualistic and sensitive as the warmhearted preserver of pride in the black family. Her comment to Lutiebelle bears this out, after the latter has enumerated all the good things that Purlie reminds her of: "Oh, child, being colored can be a lot of fun when ain't nobody looking."[98] In her comment lie both the joy and difficulty of being oneself in a white-dominated society.

Initially, Chester Hime's assortment of Harlem characters, in his popular police novels of the 1950's and 1960's, also seem reminiscent of stock buffoons. *A Rage in Harlem* (1965) was the first of these novels, published in France in 1957 under the original title, *For Love of Imabelle*. A sampling of its "colored" types, so designated by Himes, includes Beau Diddley, a taxicab driver; H. Exodus Clay, funeral director who is fond of counting his money and of wearing formal morning clothing and pince-nez; Jackson, his gullible assistant who can be duped by an obvious charlatan with promises of raising the denominations of paper money; Imabelle, Jackson's not entirely to be trusted mulatto woman with "ball-bearing" hips whom Jackson wants desperately to marry if and when she obtains a divorce; and The Reverend Gaines, booming-voiced, fire-and-brimstone preacher who wears a large diamond ring, is more than a little fond of fine clothes, and asks the Lord to deliver him from "squares" like Jackson. Some place names are as comical as Cohen's. Meat markets are named Hog Maw, Chitterling Country, Pig Foot Heaven.

On closer examination, one soon realizes that the resemblance between these characters and earlier buffoons is superficial; further, that Himes delineates a broad spectrum of black characters which may more accurately be classified as Harlem grotesques combining caricatured appearances and motives with nightmare-like situations and sequences.

In *A Rage in Harlem*, there are three characters called black widows, who appear to be respectable middle-aged women sharing an apartment and a housekeeper named Mother Goose in a middle-class section of Harlem. When one considers what they actually do for a living, they seem as deadly as black widow spiders. All are male dope addicts surviving by their wits and impersonating women in order to camouflage their true identities and illegal activities in support of their drug habits. One is known as Lady Gypsy, a fortuneteller and dispenser of "lucky numbers"; another is called Big Kathy, who is the "madam" of a house of prostitution called The Circus; the third is known as kindly Sister Gabriel, who wears the habit of a Sister of Mercy, collects alms, sells admission cards to heaven to the relatives and friends of people who are dying. Sister Gabriel is really Goldy, Jackson's ruthless and dangerous brother who leads a triple life as Sister Gabriel, a police informer, and as respectable husband of a wife who is a domestic and lives at her job and with whom he shares an apartment in another section of Harlem. On his wife's free Thursdays and every other Sunday afternoon, Sister Gabriel is noticeably absent from her customary stations along 125th Street.

Some unusual as well as grotesque characters included in Himes's other police novels, such as *The Heat's On* (1966) and *Hot Day, Hot Night* (1969), originally titled *Blind Man with a Pistol,* are Wop, a straight-haired black drug addict; Sugartit, a juvenile delinquent; Johnson X and Michael X, symbols of the new black militancy; Pinky, a giant black albino and drug addict; Daddy Haddy, the leprous-looking operator of a tobacco shop, really the receiving center for gambling bets and narcotics; Dr. Moore, an expert fund-raiser who advocates black power among the lower class and brotherhood among the middle-class Harlemites; Sister Z, gold-toothed guardian of street contributions for the coming revolution; Dr. Sam, a black Mormon with a harem of wives, all dressed as nuns, and their innumerable progeny; Billie, a hermaphrodite; Jonas "Fats" Little, homosexual; his lesbian wife Catherine; her lover Patricia; and spurious virility rejuvenator, Dr. Mubuta, whose noisome elixir is no more difficult to believe in, according to the author, than the eventuality of black social equality. In addition to these, Himes, in *Hot Day, Hot Night,* creates Black Jesus Baby, a huge, gruesome replica of a lynched Negro which symbolizes the cultural mutilation of blacks. These are a sample of the literary figures who have their existence in a Harlem created by Himes, reeking of greasy food, cheap liquor, hair "frying," of garbage-filled streets and all imaginable forms of human excrement. It is a Harlem resounding with laughter, shouts, curses, blaring radios, cat "spasms," and the sinister sounds of mugging, rape, arson, riot, murder; a damp-rotten Harlem, of graffiti-decorated walls and streets with names like Bucket of Blood. His Harlem is a counterpart of *Le Grand Guignol,* replete with gore, horror, and sensationalism.

Two characters who appear regularly in Himes's novels are a pair of detectives named Ed Johnson and Digger Jones, better known as Coffin Ed and Grave Digger because of their admonitions to suspects to keep cool and avoid filling their own coffins and digging their own graves and because of their trigger-happy inclinations, particularly in the earlier novels, to control dangerous situations by shooting first and asking questions afterwards. Their scarred faces attest to numerous violent encounters, such as the time, in *A Rage in Harlem,* when acid is thrown into Ed's face, necessitating a skin graft and resulting in a permanent muscular twitch. Built like athletes—big, broad-shouldered, loose-jointed men in dark clothing—they are prime specimens of black and burly virility as they nightly cruise or fearlessly lope through the dark streets of Harlem.

In the earlier novels Ed and Digger are typical of New York policemen prior to the heightened civil rights sensitivity of the 1960's. They live in a suburban community, send their children to summer camp in the Catskills, support strict enforcement of law and order. As rough tough detectives, they are seldom seen without guns drawn, cocked, and ready to be used. In *A Rage in Harlem* they slap the head of a confidence man, as if it were a Ping-pong ball, until he is insensible. In *The Heat's On*, they punch a narcotics peddler so savagely in the stomach, to make him disgorge the packets of narcotics that he has swallowed, that they kill the man. For this they are suspended. In retaliation they accuse their superiors of being soft on white narcotics peddlers in black neighborhoods. They are not always such strict law enforcers, not always enforcing laws against pimps, prostitutes, homosexuals, or operators of houses of prostitution, from whom they take graft. They do not consider themselves arbiters of other people's sexual practices and can find no sensible reason for putting such people out of business and forcing them to become welfare recipients.

Similarly, when the prejudicial attitudes of white officers endanger black criminals, Digger and Ed cannot avoid getting involved and disregarding the law while at the same time trying to behave fairly to both. For example, in *The Heat's On*, when white firemen discover that Pinky, the giant albino, who has turned in a false alarm, is really a Negro, they turn hostile and abusive. Pinky, becoming violent, starts choking the white captain. To subdue Pinky, a fireman hits him with the back of his ax. Just as another fireman lifts his ax, Digger interrupts its descent with one hand and with the other hits Pinky's hand with his revolver so forcefully that Pinky's grip spasmodically tightens on the captain's neck, then as quickly slackens. Seeing the captain unconscious on the ground, the fireman moves to hit Digger, but is stopped by Coffin Ed, whose revolver is aimed at him. Attention removed from him, Pinky starts running away. Ed and Digger agree to let him escape; and, as a white policeman starts to shoot him, Coffin Ed ruins his aim by hitting his arm.

In lighter moments, they behave as mischievously as children. While on late duty one night, they decide to eat at a night club featuring a line of chorus girls. For dessert they have watermelon. Ed begins making a game of spitting out the seeds at the chorus girls, causing them to jump about as if stung by insects. Angered, the girls spread out through the club searching for those responsible, never suspecting the detectives because Ed has hidden the plates containing rinds and seeds underneath their table. This kind of horseplay, free from tension, is in direct contrast with Digger's and Ed's relationships with whites, with whom they can never forget skin color differences. Moreover, whites, as delineated by Himes, are so ignorant of culturally induced sensitivities inherent in the black American experience that even their unpatronizing efforts at friendship bring "knowing" smiles to the detectives' faces, shared sometimes, even in earlier novels when they are delineated as firm law and order advocates, with black suspects during investigations and interrogations. In these ways the author demonstrates the failure of reciprocal black-white relationships.

Two character types that have appeared frequently in the drama of the 1960's and may become contemporary stock characters are the professional Negro who makes a vocation of his blackness and, in direct contrast, the white-veneered Negro whose blackness is so submerged in white modes of thought and living that he has lost whatever mother wit he was born with. Both are fictional symbols of people who have lost contact with reality. Excellent examples are Foxtrot in *Scuba Duba* (1967) by Bruce Jay Friedman and two characters, Jack in *Clara's Ole Man* (1965) and Carpentier in *The Electronic Nigger* (1968), both by Ed Bullins.

Foxtrot, also known as Frogman and Scuba Duba, is the character with whom the white protagonist believes his wife has eloped. One never learns what he is really like; for just as he never appears on stage in any costume other than a totally concealing skin-diving outfit, so is he always "on stage" as an ever-smiling, "hip"-talking, cutely militant type. In his portrait, all the clichés have been included: he talks about "working roots" and eating "chit'lin's"; offers a gift in the name of civil rights leaders; feigns rhapsodic ecstasy in the word "whoooooeeee"; boasts of black sexual prowess, among other things. Actually he is not the wife's lover. She chooses, instead, Ambrose Reddington, a soft-spoken black man, the absolute opposite of Foxtrot.

Twenty-year-old Jack, not long out of the Marines, works

at the post office and, with government assistance, attends
college preparatory school. He has been invited by Clara to
visit her house one afternoon when, as she puts it, her "old
man" will be at work. The "old man" turns out to be the
lesbian, Big Girl, with whom Clara lives. Big Girl, evidently
suspicious of Clara, stays home from work on the day in
question and helps entertain Jack. The audience is expected
to believe that service in the Marines, the pursuit of higher
education, and steady work—or the acquisition of middle-
class values—have made Jack forget the realities of Philadelphia slum life in which he was reared. Something of an
exhibitionist, he uses a speech pattern that is inappropriate
for the situation and that attracts unnecessary animosity.
Further, he completely ignores evidence, revealed bit by bit,
indicating the relationship between Clara and Big Girl. As
the afternoon wears on, he tries to change, to become a
member of the group, but by then the damage is done. Big
Girl gives orders for him to be beaten by a group of young
hoodlums.

Mr. A. T. Carpentier is the completely artificial man. His
speech is more sophisticated than Jack's but as cliché-ridden,
casually dropping expressions like "cybernetic generation,"
"theatrical-literary community," and "adolescent necrophilia."
As if he were a computer, a word, an idea, or fact elicits
vast amounts of information and numerous theories and
personal opinions. Totally insensitive, he monopolizes all
discussions in a black professor's class. The black professor,
though educated, has not lost sight of his black identity or of
his responsibility to other black people. Carpentier radically
opposes all ideas connected with Negritude, denies his own
blackness and any idea of black brotherhood. Bullins seems
to be suggesting that persistent blindness to life's realities
is suicidal.

The examination of aesthetic symbols, expressive of culture and of personality as shaped by culture, shows that
certain shifts in cultural attitudes can be documented even
though a basic belief in the concept of black inferiority and
white superiority remains constant and continues subtly in
the works of white writers down to contemporary times.
Names attached to descriptions of stock characters show this

clearly. Insofar as fictional personality is concerned, the overall picture, as delineated by authors, is not so clear. Except for Uncle Julius, Barber Jim, and Alfred Revere, accommodationists consider themselves so far beneath whites that they are contentedly docile in their servile dependency. As lovable domesticated mastiffs, they are merely doers of their trainers' commands and inferior extensions of their masters' personalities. When the mastiff-like character runs away from his trainer, he invariably goes wild and reverts to primitive brutishness. Appearing often in this group is the dark mulatto, in whom African and Aryan inheritances are constantly at odds. Somewhat contradictorily, the Aryan strain is shown as incapable of subduing its darker primitive coeval. Among glorified counter types, all animal has been bred out; they are idealizations and, consequently, failures as individuals. Among buffoons, as a group, we begin to see the emergence of at least one of the components of fictional personality but not of all three. If they see themselves as separate in identity from whites, they are prone to irresponsible decisions; if they possess the sense of independent responsibility, they are submissive in relations with whites.

The comic component of fictional personality remains constant also in each of the major groups, although it may have been omitted in some incidental manifestations. Among chattels and buffoons there are several elements of humor: ironic or florid namings; in some cases, caricatured appearances; and ludicrous speech, replete with mispronunciation, malapropism, and the verbosity of old-fashioned, high-flung oratory. Among the emotionally enslaved free men, humorous dialect remains constant, while ironic names and ridiculous appearances tend to be deemphasized. Depictions of brutes combine ludicrously caricatured appearances with terrifying behavior; by such a union, they are made literary grotesques. The saccharine primness of speech and the highly improbable behavior of the glorified countertypes are smile-provoking. In contrast, contemporary black writers have taken such characteristics and have manipulated them in ways that indicate a rejection of cultural attitudes and, more significantly, shifts toward attitudes of self-acceptance and black identity.

In general the stock figures, as simple fictional symbols, are like signposts charting trends in cultural attitudes toward black people. A reader might be irritated by portraits of accommodationists and wish that they had not been made so selflessly compliant, or that the lighthearted clowns, even as he laughs at them, were not such foolishly irresponsible, trivial show-offs. He might even become angry at the vicious depravity attributed to black non-conformists or culturally designated brutes. But these would be superficial reactions compared with those elicited by the complex archetypal symbols of human personality in the next chapter.

Notes

1. John Pendleton Kennedy, *Swallow Barn, or A Sojourn in the Old Dominion,* rev. ed. (New York, 1852), p. 453.
2. See Tremaine McDowell's introduction to the Modern Library edition of *The Spy* by James Fenimore Cooper (New York, 1931), p. xxv.
3. James Fenimore Cooper, *The Spy, A Tale of the Neutral Ground* (New York, 1931), p. 16.
4. *Ibid.,* p. 44.
5. *Ibid.*
6. *Ibid.,* pp. 44ff.
7. *Ibid.,* p. 45.
8. *Ibid.,* p. 39.
9. *Ibid.,* p. 102.
10. *Ibid.,* p. 45.
11. *Ibid.,* p. 306.
12. *Ibid.*
13. James Fenimore Cooper, *Satanstoe, or the Littlepage Manuscripts: A Tale of the Colony* (New York, 1945), p. 70.
14. Edgar Allan Poe, "The Gold Bug," *The Viking Portable Edgar Allan Poe* (New York, 1957), p. 463.
15. William Gilmore Simms, *The Yemassee, A Romance of Carolina,* new and rev. ed. (New York, 1882), p. 438.
16. *Ibid.*
17. (Nathaniel) Beverly Tucker, *The Partisan Leader, A Key to the Disunion Conspiracy,* I (New York, 1861): 97–98.
18. *Ibid.,* p. 98.
19. *Ibid.,* pp. 98ff.
20. *Ibid.,* p. 99.
21. *Ibid.,* II: 98.
22. William Gilmore Simms, *The Forayers, or the Raid of the Dog Days* (New York, 1864), p. 14.

23. *Ibid.*
24. Dion Boucicault, *The Octoroon; or, Life in Louisiana* (London, n.d.), p. 32.
25. William Alexander Caruthers, *The Cavaliers of Virginia, or the Recluse of Jamestown,* I (New York, 1834): 151.
26. Herman Melville, *Moby Dick or, The Whale* (New York, 1950), p. 8.
27. *Ibid.,* p. 294.
28. *Ibid.,* p. 296.
29. *Ibid.,* p. 298
30. Simms, *The Forayers,* pp. 73ff.
31. *Ibid.,* p. 76.
32. Sophia L. Little, *Thrice Through the Furnace, A Tale of the Times of the Iron Hoof* (Pawtucket, R.I., 1852), p. 4.
33. *Ibid.,* pp. 12ff.
34. *Ibid.,* p. 23.
35. *Ibid.,* p. 100.
36. *Ibid.,* p. 75.
37. *Ibid.,* p. 1.
38. *Ibid.,* p. 9.
39. J. T. Trowbridge, *Cudjo's Cave* (Boston, 1895), p. 117.
40. *Ibid.,* p. 122.
41. *Ibid.*
42. *Ibid.,* p. 288.
43. *Ibid.,* p. 215.
44. *Ibid.,* p. 225.
45. *Ibid.,* p. 226.
46. *Ibid.,* p. 498.
47. *Ibid.,* p. 52.
48. *Ibid.,* pp. 232ff.
49. *Ibid.,* p. 293.
50. *Ibid.,* p. 493.
51. Joel Chandler Harris, "A Story of the War," *Uncle Remus, His Songs and Sayings* (New York and London, 1929), p. 208.
52. *Ibid.,* p. 212.
53. *Ibid.*
54. Joel Chandler Harris, "Ananias," *Balaam and His Master and Other Sketches and Stories* (Boston and New York, 1891), pp. 114ff.
55. *Ibid.,* pp. 116ff.
56. *Ibid.,* p. 119.
57. *Ibid.,* p. 120.
58. *Ibid.,* p. 148.
59. Joel Chandler Harris, "Free Joe and the Rest of the World," *American Short Stories,* Eugene Current-Garcia and W. R. Patrick, eds. (Fair Lawn, N.J., 1952), p. 241.
60. *Ibid.*
61. *Ibid.,* p. 245.
62. Frank R. Stockton, "The Cloverfields Carriage," *The Novels*

and Stories of Frank R. Stockton, Stories II, XVI (New York, 1900): 147.

63. Thomas Nelson Page, *In Ole Virginia, or Marse Chan and Other Stories* (New York, 1887), p. 5.

64. Charles Waddell Chesnutt, "The Goophered Grapevine," *The Atlantic Monthly,* LX (August, 1887): 257.

65. O. Henry, "A Municipal Report," *Strictly Business* (New York, 1910), p. 156.

66. *Ibid.,* p. 158

67. *Ibid.,* p. 159.

68. *Ibid.*

69. *Ibid.,* p. 160.

70. William Faulkner, "A Rose for Emily," *The Portable Faulkner,* Malcolm Cowley, ed. (New York, 1956), p. 499.

71. Thomas Nelson Page, *Red Rock, A Chronicle of Reconstruction* (New York, 1898), p. 293.

72. *Ibid.,* p. 292.

73. Sarah Barnwell Elliott, "An Incident," *An Incident and Other Happenings* (New York, 1899), p. 39.

74. Thomas Dixon, *The Leopard's Spots: A Romance of the White Man's Burden, 1865–1900* (New York, 1902), p. 380.

75. Thomas Dixon, *The Clansman, An Historical Romance of the Ku Klux Klan* (New York, 1902), p. 216.

76. *Ibid.,* p. 313.

77. *Ibid.,* pp. 57 and 157.

78. *Ibid.,* p. 93.

79. E(ldred) K(urtz) Means, "The Late Figger Bush," *E. K. Means* (New York and London, 1918), p. vi. Reprinted by permission of G. P. Putnam's Sons.

80. *Ibid.,* p. 1.

81. *Ibid.,* pp. 2ff.

82. *Ibid.,* p. 6.

83. *Ibid.,* p. 7.

84. *Ibid.,* pp. 7ff.

85. Irvin S. Cobb, "J. Poindexter, Colored," *The Saturday Evening Post,* CXCIV (June 10, 1922): 12. Reprinted by special permission of *The Saturday Evening Post.* © 1922 by the Curtis Publishing Company.

86. *Ibid.,* CXCV (July 1, 1922): 54.

87. *Ibid.,* CXCIV (June 10, 1922): 12.

88. *Ibid.,* CXCIV (June 24, 1922): 50.

89. *Ibid.,* CXCIV (June 10, 1922): 122.

90. *Ibid.,* CXCV (July 1, 1922): 54.

91. See H(enry) L(ouis) Mencken, *The American Language,* 4th ed. (New York, 1936), pp. 524ff.

92. Octavus Roy Cohen, "Horse-and-Buggy Daze," *The Saturday Evening Post,* CCXV (August 29, 1942): 29.

93. Glenn Allan, "Boysi's Yaller Cha'iot," *The Saturday Evening Post,* CCXV (December 27, 1941): 48. Reprinted by special

permission of *The Saturday Evening Post.* © 1941 by the Curtis Publishing Company.

94. James Gould Cozzens, *By Love Possessed* (New York, 1957), p. 357. Reprinted by permission of Harcourt, Brace and World, Inc. and Longmans Group Ltd.
95. *Ibid.,* p. 360.
96. *Ibid.,* pp. 517ff.
97. Ossie Davis, *Purlie Victorious* (New York, 1961), p. 81. Reprinted by permission of Ossie Davis.
98. *Ibid.,* p. 20.

CHAPTER

3

ARCHETYPAL PATTERNS

An archetype, as defined earlier, is the dominant embodiment of an idea or kind of person that rises in literature, attracts conscientious responses, recurs as thematic motif in subsequent manifestations, and acquires mythic dimensions as demanded by cultural needs. Black archetypes cluster in five major configurational patterns: as tragic mulatto or visible symbol of lust and what the culture deemed, pejoratively, miscegenation; as sacrifice symbol or victim of environmental determinism; as beloved mammy or black, hence inferior, representative of the powerful mother symbol; as natural primitive or symbol of freedom from cultural taboo; as alter-ego symbol or the affirmation of brotherhood. All are designed to probe consciences and to channel emotions in particular ways.

Some recent portraits within each major category contain attributes of individuals as defined in this investigation. Because these shifts in portraiture exist, the order in which archetypes are examined is designed to dramatize the changes, beginning in each pattern with an early delineation and tracing its dominant character through a sample of subsequent portraits.

Mulattoes

The tragic mulatto is probably the oldest archetype in our literature, indicating early conscientious feelings among whites about the enslavement of people who, like themselves, were observably white. The idea of subjecting them to the indignities and rigors blacks were forced to endure resulted in a number of early nineteenth-century works dealing with the subject. These literary figures are usually children begotten by white masters with quadroon or octoroon concubines. The quadroon's ancestry contains one black grandparent; the octoroon's one black great-grandparent. Usually they are lighter in skin color and handsomer or more beautiful than other people who are accepted as white; but because their black ancestry is known, they are classified as black. On every hand their lives are circumscribed by the known fact of their black ancestry.

Probably the first of the mixed-bloods is Archy Moore in *The White Slave* (1836) by Richard Hildreth. The time of the novel is just before the Revolutionary War. Archy is the son of Colonel Moore, who is also his master. The father is a Virginia aristocrat who "especially prided himself upon owning the swiftest horse, the handsomest wench, and the finest pack of hounds."[1] His handsomest wench is Archy's bright mulatto mother, who is the illegitimate daughter of a neighboring aristocrat. Yet she tries to instill pride of white ancestry in her son, and both are convinced that "one drop of blood imported from Africa—would be enough to taint the whole pedigree."[2] To his "white drop" he attributes his "proud spirit, sensitive feelings, and ardent temperament." To this inheritance also can be attributed his refusal to adjust to personal indignities, his decision to seek superior advantage as a white in England, and his conscientious return years later to rescue his wife and son from slavery.

Before his escape, Archy incurs the colonel's hatred, first, because he dares mention their kinship publicly, and, second, because he secretly marries his half-sister whom their father-master has incestuously designated as his next concubine. After many such humiliations, he manages to make his way to Boston where he joins the crew of a ship headed for Bordeaux. War is declared before the ship reaches its destination. Archy's ship is captured by an English brig. He feels no compunction about joining the crew of the enemy ship.

> I had renounced my country; if indeed that place can be fitly called one's country, which, while it gives him birth, cuts him off, by its wicked and unjust laws, from everything that makes life worth having. Despite the murmurs and hisses of my companions, I stepped forward, and put my name to the shipping paper. Had they known my history they would not have blamed me.[3]

This archetypal image appears to have been set by the middle of the nineteenth century. Some of Harriet Beecher Stowe's mulattoes in *Uncle Tom's Cabin* (1852), particularly George Harris and Cassy, the slave concubine of Simon Legree, bear a striking resemblance to Hildreth's characters in ancestry, physical appearance, kinds of decisions reached, and relationships with others.[4] During the latter half of the century this image was kept alive by many writers.

The next year, in 1853, *Clotel; or, the President's Daughter,* by William Wells Brown, a fugitive slave, was published in London. Its purpose was to dissuade Christians from buying and selling human flesh: "Were it not for persons in high places owning slaves, and thereby giving the system a [good] reputation, and especially Christians, Slavery would long since been abolished."[5] The main characters of the novel are all tragic mulattoes: Currer, a quadroon, has been, prior to the beginning of the novel, the housekeeper of Thomas Jefferson, the father of her octoroon daughters, Clotel and Althesa. It was accepted practice, under certain circumstances, for slaves to be hired out or allowed to hire themselves out for profit. Brown notes that the following scene was also customary and accepted practice: "Society does not frown upon the man who sits with his mulatto child upon his knee, whilst its mother stands a slave behind his chair."[6]

When her employer is called to government service, Currer supports herself and her daughters as a laundress, giving them the necessary training to attract admirers at "negro balls" as a first step toward becoming the concubines of whites. After the death of their owner, they are auctioned along with the other slaves. The merchandise was attractively advertised:

> The Negroes are in good condition, some of them very prime; among them are several mechanics, able-bodied field hands, ploughboys, and women with children at the breast, and some of them prolific in their generating qualities, affording a rare opportunity to any one who wishes to raise a strong and healthy lot of servants for their own use. Also several mulatto girls of rare personal qualities: two of them very superior. Any gentleman or lady wishing to purchase, can take any of the above slaves on trial for a week, for which no charge will be made.[7]

Only Clotel is bought by an admirer; Currer and Althesa are sold to a slave speculator.

Clotel's new owner establishes her in a pleasant house not far from Richmond. After the birth of a daughter, named Mary, Clotel begs him to take her and the child to Europe where they would be safe from persecution. He is agreeable, but circumstances force him into a marriage of convenience. When his wife learns of his relationship with Clotel, she demands that the concubine be sold out of the state; and "as if to make her husband drink the cup of humiliation to its dregs," she retains Mary, his daughter, as a slave in her own father's household.

Sold to a Mississippian, Clotel is subjected to the cruelty of her owner's wife and the spitefulness of the other slaves because of her appearance and ladylike ways and speech. One slave, William, treats her kindly. Together they manage to escape to Ohio. William unsuccessfully tries to persuade her to continue on to freedom in Canada; but she is determined not to leave Mary. Disguised as a man, she returns to Virginia. Her arrival coincides with the capture and execution of Nat Turner and his revolutionaries, a time when all slaves and newcomers to the community are carefully watched and searched. Her identity discovered, she is arrested and sent to the "negro pens" in the District of

Columbia where fugitives await transportation back to their owners.

Once again, however, she manages to escape, successfully reaching the Long Bridge that crosses the Potomac. At the end of the bridge lies comparative safety in the dense Arlington woods. Halfway across the bridge, she sees three men approaching from the Virginia side. Her pursuers

> . . . called to them to arrest the fugitive whom they proclaimed a runaway slave. True to their Virginia instincts as she came near, they formed in line across the narrow bridge, and prepared to seize her. Seeing escape impossible in that quarter, she stopped suddenly, and turned upon her pursuers. On came the profane and ribald crew, faster than ever, already exulting in her capture, and threatening punishment for her flight. For a moment she looked wildly and anxiously around to see if there was no hope of escape. On either hand, far down below, rolled the deep foamy waters of the Potomac, and before and behind the rapidly approaching step and noisy voices of pursuers, showing how vain would be any further effort for freedom.[8]

She commits suicide by jumping from the bridge. Her body, when washed ashore, was buried in a grave in the sand without an inquest or religious ceremonies.

John Townsend Trowbridge's Camille in *Neighbor Jackwood* (1856) is the daughter of a French merchant and a mulatto slave in New Orleans. When she is ten years old, her father dies and she learns of her "black blood." Rather than become the concubine of a dissolute white, she runs away, becoming a fugitive slave like Clotel. Using the alias Charlotte Woods, she escapes to Vermont where the Jackwoods befriend her without knowing she is a mulatto. While there she falls in love with a white man, Hector Danbury, who proposes marriage. She refuses the proposal.

> If you knew my history, you would put me from you. It is the consciousness of this that shoots me through with pain, when I remember myself—you—and the gulf between us![9]

Hector buys her from her owner and marries her. In the end, she accepts herself in the new role.

Dion Boucicault's Zoe in *The Octoroon*—a melodrama published first in 1859—is the daughter of a mulatto slave and of Judge Peyton, the deceased former owner of Terrebonne, a plantation in the Mississippi Delta. She has been reared by Mrs. Peyton as if she were the judge's legitimate child. Her cousin George Peyton, having lived most of his life in Europe and not knowing her ancestry, asks her to marry him. True to the archetypal pattern, Zoe refuses because of the "inefficable curse of Cain" that separates them.

> ZOE: Of the blood that feeds my heart, one drop in eight is black—bright red as the rest may be, that one drop poisons all the flood; those seven bright drops give me love like yours, hope like yours—ambition like dewdrops on the morning flowers; but the one black drop gives me despair for I am an unclean thing—forbidden by the laws—I am an Octoroon.

> GEORGE: Zoe, I love you none the less, this knowledge brings no revolt to my heart, and I can overcome the obstacle.

> ZOE: But *I* cannot.[10]

When Terrebonne and the slaves are sold, Zoe is bought by Jacob McLoskey, who plans to make her his concubine. Boucicault wrote at least two endings to the play. In one, Zoe commits suicide rather than be owned by McLoskey. In another, she marries George and returns with him to Paris.

In *A Royal Gentleman* (1874) by Albion W. Tourgée, there are two tragic octoroons, a mother whose name is Belle and her daughter 'Toinette. In a flashback, the reader learns that Belle killed her master-lover in a jealous rage, believing that he planned to cast her aside in favor of a white wife. Actually he had been making sure that she and their three children would be freed after his death. Killing him precipitated what he tried to prevent: she and all of the children except 'Toinette were sold to different masters. 'Toinette was allowed to remain with the mother.

Tourgée's treatment of the tragic octoroon differs from

earlier treatments. Belle does not passively accept what happens to her. She reacts violently against those who try to abuse her or her daughter. When 'Toinette reaches adolescence, her beauty catches the eye of her master's son, Geoffrey Hunter. He requests and obtains her as a Christmas gift. Belle, fearing that 'Toinette will become his concubine, decides that the girl will be better off dead. She stabs her daughter, but the wound is not fatal. 'Toinette recovers, becomes Geoffrey's mistress, and is rejected by her mother. Geoffrey is more honorable than some of his predecessors in literature. He trains 'Toinette to behave and speak as a lady, manumits her, and carries her off to live with him in Ohio where their son is born.

When the Civil War breaks out, he returns South to fight. She, as Mrs. Geoffrey Hunter, passes for white, becomes a respected nurse in a government hospital, and is instrumental in saving his life. On learning what she has done, he is incensed. Vengefully, he insults and embarrasses her in front of those who respect her. When he realizes how unworthy his behavior is, he begs her to resume their former relationship. Now a self-respecting woman, she refuses to be lured back into a slave-concubine relationship no matter how deeply she loves him. Moreover she can no longer justify his stubborn pride of race and caste.

> It was the knowledge that he would . . . offer a love which could debase its object, that he would persuade her to yield herself to shame, which cut her to the quick. She would go away before her idol shattered himself completely at her feet.[11]

George Washington Cable and Charles Waddell Chesnutt widen the dimensions of the tragic mulatto with sensitive portraits of the quadroon mothers and male mixed-bloods. Two of the former appear in Cable's " 'Tite Poulette" and "Madame Delphine" (1874). Exotically named Zalli and Delphine are physically of "hyperion excellence and nymphean beauty" that have been "culled out of the less negroidal types of African live goods . . . through seventy-five years devoted to the elimination of the black pigment."[12]

In their youth, like Clotel, they were selected as mistresses by white *patrones,* established in little houses, and talked about in whispers by their Creole neighbors. They bore children and remained faithful to their *patrones.* When "widowed" they lived circumspectly in shabby gentility on whatever remained of the gifts bestowed upon them by their lovers. Marriage between quadroons and whites was illegal. In the stories, Delphine and Zalli are determined that their children will marry white men. This can be accomplished only if the mothers deny their parenthood. Each swears that her daughter is the child of two white parents so that the young women can enjoy the privileges of whites.

In "Her Virginia Mammy" (1899), Charles Waddell Chesnutt, himself a mulatto, creates a character similar to Delphine and Zalli. Mrs. Harper, the main character of the story, bears a daughter for her master who loves and wants to marry her. Knowing that such a union is impossible in the South and difficult in the North, he decides to leave America and is running away to Europe with her and the child when the Mississippi steamboat on which they are traveling explodes. He is killed; she is returned to slavery; and their daughter Clara is adopted by Northern whites who do not know her ancestry.

Years later, after the Civil War, Clara's foster parents die and she supports herself by teaching dancing lessons to segregated groups of Negro and white children. She is engaged to a white man but hesitates to marry him because she does not know who her real parents are. Believing herself white, she is more concerned about passing on insanity or criminal tendencies to her children than Negro ancestry. She relates her dilemma to a sympathetic mulatto, Mrs. Harper, who brings some children to dancing school. When Mrs. Harper hears about the ship's explosion and sees the clothing Clara was wearing at the time, she knows that the girl is her daughter. Without hesitation she denies her parenthood in order to insure the happiness of her daughter. She reassures the girl that her ancestry on both sides includes members of proud Virginia families. When Clara questions, "And how did you know about them?" Mrs. Harper replies, "I was one of the party." The girl assumes, "You were my colored nurse?—my 'Mammy'?" The woman answers, "Yes child, I was your mammy." Later, Clara's fiancé notices the resemblance between the two. "Something in his expression caused Mrs. Harper's eyes to fall, and then glance up appealingly." He keeps her secret.[13]

In "The Wife of His Youth," Chesnutt delineates a male mulatto in relationship with a darker-skinned woman. The story takes place shortly after the Civil War. A group of mulattoes organize a society which they call the Blue Veins. Membership is restricted to those "white enough to show blue veins." Its purpose is "to establish and maintain correct social standards among a people whose social condition presented almost unlimited room for improvement." Snobbish and self-isolating, the Blue Veins find it difficult to accept darker Negroes in reciprocal relationships.

Many years earlier, while still enslaved, Mr. Ryder, dean of the Blue Veins, was married to a black woman, but slave marriages were not binding on either person after emancipation. Throughout the intervening years, his wife searched for him. Both are changed in appearance, and neither recognizes the other when they finally meet. When she tells him her story, he knows who she is. His dilemma is a moral one: whether or not he should acknowledge her and jeopardize his social position or simply keep his mouth shut. He introduces her to his friends as his wife.

An excellent portrait of the tragic male mulatto is delineated in Joel Chandler Harris's "Where's Duncan?" (1884). Willis Featherstone, so white that no one recognizes him as a Negro, enters the story when he joins a caravan of farmers taking cotton to market. Willis keeps his identity secret but tells them that he is headed for the Featherstone plantation. That he is emotionally distressed is noticeable from his moodiness and taciturnity. On rare occasions, he plays his banjo with a skill that entrances his audience. When the caravan reaches the plantation, he reveals a clue to his personal tragedy.

> I'll give you a riddle. If you can't unriddle it, it will unriddle itself. A father had a son. He sent him to school in Augusta, until he was fifteen. By that time, the father grew to hate the son, and one day, in a fit of anger, sold him to a nigger speculator.[14]

It becomes obvious that he is consumed by bitter hatred not only for his father but also for his mother because she did nothing to prevent his being sold; nor has she avenged that inhuman act. He makes himself known to her by playing a tune that she used to sing to him. On hearing it played, she cries fearfully, "Who de name er God is dat man?" In reply, Willis demands, "Where's Duncan?" Running away like a madwoman, she screams, "He sold 'im!—he sold Duncan! He sold my onliest boy."

All three—father, mother, and son—are trapped in one of the tragic outcomes of slavery. Their deaths are recorded through the eyes of two spectators, a white boy and his slave, Crooked-leg Jake. Through a window of the mansion, ablaze with fire, they see the mother struggling with the father.

> . . . she had her carving-knife raised in the air in one hand, and with the other she had the white man by the throat.
> "Where's Duncan?" she shrieked.[15]

As in Greek drama, the events move inexorably toward a tragic climax. She stabs Featherstone twice; both fall out of sight of the horrified spectators. Crooked-leg Jake notices Willis sitting calmly at a table "enjoying the spectacle." Hating both parents he thus avenges their misuse of him.

Rhoda Aldgate, in *An Imperative Duty* by William Dean Howells (1891), is legitimate, the product of a mixed marriage. When his mulatto wife dies, Rhoda's father places her in the care of his sister. Later he dies, and Rhoda, reared as white, knows nothing about her Negro background. In young womanhood, she becomes engaged to a white minister. Her aunt feels it her duty to tell the girl that she is not white. With this knowledge, Rhoda makes the decision required of her as archetypal mixed-breed: renunciation of her right to marry a white man. Actually she does not love the minister, and the tragedy of her decision is tempered by growing attachment to another white man, who is a doctor. When he proposes marriage, she blurts out her dark secret. He does not recoil because, as Howells puts it,

> . . . It was the elder world, the beauty of antiquity which appealed to him in the lustre and sparkle of this girl; and

the remote taint of her servile and savage origin gave her a
kind of fascination which refuses to let itself be put into
words: it was like the grace of a limp, the occult, in-
definable lovableness of a deformity, but transcending
these by its allurement in infinite degree, and going for
the reason of its effect deep into the mysterious places
of being where the spirit and the animal meet and part
in us.[16]

The doctor convinces her that they should marry and
live in Europe where she can pass for an Italian or a Spaniard. But they are not happy together; he can overlook her
drop of black blood. Like Zoe, she cannot.

Kate Chopin's story, "Desirée's Baby" (1893), goes
straight to the dominant fear in such liaisons: the probability
of producing dark-skinned offspring. Desirée, an orphan,
becomes the wife of "imperious and exacting" Armand
Aubigny. His love for her demands no knowledge about her
background until their son is born. Everyone except Desirée
notices that her child is a mulatto. Armand's love turns to
hate. When he can stand the sight of her no longer, he
repudiates their marriage and sends her and the child away
because he is convinced that she is not "pure" white. While
destroying everything that might remind him of her, he finds
a letter written by his mother to his father many years earlier.

But above all, she wrote, night and day, I thank God
for having so arranged our lives that our dear Armand
will never know that his mother, who adores him, belongs
to the race that is cursed with the brand of slavery.[17]

In this century, the mulatto's problem of identity continues. One of Chesnutt's novels, *The House Behind the
Cedars* (1900), examines the consciences of two intelligent
mulattoes. In this novel Chesnutt achieves a higher level of
perception about this subject than any other writer prior to
James Weldon Johnson in *The Autobiography of an Ex-
Coloured Man* (1912). *The House Behind the Cedars* tells
the story of John and Rena Walden, the octoroon children of
a Southern aristocrat. In young manhood, John, the elder
of the two, decides to leave the community that classifies him

an inferior human being, change his name, and enjoy elsewhere the privileges of a white man. He marries a white girl
who dies soon after the birth of their son, conveniently leaving
John sole heir to her estate and a respected man in the community. Qualms of conscience do not bother him in the least.
In his conviction, Chesnutt writes phrases reminiscent of
the Declaration of Independence.

> Once persuaded that he had certain rights, or ought to
> have them, by virtue of the laws of nature in defiance to
> the customs of mankind, he had promptly sought to enjoy
> them.[18]

Rena is different. She yearns for the privileges of whites
but is not an opportunist. After John's wife dies, she goes to
live with him, passes for white, becomes engaged to a white
man who presses for an early wedding date. More sensitive
than her brother, she is tortured by the deception he practices
and advocates.

> I am afraid to marry him, without telling him. If he
> should find out afterwards, he might cast me off, or cease
> to love me. If he did not know it, I should be forever
> thinking of what he would do if he *should* find out; or,
> if I should die without his having learned it, I should not
> rest easy in my grave for thinking of what he would have
> done if he *had* found out.[19]

When her fiancé learns the truth, he repudiates her as his
prospective bride but continues to want her as his mistress.
Rejection of the base proposal is certain in a character like
Rena.

In his portrait of George Harris (*The Leopard's Spots*,
1902), Thomas Dixon extends an image of mulattoes that
was first created by Harriet Beecher Stowe in *Uncle Tom's
Cabin*. He is the child of George and Eliza Harris, the one
Eliza held in her arms as she jumped, with bleeding feet,
from one fragment of ice to another in order to escape her
pursuers. In later life, according to Dixon, instead of
migrating to Liberia with his parents as Mrs. Stowe forecast,
he lives in New England—"a modest, handsome, almost
white" young man, the protégé of a white benefactor. As

proof of Dixon's thesis, refuting the abolition of slavery and the educating of freedmen, George presumes to ask the patron for his daughter's hand in marriage. When refused, George persists,

> "Am I not a graduate of the same university as you? . . . am I not your equal in culture?"
> "Granted, nevertheless you are a Negro and I do not desire the infusion of your blood in my family."
> "But I have more white than Negro blood, sir."
> "So much the worse. It is the mark of shame."[20]

His patron would rather see his daughter dead than married to a Negro.

> I happen to know the important fact that a man or woman of Negro ancestry, though a century removed will suddenly breed back to a pure Negro child, thick-lipped, kinky-headed, flat-nosed, black-skinned.[21]

Thus shamed, George reverts to type, becoming a gambler and murderer.

Perhaps the best interpretation of the intelligent mulatto's dilemma in American society is contained in *The Autobiography of an Ex-Coloured Man* (1912) by James Weldon Johnson. The nameless narrator is forced to make three important decisions in his search for self-identity and fulfillment. After his mother's death he enrolls in a Negro college because he has decided to reject his white ancestry and to identify with those who are more likely to accept him. On his way to the college, the money he has managed to scrape together for tuition fees and board is stolen by a Pullman porter. He goes to work in a tobacco factory, hoping to save enough money to enter college later. After a time, the factory closes and the youth returns North to work as a piano player in a night club. A murder is committed in the place and, thinking that he might be implicated, he runs away to Europe with a white patron who admires him. There, as the pampered protégé of an affluent white, he gets a taste of living and being accepted not as a Negro but as a musically gifted human being. He is tempted to remain in Europe; but still wishing to identify with his people and to perform a service for them by recording and preserving folk tunes, he returns to a Southern state to carry out that ambition.

While there, he witnesses the brutal lynching of a Negro, an event that leads him to his second decision. "A great wave of humiliation and shame swept over me. Shame that I belonged to a race that could be so dealt with."[22] He rejects his race, because he no longer wants to be identified with a group that "could with impunity be treated worse than animals."

> I finally made up my mind that I would neither dis-
> claim the black race nor claim the white race, but that
> I would change my name, raise a mustache, and let the
> world take me for what it would; that it was not neces-
> sary for me to go about with a label of inferiority pasted
> across my forehead.[23]

He realizes the alternatives involved in passing for white. On the one hand he will deny himself the companionship of Negroes; on the other, he must live in constant fear of being recognized by someone who knows him.

His search for identity and fulfillment involves not merely himself but understanding of himself in relation with others. In casual contacts with whites, his deception proves no obstacle. His relationship with a girl who later becomes his wife is different. It seems to him that deception in some relationships can be condoned but not when the deception involves the girl's right to know facts and especially when she is confronted with a decision as important in our society as marrying a Negro. He gives her the opportunity to decide with full knowledge of the difficulties that may arise. He never doubts the wisdom of this third decision; he is not so sure about the second.

> . . . I cannot repress the thought that, after all I have
> chosen the lesser part, that I have sold my birthright for
> a mess of pottage.[24]

The portrait of Jean Toomer's Louisa, in "Blood-Burning Moon" (*Cane*, 1923), presents an interesting variation from the more familiar mulattoes in our literature who overexalt white and undervalue black ancestry. In one way, her dilemma bears a striking resemblance to that of Langston Hughes in the poem "Cross," for she is the true mixed-blood or crossbreed: neither black nor white as defined in American society, but a mixture the "color of oak leaves on young trees in fall."[25] But there is more than simple external evidence. At the same time that that which is black and that which is white are exerting something like positive and negative (no value judgment intended) forces upon her, she is reaching out for both of these at the same time, creating a situation and a sensation of almost unbearable tension.

The symbols of her dilemma, with regard to her identity, are two young men who love her: one black, the other white —both of whom she loves equally. Technically her relationship with Bob Stone, the white one, has progressed farther than her relationship with Tom Burwell, the black one. For one thing, as cook in Bob's house, she sees him more often and regularly than she does Tom, who works all day long in the fields. Another thing is that Tom has neither Bob's arrogance nor his assurance of Louisa: "Strong as he was with hands upon the ax or plow, he found it difficult to hold her. Or so he thought."[26] Actually, he exerts as much influence on her as Bob. Each is in dynamic equilibrium with her. "His black balanced and pulled against the white of Stone, when she thought of them."[27] When she tries to think of them separately she comes to the conclusion that neither has any special significance apart from the other. Both, as extensions of Louisa, are needed to complement her. Louisa is considered in this category instead of among the sensualists, for Toomer seems to be emphasizing more than promiscuity in her portrait.

We see that some of these portraits have advanced from characters dominated by hatred of their black blood toward an assertion of certain rights as human beings. Later portraits, during the 1930's, 1940's, and 1950's, show even greater advancement. T. S. Stribling gives a sharp image of a mulatto woman in his trilogy: *The Forge* (1931), *The Store* (1932), and *Unfinished Cathedral* (1934). Her name is Gracie. In the three novels, she progresses from traditionally abused octoroon to a character possessing some traits of an individual. In *The Forge* she is obscenely raped by her white

half-brother, Miltiades Vaiden. Despite such abuse, she remains emotionally attached to her white family. When she
contemplates running away to avoid being sold in settlement
of her father's debts, she hesitates as she realizes what separation from them will mean to her. Never again would she be
able to "lose her heart in the gray eyes of her young mistress
and half sister, never to brush her hair, never again, in the
person of the white girl, to go to dances and waltz with
white men."[28] She leaves but returns after the war, bringing
with her the son she has borne as a result of the episode
with Miltiades. In *The Store*, Gracie, though married to a
Negro, is mistress of a white merchant. She dreams that her
blond, blue-eyed son, Toussaint Vaiden, will marry a white
girl and thereby keep the family moving closer to her ideal
of whiteness and recognition as white. As stubborn as the
white Vaidens, Toussaint marries a ginger-colored mulatto
whom he loves. In addition, he refuses to perform the servile
rituals demanded of Negroes. As a result, he attracts the
animus of whites and is lynched. Gracie protects Miltiades
from gossip by not revealing to anyone, not even to him, that
Toussaint is his son. She migrates north with Toussaint's
widow and baby daughter. Years later, in *Unfinished Cathedral*, she precipitates the near tragedy that overtakes her
great-grandson by instilling pride and love in him for the
white Vaidens. The fourteen-year-old youth runs away to
Alabama so that he can see the white members of the family.
On the way, he is arrested with several other Negro youths
and accused of raping a white woman. Gracie goes to
Miltiades and demands that he help their great-grandchild.
Enraged that she should openly mention that fact even in the
privacy of his office, he berates her for influencing the youth
to identify with the white side of the family and asks why
she did not tell him about his Negro kinfolk. Thus goaded,
Gracie brings all of the disgusting implications of their
relationship into the open; and for the first time in their
lives, there is straight talk between them.

> Colored relation! What colored relations? I was born
> to my mother, Old Hannah, long after Old Pap sold off
> her husband Jericho! I'm not white for nothing! . . .

Toussaint, the son I had by you was nothing but Vaiden on both sides. . . . Who would my great grandchild come back to see except white people, Miltiades?[29]

Shocked by her outburst, Miltiades helps free his great-grandson.

Lillian Smith's portrait of Nonnie Anderson in *Strange Fruit* (1944) probes deeply into the motivation of the mixed-blood female whose only happiness lies in giving herself to an upstanding white man. In so doing she can redeem the white in her and thereby wash out the strain of black ancestry. In an episode that blends erotic and religious overtones, Nonnie finds sensual pleasure in the words of a gospel hymn that she hears while waiting in the woods for her lover, Tracy Dean. *"Whiter than snow. . . . Yes, whiter than snow. . . . Oh wash me and I shall be whiter than snow."*[30]

Unlike Gracie's non-reciprocal relationship with Miltiades, until late in life, Nonnie and Tracy, from childhood, have exercised reciprocal support in the form of emotional crutches for each other. Each feels that it is only the other who can provide the understanding and strength necessary for personal stability. Bound in mutual dependence in a relationship that is condemned by whites and bitterly resented by blacks, the two are doomed never to achieve mature, independent individuality.

Their affair sets off a chain reaction that reveals how both whites and blacks are controlled by intergroup hostility, particularly with regard to sexual liaisons between blacks and whites. Goaded by what he assumes is just another case of a black woman's defilement by a white man, Nonnie's brother murders Tracy. In retaliation, vengeful whites forcefully take an innocent black from jail and lynch him. The mutilated body of a black man violently killed in this manner is the "strange fruit" that grows on American trees and recalls the long history of white violence. Fair-minded individuals of both races are powerless either to prevent injustice to an innocent man or to prevent similar tragedies in the future.

A more recent portrait of the male mulatto appears in Hamilton Basso's novel of the Civil War, *The Light Infantry*

Ball (1959). His name is Allbright, and he is proprietor of a
barber shop in Pompey's Head, Basso's mythic Southern community. In appearance he is different from other tragic mulattoes in fiction. He is a thick-necked man with coarse features and yellow skin marred by liver spots. His pompous
speech and "airy high-tonedness" make him the laughing
stock of Pompey's Head. When greeting customers, he behaves like an overeager hound straining at the leash. His
bow is too elaborate; it would have been "more in place in a
minstrel show." As John Bottomley, his white nephew, remarks, "His name might just as well be Pork Chops or Ham
Gravy," two popular figures in such shows.

Allbright enjoys certain privileges as a free man of color
before the general emancipation of Negroes. He could walk
the streets after curfew, marry without obtaining special permission, and travel outside the state whenever he wished.
But he could not vote, serve on a jury, or join the militia. To
own his shop, a petition, signed by four prominent whites,
needed the approval of the state legislature. But he took advantage of his opportunities. During his forty years of
freedom he established a lucrative business and became a
wealthy man compared with other free Negroes in the community. One might wonder why he did not migrate north
where he could have enjoyed even more privileges. His portrait suggests that he stayed there because he loved his white
family, found his identity in them, and wanted to be of service to them.

To them he is the shameful substantiation of their grandfather's lust. They try to pretend even among themselves that
he does not exist. Only one Bottomley, young dissolute Cameron, appreciates his devotion. Allbright extricates him from
many wild escapades and saves the family from embarrassment. On one occasion, Allbright becomes an accessory to
murder by helping Cameron escape punishment. When John
tries to command Allbright's silence about the murder, by
threatening to send him to the chain gang, the mulatto asserts himself with dignity and a sense of family pride.

> You hate old Allbright, don't you, Mister John. . . .
> You wish he had never been born. . . . You hate him for

being who he is. . . . But I was born . . . and I is who I
is. There ain't nothing you can do about that, not you or
nobody. . . . It ain't for me to fly with eagles, that I know,
but that don't mean I have to peck with crows. I can't be
made to peck, Mister John. . . . If what you want is for
me to keep my mouth shut, yes sir, Mister John, I'll keep
it shut. And it ain't just because you'd go to the sheriff
and make things hard for me. That ain't the reason.
The real reason, like you must know like you *ought* to
know—[31]

In this speech there is no evidence of the stock minstrel
characters, Pork Chops and Ham Gravy.

From Archy Moore to Allbright, the tragedy of the mulatto shifts from the fatal infusion of one drop of "black"
blood to the problem of identity for the individual who is
neither white nor black. He occupies a halfway point between
the polar extremes of the black-white value system, unable
to "fly with eagles" and refusing to "peck with crows," a
tragic situation—the tragedy of the submerged self.

A contemporary mulatto, perceptively delineated by Lorraine Hansberry in *The Sign in Sidney Brustein's Window*
(1964), has no such problem; but he has another which is as
tragic. Black identity for Alton Scales is a state of mind, having nothing to do with the color of his skin and prompting
another character in the play to accuse him of playing fast
and loose with reality and of living a life of fantasy: "white
boy playing black boy all the time." Despite his "black" state
of mind, he loves Gloria, a white girl whom he asks to marry,
not knowing that she is a high-priced prostitute. She wants
to marry him too. His overreaction on learning the truth
appears juvenile on the surface until we recognize the cultural factors that have made him who he is and have influenced his rejection of Gloria.

When he thinks about the things that such women are
required to do and about the fact that Gloria has allowed
herself to be used as if she were an inanimate object, a piece
of property that can be bought and sold, his response is pre-
determined by the knowledge of similar uses to which his
female ancestors were put during slavery. Further, he re-

members his father, a railroad porter, and his mother, a domestic, and how, even though his father was galled by it, their family survived on the leftovers and hand-me-downs of whites. In his mind, Gloria, because of her occupation, is in the same category; and any alliance with her is impossible. As he gives Sidney a note for Gloria, Sidney asks two crucial questions: whether or not Alton would feel the same if Gloria were black; and whether or not his leaving a note for her, instead of seeing her face to face, is an indication of fear that if he sees her, he will realize how much he loves her and relent. Alton answers neither of the questions directly; his silence with regard to the first one indicates to Sidney that he is a racist. Alton's decision contributes to Gloria's suicide.[32]

Sacrifice Symbols

An archetype that shares prominence with the tragic mulatto is the sacrifice symbol or victim of cultural and environmental determinism. Harriet Beecher Stowe's Uncle Tom is the classic archetypal figure of this category. His history in national consciousness is evidence of the archetype's autonomy, its ability to "lead its own life" in extended meaning that differs from its creator's intent. Mrs. Stowe's purpose is similar to Mrs. Little's in *Thrice Through the Furnace*, published later the same year. Mrs. Stowe writes,

> The object of these sketches is to awaken sympathy and feeling for the African race, as they exist among us; to show their wrongs and sorrows, under a system so necessarily cruel and unjust as to defeat and do away the good effects of all that can be attempted for them, by their best friends, under it.[33]

All of Mrs. Stowe's characters are constructed to support that purpose in one way or another. Uncle Tom is drawn on an heroic scale to move minds and channel consciences in ways that she wanted them to go.

> He was a large, broad-chested, powerfully made man, of a full glossy black and a face whose truly African fea-

tures were characterized by an expression of grave and steady good sense, united with much kindliness and benevolence. There was something about his whole air self-respecting and dignified, yet united with a confiding and humble simplicity.[34]

Unlike his apostolic namesake, Tom's faith in God and man is never shaken despite the careless inefficiency of two masters and the brutality of the third. As exemplar of the Beatitudes, he never loses his meekness, for which he should have inherited the earth, nor his evangelical zeal to lead men back to the fold. Mrs. Stowe makes him a "light of the world" by which men may be challenged to recognize the evils of slavery; and in line with her belief, he does "inherit the kingdom of heaven."

Tom's original owner, Mr. Selby, a poor manager of financial matters, arranges to sell Tom and the young son of the quadroon slave named Eliza in order to pay his debts. Eliza urges Tom to run away, but Tom refuses, preferring to become a sacrificial lamb.

> "If I must be sold or all the people on the place, and everything go to rack, why let me be sold. I s'pose I can b'ar it as well as any on 'em," he added, while something like a sob . . . shook his broad, rough chest convulsively. "Mas'r always found me on the spot—he always will. I never have broke trust, and I never will."[35]

He is, in addition, an emotionally attached father-daddy accommodationist. When Tom's wife Aunt Chloe (another Aunt Jemima) berates both God and Shelby for allowing him to be sold, he apologizes for the master's misuse of him and mildly chastizes Chloe.

> ". . . it goes agin me to hear one word agin mas'r. Warn't he put in my arms a baby?—it's nature I should think a heap of him. . . . Mas'rs is used to havin' all these things done for 'em and nat'lly they don't think so much on't."[36]

When sold, he becomes the property of Augustine St. Clare and transfers his fatherly solicitude to his new master when he discovers that St. Clare never goes to church or reads the Bible, that he carouses with questionable company in wine-halls, and worst of all, that he does not believe in God. One morning after St. Clare has been brought home drunk, Tom begins working on him. It is not the platitudes that Tom utters but his humble, selfless concern that influences the owner.

> "Mas'r allays been good to me. I haven't nothing to complain of, on that head. But there is one that Mas'r isn't good to. . . . Mas'r isn't good to *himself*" . . . St. Clare felt his face flush crimson, but he laughed.
> "Oh, that's all, is it?" he said gaily.
> "All!" said Tom, turning suddenly round and falling on his knees. "O, my dear young Mas'r! I'm 'fraid it will be *loss of all—all*—body and soul. The good Book says, "it biteth like a serpent and stingeth like an adder,' my dear Mas'r!"
> Tom's voice choked, and the tears ran down his cheeks.
> "You poor silly fool!" said St. Clare, with tears in his own eyes. "Get up, Tom. I'm not worth crying over."
> But Tom wouldn't rise, and looked imploring.[37]

St. Clare promises to curb his drinking. The old slave's next evangelical effort is to convert his master to Christianity. As Tom struggles, offering ideas that can be accepted only if one has faith, it is again his humility and compassion that argue the more convincingly.

> Tom spoke with fast-running tears and choking voice. St. Clare leaned his hand on his shoulder, and wrung the hard, faithful, black hand.
> "Tom, you love me," he said.
> "I's willin' to lay down my life, this blessed day, to see Mas'r a Christian."[38]

The reader knows, by this time, that Tom is a black Christ symbol in the novel.

Tom converts his master to Christianity but fails miserably with a slave named Prue. She has been misused too obscenely to be influenced by either his compassion or his platitudes. Most of her life was spent breeding children for the slave market. Each child, except the last, was taken from her at birth and sold, and that one died from malnutrition. Grief-stricken, she has been drinking in order to forget the hunger cries of her baby. Tom is the only person who tries to console her.

> "O ye poor critter!" said Tom, "han't nobody never told ye how the Lord Jesus loved ye, and died for ye? Han't they telled ye that he'll help ye, and ye can go to heaven, and have rest, at last?"
> "I looks like gwine to heaven," said the woman; "An't thar where white folks is gwine? S'pose they'd have me thar? I'd rather go to torment, and get away from Mars'r and Missis."[39]

Her reaction is almost prophetic of contemporary rejection of the Tom image.

After St. Clare's death, Tom is sold to Simon Legree, at whose plantation he continues his missionary zealousness. Legree provides only one mill for the slaves to grind corn for their evening meal. The stronger preempt the places of the weaker in the line of waiting slaves. Tom, weak and hungry, having just arrived from the slave mart, grinds corn for two tired women before tending to his own needs, performing

> . . . a deed of charity, small as it was; but it woke an answering touch in their hearts—an expression of womanly kindness came over their hard faces. They mixed his cake for him, and tended its baking.[40]

While they cook, Tom reads the Bible aloud to them, but the women, like Prue, cannot believe that God cares what happens to them.

Two other incidents round out the Tom image. Each slave is expected to pick a specified amount of cotton each day. Standing over them are two burly Negro "drivers" who beat them if they stop to rest. To protect a woman from the whip, Tom transfers some of the cotton from his sack to hers, thereby incurring the anger of the driver, who reports the incident to Legree. Legree, desirous of turning Tom from his virtuous ways, promises him special privileges, as a driver, if he will flog a female slave. Tom refuses. Angered, Legree

orders his drivers to beat the old man repeatedly and unmer-
cifully. Still Tom refuses to compromise in any way. Even
when he is near death, he forgives his tormentor and tries to
save his soul.

> Tom looked up to his master, and answered, "Mas'r, if
> you was sick, or in trouble, or dying, and I could save ye,
> I'd *give* ye my heart's blood; and if taking every drop of
> blood in this poor old body would save your precious soul,
> I'd give 'm freely, as the Lord gave his for me. O mas'r,
> don't bring this great sin on your soul!"[41]

Obviously Tom is Mrs. Stowe's cultural oblation, delineated to reinforce her argument against the evils of slavery.
In *Goodbye to Uncle Tom*,[42] J. C. Furnas shows how the Tom
image has infiltrated national consciousness and been ex-
ploited since the novel was first published. Instead of endur-
ing as a symbol of that which is best in Christian society, the
image has become symbolic of servile passivity and accommodativeness, and has helped to stereotype black images in
literature. Tom's overwillingness to "turn the other cheek"
and to allow his head to be beaten to a pulp has caused his
name to become a "snarl word" in contemporary life.

Demonstrating the persistence of this figure into this century, Sam Fathers, created by William Faulkner, is a modern
black father and sacrifice symbol; but nothing remains of
slave servility in his portrait. His description ("A Justice,"
These Thirteen, 1931) separates him from other caricatures
of Negroes, a differentness attributable in part to Sam's
Chickasaw ancestry. He was not, in skin color or in bodily
configuration or in relationship with others, what Faulkner
calls "a blue-gum, or nigger."[43] In "The Bear" (*Go Down,
Moses, and Other Stories*, 1942) he is called "taintless and
incorruptible" along with Old Ben, the bear, and Lion, the
mongrel dog.

As black father symbol, he teaches Ike McCaslin the best
that is in his culture, and it is assumed that if Ike learns the
code of an honorable hunter, he will never thereafter be
false to himself or behave dishonorably with others. From
the moment that Sam takes the boy under his "Negro rank
quilt" to protect him from the cold November drizzle in the

wilderness, Ike senses that he is "witnessing his own birth." Under Sam's tutelage, Ike learns humility, courage, and fortitude. This trinity of ideals influences his behavior for the remainder of his life, as he tries to make right the evils he has inherited from slaveholding ancestors.

Although Sam is not a black Christ in the sense that Tom is, he is nonetheless a sacrificial symbol in a society controlled by ideas of white supremacy. When Ike discovers the old journals that record slave births and deaths and unveil sordid details of concubinage, incest, and denial of black offspring, he realizes the meaning behind his grandfather's thousand-dollar legacy to Turl: "*So I reckon that was cheaper than saying, My son is a nigger. . . . Even if My son wasn't but two words.*"[44] All of Sam's life has been spent under a shadow, because he belongs to a group that is denied equality of opportunity, and social acceptance. After Old Ben's death, symbolically marking the end of Ike's education in the wilderness, Sam senses that he will soon die, and is not sorry, for his life among American whites has been lonely and miserable.[45]

Other twentieth-century characters sacrificed by cultural attitudes are black protest symbols that support authors' theses for reform. In their search for whatever, for them, would be the "good" life, protagonists are invariably thwarted by stultifying economic and social conditions. No matter how hard they struggle against these influences, environment— the real villain—prevails in the end. In addition, a protagonist may be forced to wrestle with some personality trait that he possesses, but here again, both inception and nurture of the trait are due to environmental evils against which an individual is the pawn of natural and social forces. Paul Green's note prefacing his volume of plays, *Lonesome Road: Six Plays for the Negro Theatre* (1926), shows implicit ecological imbalance precluding success in interactions with the environment.

> *Living in the vilest of huts, the prey of his own superstition, suspicions and practices, beaten and forlorn before God Almighty himself—he* [the Negro] *has struggled helplessly in the clutch of affliction and pain. He has*

*perished by the thousands in the long servitude of his
white master. Unceasingly he has matched his strength
with the earth that bore him, going forever in the end to
rot unnoticed in the land he's tilled.*[46]

Though Paul Green writes about the rural South, the impotence of Negroes in conflict with natural and cultural
forces appears in fiction depicting other places: a city slum,
a Western ranch, a Tennessee backwater.

Mulatto Peter Siner in T. S. Stribling's *Birthright* (1922)
is an example of this literary figure. Four years before the
start of the novel, Peter's ambition and altruistic concern for
his people had driven him away from Hooker's Band, Tennessee, up north to Harvard for an education. His ambition
and altruism, according to Stribling, are attributable to his
"white" blood.[47] He returns with a "flame in his heart" to
improve economic and social conditions but finds that he is
no longer able either to understand the peculiarities of his
own culturally deprived black people or to deal realistically
with black-white relations. Only at Cairo, Illinois—the mythical line dividing South from North—when he is ordered into
the Jim Crow railroad coach, does he begin to remember
what it means to be black in the South.

From the moment of Peter's arrival home, everything
connected with his dream of uplifting his people goes wrong.
First, instead of being welcomed as savior, he is looked upon
with suspicion. Incomprehensible to the townsfolk are his
acquired habits of taking a bath every day and of wasting
time with books instead of enjoying the more normal youthful pastimes—gambling, carousing, and chasing women. In
contrast, Tump Pack, who returns at the same time, the
local boy who-really-made-good, is welcomed heartily. Tump,
a loud-mouthed, hard-liquor-drinking ex-soldier, has received
a Congressional Medal for bravery during the war and values
it as a good luck amulet in crap games. Second, Peter's idealism interferes with his common sense. He obtains money
from the Sons and Daughters of Benevolence to buy land for
a black school. Because he fails to read the fine print in the
deed of sale that a white clerk hoodwinks him into signing,
he loses the respect of the entire community. The deed for-

bids blacks from entering upon, occupying, or removing timber from the property. As a result both whites and blacks, including his mother, believe that his education has irrevocably addled his brains.

The only people who sympathize with him are a girl named Cissie, whom Tump Pack appropriates as his woman, and a white alumnus of Harvard, who is as impractical and idealistic as Peter. Cissie, like Peter, had tried to lift herself out of the stagnation of Hooker's Bend by obtaining an education at a Negro college. On returning home, she discovered that the only employment available to her is as the domestic servant of whites. Stribling attributes her ambition to white ancestry that is buried futilely and wastefully in the inert blackness of Niggertown, the black belt of Hooker's Bend.[48]

She and Peter, drawn together by frustration, decide to forgo their dreams, escape from the stagnation of Hooker's Bend, and try to find happiness together in the North. Two events stop them. A black minister refuses to perform the ceremony. "You an' Miss Cissie acts too much lak white folks fuh a nigger lak me to jine you, Mr. Peter."[49] Shortly afterwards, Cissie discovers that she is pregnant. Peter is not the father of her child. The reader is expected to believe that four years at Harvard have bred out of him all temptation to indulge in premarital sex relations or to break any other cultural taboo. The man responsible for Cissie's condition is either Tump Pack or the son of her employer who earlier accused her of stealing and then blackmailed her into becoming his mistress by promising to keep silent about the theft. Peter, though shocked, is willing to marry her but accepts her reason for refusing to marry him: ". . . if you were Tump Pack . . . it wouldn't have made any difference; but—you went off and learned to think and feel like a white man."[50]

In desperation, Peter takes refuge in another Messianic scheme. He convinces himself that he, as a mulatto, is the chosen evangel to teach the pure and simple doctrines of love and justice and to bring about better relations between the races. One morning, like a knight of old, he ventures forth, urging blacks to love their white employers and to stop stealing from them. He urges whites to pay their servants higher wages and to recognize that by dehumanizing blacks, they are harming themselves and the South. By nightfall, he succeeds only in increasing the basic mistrust of both groups. It had long been mutually accepted that blacks would steal from their employers and that whites would close their eyes to the petty thievery so long as it suited their purposes. Defeated, he relinquishes his dream of black social advancement and leaves Hooker's Bend with Cissie as his wife.

Abraham McCranie, a mulatto in two of Paul Green's one-act plays, *In Abraham's Bosom* (1926) and *Your Fiery Furnace* (1926),[51] is a literary figure who is driven to destruction by his desire to educate himself and his people in North Carolina. Like Peter's and Cissie's, his desire is attributed to "white" blood that must contend with the "black" for supremacy over his personality. Both whites and blacks disapprove of his desire. His white father, proud of him as one might be of a clever animal that has learned a few tricks, encourages him to master the rudiments of literacy but refuses to help to start a school. Frustrated, Abe gets into a trivial argument with his white half-brother and wins the fight that ensues, a crime punishable by death in that time and place. Abe's punishment is the lesser but more galling one of being horsewhipped publicly by his father. Burning with rage, he finds release from violent emotions in excessive sex activity.

In *Your Fiery Furnace*, thirty years devoted unsuccessfully to the realization of his dreams have passed. He has fought futilely against the opposition of whites and the fear-ridden inertia of blacks. Most distressing of all is the attitude of his mother and his son. His mother has accommodated too well to caste demands:

> Time you's learning dat white is white and black is black, and God made de white to allus be bedder'n de black. It was so intended from de beginning.[52]

His son, having lived his life under the threat and actuality of the community's opposition to Abe's dream, rejects him and the dream, and informs the Ku Klux Klan of his father's continued activity in defiance of warnings from whites. With Abe's death the chance for black advancement is dissipated and the caste system entrenched.

In one sense, Abe is luckier than Parry Clay in Ellen

Glasgow's novel, *In This Our Life* (1941). Abe does not live to witness the death of his dream. Parry Clay, in contrast, is saved from physical death but succumbs to spiritual death when his dream of becoming a lawyer is shattered by social constrictions. His family and other sympathetic Negroes are either too poor to help him or too conditioned by cultural belief to see the necessity of more than elementary education for a black boy. Here again, the one white man who might help believes that there is no need for Negro lawyers in the small Virginia community. Later, Parry is accused and jailed on a charge of hit-and-run driving. Justice before a white judge and jury with a white lawyer defending him is the last thing he can be assured of getting. Parry is exonerated only by the effort of a Southern liberal who forces the real culprit to confess. The youth forgoes his dream because the environment, offering only unsurmountable obstacles, is too powerful a force for him to overcome.

Similar stultifying effects of external pressures frustrate each succeeding generation of characters in Waters Turpin's three novels dealing with social injustices in rural and urban localities. In *Rootless* (1957), the last published but the first in time sequence, Jim Prince, slave descendant of African tribal headmen, refuses to endure the indignities of slavery and runs away to Santo Domingo where black men have risen from slavery to freedom and self-rule. This is the atmosphere in which he wants to put down his roots and insure freedom for his wife and the child that is soon to be born. He is a self-determining individual; but, in the end, he and his wife die tragically without achieving their goal. His son continues enslaved. Prince's descendants in *These Low Grounds* (1937), though physically free, are equally frustrated in their attempts to cast off the effects of caste and caste psychology, such as the ease and impunity with which a white mob can murder a black man when the latter tries to defend himself in an altercation with a white man; the abject, paralyzing fear among blacks that prevents their protecting a man from mob violence before his guilt has been proved; the unequal opportunities for education; the apathy among blacks regarding education; and, most insidious of all, the philosophy of Booker T. Washington, postulating that blacks must be twice as efficient as whites to do a comparable job. In *O Canaan* (1939) the focus shifts from the Princes living on the eastern shore of Maryland to the Bensons living in a Chicago slum. The Bensons fare no better in an urban scene than do the Princes in a rural one. Bad housing, gambling, prostitution, disease, a race riot, an economic depression create an environment that adversely controls their lives.

Another powerful protest symbol is the Negro protagonist in *Deep Are the Roots* (1945), a drama written by Arnaud D'Usseau and James Gow. Brett Charles, a war hero, returns to his home in the South after experiencing more humane treatment abroad. A female Southern liberal obtains a scholarship for him at a Northern university, hoping that if he succeeds there, he will remain in the North and escape the virulence of Southern prejudice. But Brett refuses the scholarship as he is determined to become principal of the black high school. He wants to secure superior advantages for his people and to assist in preparing them for social integration. When his benefactress discovers that her younger sister and Brett are in love, her liberalism vanishes and she reverts to race-baiting behavior. Ironically, the young people recognize the futility of their situation. The pattern of dealing with a "bad" Negro follows a typical pattern. Brett is falsely accused of stealing, imprisoned on insufficient grounds, and denied the right of counsel. Two whites, realizing that the case against him cannot be prosecuted successfully, secure his release and put him on a northbound train. He, though defeated by environmental constrictions, returns to face his accusers but not to avenge the wrong done him. His decency fosters some small beginning of self-understanding in his former benefactress.

Some writers of sociological fiction during the 1930's and 1940's go a step farther than those mentioned above in showing the effects of social constrictions on black people in American culture. Notable among these are John Steinbeck's character named Crooks in *Of Mice and Men* (1937), Richard Wright's Bigger Thomas in *Native Son* (1940), and Ann Petry's Lutie Johnson in *The Street* (1946).

Crooks, as his name suggests, is a cripple. His deformed

spine, glittering eyes, and pain-tightened mouth are outer, visible signs of a personality deformation resulting from years of sublimating his aggressive hatred and anger for what society has done to him, making him less than a forth-right, upstanding human being. As stable buck on a California ranch, he is part of a team that is essential for getting the work done, yet he is rejected by his teammates who are white. In defense, Crooks's resentment takes the form of excluding all whites from his isolated sleeping quarters. For a while he lowers his guard, becoming less rigid, as he begins to dream of sharing Lennie's and George's plan for a new and better life. The dream is shattered by a white woman. One night while her husband is away she comes to the barn to flaunt herself before two white men who are discussing the plan with Crooks. He orders her out, threatening to tell Curley of her misbehavior. Without compunction, she squelches him and his dream.

> "Listen, Nigger, . . . You know what I can do to you if you open your trap?"
> Crooks stared helplessly at her, and then he sat down on his bunk and drew into himself.
> She closed in on him. "You know what I could do?"
> Crooks seemed to grow smaller, and he pressed himself against the wall. "Yes, Ma'am."
> "Well you keep your place then, Nigger, I could get you strung up on a tree so easy it ain't even funny."[53]

Knowing the tendency of lynch mobs to act without first determining the validity of accusations, Crooks draws his seething rage inside his crooked body, like a turtle drawing its vulnerable parts into its shell. Nothing of the man's personality remains as he answers tonelessly, "Yes, Ma'am."

In Richard Wright's *Native Son* (1940), the scene is urban and the problem of environmental constriction and internalized aggression is similar. Like the rat trapped in the Thomases' one-room slum apartment and smashed to death with a frying pan, Bigger Thomas is caught between restrictive inequities imposed upon him by society and personal inability to handle his hatred for whites. His mother, older and more passively adjusted to caste status, finds release in

other-worldly religious conviction. But Bigger is male-assertive
and rebellious; his needs are of the here and now. For him,
it is galling to be denied opportunities that whites take for
granted. Unlike his friends, Gus and Jack, Bigger is unable
to sublimate his aggressions by getting drunk or vicariously
living as a white while watching motion pictures. In contrast,
his rage explodes, clearly revealing the extent to which his
personality is being mutilated by the caste position assigned
to black males in the culture: "Goddammit! . . . They don't
let us do nothing." Moreover, as a black, he is denied even
the ordinary avenues of redress afforded white males and is
expected to swallow his resentment which he compares to
"a red hot iron" being rammed down his throat. Wright establishes, in this passage, the neurotic alienation of blacks from
whites in society, for Bigger feels as if he is "outside the
world peeping in through a knot-hole."[54]

During early adolescence he vacillates between extremes
of poorly suppressed rage and indecision, with indecision
more frustrating than rage. Later, in desperation, he begins
to feel that he will never have confidence in himself unless
he commits an act "so violent that it would make him forget"
society's constricting isolation of him. Only by brutally mur-
dering twice is his suppressed anger dissipated. In the final
scene before his execution, he admits, "I didn't know I was
really alive in this world until I felt things hard enough to
kill for 'em. . . ."[55]

Ann Petry, in *The Street* (1946), shows how natural and
cultural forces work together to mold the personality of a
woman who has some characteristics of an individual. The
story opens with a cold November wind sweeping through a
trash-littered slum situated between two rivers.

> It did everything it could to discourage the people
> walking along the street. It found all the dirt and dust
> and grime on the sidewalk and lifted it up so that the dirt
> got into their noses making it difficult to breathe; the dust
> got into their eyes and blinded them; and the grit stung
> their skins. It wrapped newspapers around their feet en-
> tangling them until the people cursed deep in their
> throats, stamped their feet, kicked the paper. The wind

blew it back again and again until they were forced to stop and dislodge the paper with their hands. And then the wind grabbed their hats, pried their scarves from around their necks, stuck its fingers inside their coat collars, blew their coats away from their bodies. . . .[56]

Into this setting comes Lutie Johnson to find decent housing for herself and her young son. She aspires to middle-class standards and is determined not to fall into the customary pattern of life in slum areas: first, marriage; then, desertion by the husband; and finally, prostitution as the only means of supporting herself and her children. Almost immediately Lutie becomes the prey of Junto, white vice-lord of the neighborhood, and Boots, his Negro pander. Between the two, she is trapped. If she refuses to sleep with Junto, she becomes fair game for Boots. In anger she kills Boots and runs away to another large city, leaving her son in police custody for stealing. Her violent action represents the futile attempt of an individual to evade the destiny toward which her environment channels her.

A group of novels published more recently, during the 1960's, delineate various figures that fall within this archetypal category—portraits that exemplify the persistence of environmental determinism as a thematic influence on black portraiture in fiction. Among these are Rufus Scott in James Baldwin's *Another Country* (1962), Clay Williams in LeRoi Jones's (now Amiri Baraka's) *Dutchman* (1964), Calvin Coolidge Johnson in William Melvin Kelley's *dem* (1964) and Ludlow Washington in *A Drop of Patience* (1965) by the same author, also Nat Turner in William Styron's *The Confessions of Nat Turner* (1966) and Jack Jefferson in Howard Sackler's *The Great White Hope* (1968). All portraits focus, first, on the absence of reciprocal relations between blacks and whites, especially between black men and white women, and, second, on personality defects resulting from the cultural "castration" of black men. In these novels it seems that black men and white women, long denied access to each other by cultural taboo, enter into sexual relationships not so much because of mutual love but in defiance of the taboo or because of other more devious and psychologically warped reasons.

The historical background of this conflict is precisely
pinpointed by Cooley, or Calvin Coolidge Johnson, named,
according to once popular custom, for a President. Speaking
about himself in the third person, he explains to a white
man, whose willing wife he has seduced and who has given
birth to a black baby, just why a black man would do what
Cooley did and why he would feel no responsibility for any
offspring resulting from the union. The black man would be
settling old scores:

> Old scores from four hundred years ago, for his great
> granddaddy and his grandaddy. That's another thing
> about Cooley. He a long grudge-holding Black man. He
> don't never forget a slight. Like what old scores? Like
> having a wife or a girl you really love and then she gets
> big with a baby, and you happy as a champ. But when
> the baby comes, God damn, it ain't yours. You can't blame
> your woman; she a slave too. And you can't do nothing
> about it yourself. So you just eat shit, and you and your
> woman take and raise that kid. Then one day, after you
> and the baby get good and attached, its natural father
> up and sells it away from you. So you lost a kid, but you
> never really had one. So, he [Cooley], says, it's your
> turn.[57]

Rufus Scott, a musician, is as "grudge-holding" and vin-
dictive as Cooley in his relations with whites but, in contrast,
is totally defeated as a person. His desire for something more
than the usual submissive-dominant relationship with whites
leads him into sado-masochistic liaisons with an emotionally
scarred white girl and with a white homosexual, both Southerners. The life Rufus leads is unexamined, utterly futile until it is too late for him to do anything about it. Before he
commits suicide by jumping off a bridge, he wishes that he
had been kinder to both whites.

When we first meet twenty-year-old Clay Williams in the
stifling heat of a New York subway car, he is a black representative of middle-class America and probably considers
himself superior to Negroes like handyman Cooley or uncon-
ventional Rufus. He wears the middle-class uniform: narrow-
shouldered, three-buttoned jacket, precisely knotted tie,
reminiscent of Prufrock's submerged self. Reinforcement

comes as we learn further that he was born of a conservative New Jersey family, that his mother is a Republican, that his father is a "booster" of his country and, politically, more idealistic than the mother, voting for the candidate not the Party designee. Clinching the image, we learn that he attended a Negro college where he learned to appreciate Baudelaire. He is a "whitewashed" Negro, with his black identity submerged.

Into the same subway car comes thirty-year-old Lulu who calls herself by the epithet, Lena the Hyena, and offers him an apple. Sneeringly, probingly, brutally, she divests him of centuries of acquired Western cultural veneer, stripping it off layer by layer, until she uncovers the black essence of the man beneath. He is no longer the polite accommodative black boy. Out flow all the suppressed anger, hostility, aggressive violence that have been so deeply internalized by him and so firmly held in check by superego forces that it is doubtful he ever fully realized the extent to which he had been brainwashed. As he is about to leave the car, Lulu, as archetypal Terrible Mother, performs a ritualistic "moment of truth" by stabbing and killing him with a knife thrust through the chest; for the "white" Negro must die so that the totally black man can be resurrected and reclaim his birthright.

In contrast with Clay Williams's upward movement in *Dutchman,* the thirty years of Ludlow Washington's life in *A Drop of Patience* follows a downward movement, documenting a pattern of rejection and inevitable stunting of the blind man's personality. The first rejection comes at age five when his parents get rid of him by putting him in a home for handicapped children where he endures the cruelty of the other children and the indifference of the adults. He proves adept in music and is given training on several different instruments. At age sixteen, he is legally turned over, like an indentured servant, to a band leader who makes him a member of the band and pays him a salary, the only difficulty being that he cannot leave the band until he is eighteen without permission of the leader. Playing with the band compensates for this difficulty.

He meets and marries Etta Sue; all goes well until their baby, Bethrah, is born. Ludlow had not wanted the child.

Something of this unspoken idea must have been communicated to Etta Sue. Born to be a mother, she ceases to be a wife. Moreover, so protective is she of Bethrah that because of his blindness, and perhaps for other reasons, she does not permit him to fondle or hold the child. Thus rejected a second time, he leaves New Marsails, Kelley's fictional community, to work with a celebrated singer, and has no further contact with his family.

In the North, he goes from one musical success and from one woman to another until he meets white Ragan who becomes for him something closely akin to a Jungian *anima*. She claims to love him, to want to marry him, to bear his children. For the first time he begins to think about entering into another marriage and about having a child of his own. He is rejected a third time, more bitterly than previously when he realizes the true nature of their relationship: that she is ashamed of him, never letting him meet her family or friends; that all she wants is clandestine and, in her warped mind, exotic sex; further, that she is almost powerless to control these almost subliminal feelings resulting also from centuries of peculiar cultural conditioning. A breakdown, hospitalization follow. When released, he is, at thirty-four, a burnt-out wreck, never able to trust or enter into a satisfying relationship with anyone again, even with Harriet, a black girl who assists him in making as much of a personal and financial recovery as it is possible for him to make. Only one plan for the future has any significance for him: to play good black music for black people, unencumbered by personal entanglements.

Nat Turner and Jack Jefferson are fictional portraits of black culture-heroes delineated by white authors. The controversy stirred up by their portraits indicates something of the extent to which the real life prototypes of these fictional symbols have become embedded in American myth.[58] An early reference to Nat Turner's insurrection appears in *Clotel; or, The President's Daughter* (1853) by the fugitive slave writer, William Wells Brown. Turner is described as a "full-blooded negro" who was "made aware, by too many proofs, that the slave could expect no justice at the hand of the slave owner." Brown goes on:

He went by the name of "Nat Turner." He was a preacher amongst the negroes, and distinguished for his eloquence, respected by whites, and loved and venerated by the negroes. On the discovery of the plan for the outbreak, Turner fled to the swamps, followed by those who had joined in the insurrection. Here the revolted negroes numbered some hundreds, and for a time bade defiance to their oppressors.[59]

Brown, a contemporary of Nat Turner, does not give much more of his story than that which is quoted here. He turns his attention to a guerrilla fighter named Picquilo whose base of operation is the Dismal Swamp and whose portrait is included among the primitives later in this chapter.

Styron's in-depth portrait of the insurrectionist does not pretend to be biography but fiction. What he has done, however, is reduce a black culture-hero to a pathetically fallible creature, although one not totally stripped of admirable characteristics. Nat remains a charismatic preacher, seized by a burning passion to free blacks from the degradation and emasculation of involuntary servitude. Yet, despite his self-assertion and altruism, he is impotent both as man and insurrectionist. The author has made him celibate and saddles him with an additional burning passion for white women, epitomized by one in particular—a girl named Margaret—and for light-skinned slave girls. Further, this passion burns without hope of assuagement because the only relief he allows himself is masturbation while he engages in erotic fantasy. At times the two passions seem to fuse into an overpowering obsession so perfectly intense that one feels that he must eventually be successful as insurrectionist if not as a man, that the monomaniacal zeal he exhibits cannot possibly be entirely wasted. But it is. In the heat of battle he cannot bring himself to kill anyone except Margaret, the object of his masturbatory fantasy.

It seems that many motives are involved in this portrait. For example, is the celibacy of the culture-hero due to some mythic belief in the necessity of sexual abstinence in order to insure the successful outcome of his superhuman task? Nat does promise himself a wife when his mission is completed.

Has Nat been conceived as a tragic hero whose failure is due to a kind of *hamartia* that precludes success both as man and insurrectionist? He has been given heroic dimensions: his purpose is praiseworthy; he acts on his own responsibility; he accepts the consequences of his actions; and he suffers like a brave man. Does the answer lie in cultural attitudes toward black men? As we have noted among earlier black images, none celebrates black sexual virility. They are usually sexless or sexually distorted figures.

The portrait of Jack Jefferson, as heavyweight boxing champion of the world, is much more vigorous; but notwithstanding the vigor, he too is doomed to defeat as the contemporary manifestation of a sacrifice symbol in literature. Although he is portrayed as a brutal fighter in the ring, traditional characteristics of the stock brute have been deemphasized in *The Great White Hope*. Only a few references to the stock brute have been retained to show the attitudes of the white crowds who consider Jefferson to be an animal, a gorilla who lives like a pig, whom they call a savage assassin. As world champion he boosts black egos and deflates white ones. More disturbing, he takes a white woman as his common law wife and because of this action must be punished at home and hounded abroad. Desperate white sportsmen conclude that he must be beaten decisively by a white boxer, by foul means if necessary, to preserve the myth of white superiority and black inferiority in defiance of evidence to the contrary. Angry and bitter at what has happened to him and the white woman, he projects his frustrations onto her, ultimately rejecting her and contributing to her subsequent suicide. In the end he too is defeated, going down gallantly but still defeated.

Mammies

An archetype that shares prominence with the sacrifice symbol in our literature is the black mammy, to whom white mothers customarily relinquished the privilege of nursing their own children. Were it not for the continued emotional response engendered by the mother image in American life and letters, these fictional symbols of inferior foster mothers could be classified as stock characters. Faulkner sentimentally dedicates *Go Down, Moses* (1940) to his mammy,[60] and as we noted earlier, Lillian Smith, in *Killers of the Dream* (1949), calls the relationship with her mammy one of the profound relationships of her life. In poetry, Stephen Vincent Benét describes this paradoxical relationship:

> The matriarch of the weak and young,
> The lazy crooning, comforting tongue.
> She has had children of her own
> But the white-skinned ones are bone of her bone.
> They may not be hers, but she is theirs,
> And if the shares were unequal shares,
> She does not know it, now she is old.
> They will keep her out of the rain and cold.
> And some were naughty and some were good,
> But she will be warm while they have wood,
> Rule them and spoil them and play physician
> With the vast, insensate force of tradition,
> Half a nuisance and half a mother
> And legally neither one nor the other,
> Till at last they follow her to her grave,
> The family despot, and the slave.[61]

Benét's description can be documented many times over in literature. Little Eva's Mammy in *Uncle Tom's Cabin* is a "decent mulatto woman" who, by comparison with Marie St. Clare, a languid hypochondriac, is the more ideal mother. Especially noticeable is the difference when Eva returns home after a trip north with her father. Marie St. Clare's greeting is cold and distant whereas Mammy ". . . hugged her, and laughed, and cried, till her sanity was a thing to be doubted. . . ."[62] In *Aunt Phillis's Cabin*, (1852), the novel written by Mary H. Eastman as counter propaganda to *Uncle Tom's Cabin*, the mammy is a paragon of virtue. A tall, dignified bright mulatto, Aunt Phillis ironically stints her own child at her breast and gives preference to the white one.[63] Two characters that merit detailed analysis are Mammy Krenda in Thomas Nelson Page's *Red Rock* (1898) and Mom

Bi in Joel Chandler Harris's "Mom Bi: Her Friends and Her Enemies" (1884).

The scene of Page's novel is set in Virginia, just before the Civil War. A lively party is in progress at Red Rock, the plantation owned by the Jacquelin Grays since early colonial days. For ten-year-old Blair Cary, child of neighbors, this is the first grown-up party she has been permitted to attend. When it is past the child's bedtime, Mammy Krenda makes her entrance in as vivid an introduction as any character in the novel receives:

> In the midst of their talk an old mammy in a white apron with a tall bandana turban around her head, appeared suddenly in a doorway, and dropping a curtsey made her way over to Blair, like a ship bearing down under full sail. There was a colloquy between the two, inaudible, but none the less animated and interesting, the old woman urging something and the little girl arguing against it. Then Blair went across and appealed to her mother, who, after a little demurring, came over and spoke to the mammy, and thereon began further argument. She was evidently taking Blair's side, but she was not commanding, she was rather pleading.[64]

Northerners at the party, not understanding Southern custom, are surprised at the liberties Krenda takes with her owners, at her mistress's submissiveness, and at the tone of Krenda's voice as she reluctantly gives permission:

> "Well, jist a little while." . . .
> "You all gwine ruin my child' looks meckin' her set up so late. How she gwine have any complexion, settin' up all times o'night?"

Her authority exercised, she walks toward the door. Several ladies spoke to her,

> . . . and they must have said pleasant things; for before she reached the door she was smiling and curtseying right and left, and carried her head as high as a princess.[65]

As Benét's paradox "matriarch and slave" indicates, this scene shows clearly her culturally accepted privilege in matters pertaining to the well-being of her foster child and her culturally required behavior in the presence of whites when they speak to her.

When next seen in the novel, Krenda is free; but, completely brainwashed, she chooses to remain with her Miss Bessie and Blair. Dr. Cary, required by law to pay wages to her, is warned by his wife that Krenda will be insulted if he tries to pay for services that are given only because she loves them. A touchy situation develops as she quietly places the money on a table.

> "How much does you pay *Miss Bessie?*"
> "How much what?"
> *"Wages."* He had no idea the word could convey so much contempt.
> "Why, nothing—of course—"
> Old Krenda lifted her head.
> "I'm gwine 'way."
> "What?"
> "I'm feared you'll charge me bode!"
> "Mammy—you don't understand—" The Doctor was never in such a dilemma. . . .
> "Won't you accept the money as a gift from me?" he said at last, desperately.
> "Nor—I ain' gwine *tetch* it!" the gesture was even more final than the tone. With a sniff, she turned and walked out, leaving the Doctor feeling like a school-boy.[66]

After a few moments he hears voices in the next room. Opening the door he sees Mammy Krenda, his wife, and Blair crying in each other's arms, and then he hears Mammy say, ". . . I didn't do it for no wages."[67] It is quite a while later before he is returned to favor among the female members of his household.

Krenda is equally forceful in protecting her white "family" from an offensive, cowardly carpetbagger named Jonadab Leech who, with occupation troops, invades the Cary home in search of concealed guns and ammunition. She berates Leech and chases him away in the presence of his soldiers, one of whom, a caricatured Irishman, relates the incident to Leech's embarrassment later.

"Bedad!" said he, "the ould woman looked like wan of theyse little black game-burruds when a dog comes around her chicks, with her fithers all oop on her back and her wings spraid. . . ."[68]

Joel Chandler Harris's Mom Bi resembles a game bird even more than Mammy Krenda. She is irritable, peevish, sometimes spiteful, but utterly devoted to the white children she has nursed. Her name is a derivative of Viola, so corrupted by the many children she has cared for. Jet black, tall, gaunt, and partially paralyzed, she moves about "with a sidewise motion and with her left arm held across her body" as a mother holding an infant. Overall, she looks like a "black Amazon."

This impression was heightened by the peculiar brightness of her eyes. They were not large eyes, but they shone like those of a wild animal that is not afraid of the hunter. Her nose was not flat, nor were her lips thick like those of the typical Negro.[69]

Being the property of Jesse Waynecroft never breaks her spirit: she remains sharp of tongue and quick to react to any and all, white or black, and is especially scornful of poor whites called "sand hillers."

De Lord know, I glad I nigger. Ef I ain't bin born black der ain't no tellin', what I mought bin born. I mought bin born lak some dese white folks what eat dirt un set in de chimerly-corner tell dee look lak dee bin smoke dried. De Lord know what make Jesse Waynecroft fetch he famerly 'mongst folk lak deze.[70]

Too old to work, she spends most of her time sitting before the picture of her white child bemoaning the fact that his parents permitted him to go off to war with the inferior sand hillers. She completely misunderstands the issues of the war, her only concern being the safety of her "child." She croons to his image as if it could understand and respond:

> Look at me, honey, . . . look at you' ole nigger mammy!
> Whut make dee lef' you fer go way down dey wey one
> folks kill turrer folks? . . . Whaffer dee no lef' dem no
> 'count san'hillers fer do all de fightin'? Whaffer you' daddy
> no sen' he niggers fer fight? De Lord know dee plenty
> un um.[71]

She is grief-stricken when he is killed in battle.

Earlier, Mom Bi's daughter was sold away from her by
the Waynecrofts. Normally one would expect a mother to
react more violently to the loss of her own child than to the
loss of a foster child. Mom Bi, however, can forgive her
master and mistress for selling Maria although she resents
what they did.

> "De Lord know I done bin fergive you-all fer sellin'
> 'Ria 'way fum me. De Lord know I is! Wun I bin see you
> set down un let dat chile go off fer git kill' "—Mom Bi
> pointed her long and quivering finger at Gabriel's por-
> trait—" 'Wun I see dis, I say 'hush up, nigger! don't
> bodder 'bout 'Ria.' De Lord know I bin fergive you!"[72]

Later literary depictions of the mammy maintain the
basic characteristics of the archetype but indicate a slight
trend toward treatment of them as individuals. Among the
numerous delineations in this group are Julia Peterkin's
Maum Hannah, William Faulkner's Dilsey, Katherine Anne
Porter's Nannie, Carson McCullers's Berenice, and Henry Van
Dyke's Aunt Harry.

Maum Hannah, in Julia Peterkin's "Ashes" (*Green Thursday,* 1924), lives a self-sufficient but lonely life on land that
was once part of her Old Master's plantation. He promised
that her cabin and the land immediately around it would
always belong to her; but after his death all of his land,
including her plot, is sold. She is notified, not unkindly, that
she must leave when a new house for whites is built near
her cabin. When the owners are ready to take possession,
she is ordered to leave. Having no place to which she can go,
she prays for a sign to guide her. As she looks up to pray,
the cold ashes from her pipe trickle through her fingers to
the floor; and through her door, she sees a flaming sunrise.

To her the ashes and the red sky signify that she must set
the new house afire so that she can keep her cabin. This
done, she walks to the village and confesses her crime. The
sheriff investigates and discovers that the new owners will
not lose money as the house is insured against fire; further,
that the neighborhood of Maum Hannah's cabin is considered
jinxed, that no whites want to live there. He resettles her in
the cabin and advises her to keep silent about what she has
done. Although Maum Hannah's relationships with whites
are non-reciprocal and subservient, she decides what is best
for herself, fully recognizing alternatives and consequences
and assuming full responsibility for her decision.

William Faulkner's portrait of Dilsey (*The Sound and the
Fury*, 1929) deviates from the general archetypal pattern.
She does not carry the designative name tag; she calls her
Miss Caroline's children by their first names even after they
have become adults; and she makes responsible decisions.
It is in other aspects of her relatedness with the Compsons
and in her appearance that Faulkner creates the mammy
image. On her head she wears the traditional turban of the
archetype but she perches a black straw hat above it.
Idealized by Faulkner as black-skinned caryatid supporting
the weaker Compsons, she is as emotionally attached to them
and as ineffectual in preventing their disintegration as other
mammies in literature.[73] She feels that the Compsons are
as much hers as are T.P., Frony, or Luster; and no matter
how diligently and devotedly she cares for them, she is powerless to reverse the loss of family integrity that has been set in
motion. Nor is she capable of understanding the reasons for
their disintegration or her failure to prevent it. All she can
do is commiserate and say "you Jason" as she defies him
by offering herself as a sacrifice instead of niece Quentin, or
"Dis long time, O Jesus" and "I seed de first en de last"
as she watches their downfall. Despite these traditional overtones, Faulkner's delineation of Dilsey's sense of independent
responsibility marks a shift toward greater individualization
of this archetypal figure.

Katherine Anne Porter's Nannie appears in two short
stories, "The Old Order" and "The Last Leaf" (*The Leaning
Tower and Other Stories*, 1934). She is a neatly turbaned

black woman who was childhood playmate of Sophia Jane, her mistress. Both were married at the same time, and, according to Southern tradition, Nannie nursed her own and the first three of Sophia Jane's children. After each woman gave birth the fourth time, Nannie fell ill and Sophia Jane became wet nurse for both children. Her developing attachment for the foster child made her understand Nannie's situation better. She vowed that thereafter she and Nannie would nurse only their own children. When Nannie is freed, she chooses to remain with her mistress. The relationship between the two women in later life is mutually supportive and comforting, and its closeness is evident in their ability to communicate with each other simply by an exchange of glances, a lifted eyebrow, or a pause in their conversation as they sit together sewing quilt pieces. Yet their relationship is never reciprocal, for Nannie "had no ideas at all as to her place in the world. It had been assigned to her before birth, and for her daily rule she had all her life obeyed the authority nearest her."[74] It is only after Sophia Jane's death that Nannie begins to acquire separate individuality. To the disapproval of Sophia Jane's children, she leaves their household and sets up living quarters in a cabin on the plantation.

> . . . she was no more the faithful old servant Nannie, a freed slave; she was an aged Bantu woman of independent means, sitting on the steps [of her new home], breathing the free air.[75]

Carson McCullers's character Berenice, in *The Member of the Wedding* (1958), is a modern representation of a long line of cooks and mammies that goes back to Aunt Chloe in *Uncle Tom's Cabin,* whom J. C. Furnas describes as "woefully like Aunt Jemima."[76] Although Berenice cooks for Royall Addams and his daughter Frankie, and serves as substitute mother to Frankie, she is neither an Aunt Chloe nor an Aunt Jemima nor a Dilsey. Mrs. McCullers makes her an individual who thinks well of herself, who can make responsible decisions, and who has a proper sense of relatedness with others.

> She was very black and broad-shouldered and short. . . . Her hair was parted, plaited, and greased close to the

skull, and she had a flat and quiet face. There was only one thing wrong about Berenice—her left eye was bright blue glass. It stared out fixed and wild from her quiet, colored face, and why she wanted a blue eye nobody human would ever know. Her right eye was dark and sad.[77]

She always thought of herself as beautiful and attractive to men, an idea that strikes a discordant note to Frankie; but Frankie learns something about self-respect and self-acceptance from this woman, who has had numerous beaux, four husbands, and is currently being courted ardently. Frankie wonders why Berenice would want to wear a blue eye. The answer lies in a passage describing Berenice's dream of how she would re-create the world if she could.

> But the world of the Holy Lord God Berenice Sadie Brown . . . was round and just and reasonable. First, there would be no separate colored people in the world, but all human beings would be light brown color with blue eyes and black hair. There would be no colored people and no white people to make the colored people feel cheap and sorry all through their lives. No colored people, but all human men and ladies and children as one loving family on earth.[78]

Selection of a blue eye gives Berenice a chance to come closer to her dream of a world in which all people are equal. Though she is able to compensate by accepting her own kind of beauty, she reveals, in her fantasy, a culturally conditioned rejection of her black skin and eyes and a tragic acceptance of the black-white value system.

Because she has not been defeated by cultural attitudes, she helps Frankie understand and accept herself in interpersonal relationships. Frankie begins to learn that each human being is an important, separate entity and that it is possible for everyone to enter into satisfactory relations with others. What Berenice cannot do is protect Frankie from the heartbreak of rejection and disillusionment. No one can. In early life, Berenice experienced what she thought was a kind of rejection when her first husband, her ideal, died leaving her to wander from man to man in fruitless search for the relationship she had had with him. Each subsequent "husband" was selected because he manifested some quality that the first had had. It is only when she accepts the fact that the earlier perfection cannot be duplicated that she takes second best and marries her dependable suitor.

In relationships with others, Berenice does not conform to the mammy archetype. She is concerned, as one sensitive being can be, about the welfare of other people; but she has a healthy regard for herself and is not so selflessly attached to whites as earlier archetypal figures. Unlike them, when she uses the pronoun "we," she means her black family, the members of her lodge or church, in addition to Frankie and the white family of whom she is as fond as her literary predecessors. Emergence of the mammy from dependence and selfless attachment seems to have taken place in Berenice.

Henry Van Dyke's Aunt Harry, full name Harriet Gibbs, in *Ladies of the Rachmaninoff Eyes* (1965) is paradoxically as individualistic as Berenice yet seemingly as devoted to the memory of her white "child" as Mom Bi. Thirty years before the start of the novel, she and her husband Gideon began working for Etta and Ezra Klein when their two sons were small and the family lived on Long Island. Later they moved west with the Kleins to Green Acorns, not far from Kalamazoo. When the story begins both women have been widows for many years; Etta's son Sargeant is dead; her son Jerome is married to a gentile and lives in Kalamazoo. The elderly women live together, sharing the responsibility of rearing Harriet's grandnephew Oliver, who is the narrator of the story and treated as if he were the beloved son of the household.

That Harriet is a respected member of the group can readily be seen in the terms of address used by other characters. Everyone calls her Mrs. Gibbs except Oliver and Etta. He calls her Aunt Harry; the two women call each other by their first names unless they are being nasty to each other. In addition, she does not look like a servant. An impressive woman with alert black face, sparkling dark eyes, and thick "fiberglass" hair, she wears colorful dresses during the day as she works or supervises the other workers. Afternoons, she changes to one of her "good" dresses for tea. On special occasions, she dons regal black lace with a high starched collar, such as the evening that Maurice Le Fleur, self-styled warlock, conducts a séance to make contact with Sargeant, who committed suicide five years earlier in New York. As far as her personality is concerned, she is a puritanical, no-nonsense, cleanliness-is-next-to-godliness character who takes pleasure in telling people all sorts of unpleasant truths about themselves, largely out of a genuine respect for truth as she sees it but also for the pleasure of seeing the culprit squirm.

Friendship between Harriet and Etta is not the idealized one that exists between Nannie and Sophia Jane. It is a love-hate relationship established deftly at the beginning of the novel when Oliver, just before daybreak and after the séance, runs out of the house down to the salt lick with Aunt Harry's heart medicine. There, Etta is bending over Harriet's body, crying, "*Look* what she's done. She did it to spite me . . . I know she did." She continues her indictment, calling Harriet by name as if to will her back to life. A few days later she dies also, and the two women are buried beside each other. The rest of the novel explores their unusual relationship as it leads to this moment.

Over the years, these women have ruthlessly played a game of "one-upmanship" or, as Oliver calls it, "squelches," with each maneuvering to get the upper hand over the other; and it was a game that had its own rules and rituals. For instance, Harriet takes sadistic pleasure in berating Etta about the latter's fondness for rum, telling her that no one will allow her body to be cremated when she dies for fear of starting a "conflagrating fire." Etta makes fun of her expression, "conflagrating fire," and announces that she may decide not to be cremated. Harriet insists that she must be cremated, that all Jews are cremated, that even their beloved Sargeant was cremated.

Mentioning Sargeant's death starts them crying, a situation that frightens Oliver, as he sees the tears flow from "their ancient eyes . . . so like old pictures of Rachmaninoff's eyes," and as he runs a relay trying to console one and then the other. For he knows what the next step in the ritual will be: like avenging Erinyes, they will find a scapegoat on whom they can project their guilty embarrassment and thereby facilitate their reconciliation. Aunt Harry's wrath usually is spent berating Oliver for giving more time to consoling Etta Klein than he gives to consoling Harriet, his own flesh and blood. She accuses him of playing up to Etta for personal gain and condemns him for letting Etta make a white boy out of him. There is just enough truth in what she says to make Oliver uncomfortable—truth corroborated by Jerome, who refers to Oliver as Etta's toy or pacifier to help her get over Sargeant's suicide.

In contrast to such spiteful moments, their relationship is extremely close, containing undertones of latent lesbianism. On one occasion Etta coquettishly recalls her former youthful beauty. Harriet, her eyes aglow, concurs. Memory of an incident in the past enraptures them to the point of caricature. They giggle, snicker, grasp each other's arms, hug each other; and for the moment they recapture their youth. Later, after the tragic séance, Oliver, having matured somewhat, can assess their relationship more precisely and with greater understanding.

> They had woven a bickering, bantering tapestry together that was stronger than husband and wife, or sisters or cousins. And this bickering and bantering, this arguing, I was beginning to learn, was not to be made light of; it was a high seriousness, their arguing; it was the way they made love.[79]

Green Acorns was their innocent Garden of Eden until they invited Maurice LeFleur to conduct the séance at which Harriet, goaded by Etta, betrayed the memory of Sargeant by openly revealing the cause of his suicide—a secret shared by them but probably never mentioned even in private. Trouble starts when Maurice makes Etta the star performer of the occasion. Etta histrionically makes the most of her opportunity to impress the others present, including Jerome and his gentile wife Patricia Jo. She begins to claim that she can feel Sargeant's presence among them, that he is coming to her, his mother. Harriet, unable to endure Etta's being the center of attention, hints that the whole thing is

fraudulent and is reminded by Etta to mind her own business, a reminder that precipitates Harriet's anguished outburst that anything having to do with Sargeant is her
business. He was Etta's in blood but hers "in spirit and heart
and soul."[80] To prove her point she reveals the cause of his
suicide, his homosexuality. Etta throws a glass of rum at
her, the contents of which spatter and run down her high
starched collar. Calmly, deliberately, she relates the details
of Sargeant's attachment to a black youth, his disillusionment, her disdain for the lover, her compassion for Sargeant.
Infuriated by this time, Etta lashes out, searches for something to say that will hurt Harriet, the ultimate obscenity.
"You're a—demented old, old evil nigger woman!"[81]

Later, as Oliver knew they would, they began their reconciliation ritual with Harriet remorseful over the betrayal of
her "baby" and Etta petting and urging her to take one after
another "bitsy nips" of rum. Finally, Oliver sees them, word-
lessly and in unison, turn their Rachmaninoff eyes on
Maurice as their scapegoat. Reconciliation this time being
more difficult than ever before, they set upon him with
fiendish vigor, beating him nearly to death with big heavy
sticks. So inhuman is their behavior that Oliver stops them
long enough for Maurice to escape. The ferocity of the punishment brings on Harriet's fatal heart seizure.

Primitives

Another persistent archetype is the primitive which mani-
fests itself in several ways: as noble savage who is unaffected
by contacts with Western culture; as atavist who reverts to
jungle primitivism; as carnal sensualist whose whole being
is dominated by violent passions. Examples of the purely
"natural" figures are Daggoo in Melville's *Moby Dick* (1851)
and Bras-Coupé in Cable's *The Grandissimes* (1880).

Names assigned to primitives tend to be exotic or suggestive of a prevailing characteristic. For example, the name
Daggoo is foreign, possessing no associative connections for
us. Its meaning is farther removed than the name Bras-
Coupé, which, translated freely as the amputee, is symbolic

of spiritual maiming by virtue of the character's having been reduced from majestic chieftain to chattel. Bras-Coupé's African name, Mioko-Koanga, is as foreign-sounding as the name Daggoo.

Equally important in signaling this archetype are observable aspects of physical superiority. Daggoo, a "gigantic, coal-black Negro savage," is so huge that he must sit on the floor of Ahab's cabin at mealtimes. Animal similes—"erect as a giraffe," "lion-like tread," "as an African elephant," or "like a pacing tiger"—point up the savage image. Add to these "an Ahasuerus to behold," and he becomes absolute lord of all he surveys.

Of the two savages, Daggoo is the nobler, having been exposed to fewer contacts with Western culture. In youth, he joined the crew of a whaler, and, since then, touched none but whaling ports, most of which, according to Melville, were pagan. In contrast, Bras-Coupé exercised no volition in his destiny. Captured in Africa, he was transported to New Orleans in the hold of a ship ironically named *Egalité,* and thereupon reduced to a salable commodity. Though manacled, he is still a giant of "herculean puissance" and "savage dignity." Animal imagery helps build his primitive qualities. He is called *"ce maudit cocodri"* ("That accursed alligator"), a symbol of voodoo witchcraft. He has the face of a rhinoceros from which his eyes shine with a "tiger glance," revealing his "untamable spirit."

In a sense both characters are inscrutable blacks, producing "dark feelings of mystery and mounting fear of the incomprehensible." Daggoo glories in his blackness and is aware of the power it gives him over men who can be terrorized by its symbolic meanings. In response to the old Manxman's fear, he boasts, "Who's afraid of black's afraid of me! I'm quarried out of it!" Yet Daggoo is sensitive about his color. When pushed too far by the Spaniard's teasing, he insults the white, calling him "mannikin," impugns his valor—"white skin, white liver"—and surges instinctively to the fight. Daggoo's blackness is integral to Melville's symbolism that challenges and manipulates cultural values assigned to blackness and whiteness. Another characteristic, one that raises Daggoo above the savage, is his humanitarian

concern for others. Along with Queequeg, he moves instinctively to save Tashtego from drowning in spermaceti,
disregarding his own safety and the other seamen's warnings
to be careful.

Bras-Coupé's reactions are as instinctive as Daggoo's
but he is not as essential to Cable in *The Grandissimes* as
Daggoo is to Melville in *Moby Dick*. His story is part of
American myth and legend; and, according to Cable scholar
Arlin Turner, the Bras-Coupé story has been told by other
authors.[82] There is nothing artificial about Cable's use of it,
however, as he weaves it skillfully into the main plot of the
novel.

When Bras-Coupé learns that he is expected to work in
the fields he rebels, knocks down the slave driver "with a
sweep as quick as instinct," and simultaneously makes one
grand leap for freedom, only to be stopped by a bullet from
the overseer's gun. The owner, realizing that he cannot force
this slave to work as a common laborer, makes him a driver
of the other slaves. Bras-Coupé agrees to the new job only
after extracting a promise that he will be allowed to marry a
beautiful octoroon, named Palmyre, the maid of his master's
fiancée. Love does what force cannot. Humbled by his love,
he sings mournfully, "*Ah Palmyre, Palmyre, mo' piti zozo,
mo l'aimé' ou'—mo l'aimé, l'aimé ou' *"[83] His passion for
Palmyre touches the hearts of the Creoles; for they know
that she loves a white man and will do anything, even resort
to the fearful *gris-gris*, to circumvent the marriage.

She is one of two people who can restrain the noble
savage. The other is the fiancée of his master, a pallid white
girl. To him she is a terrifying manifestation of the living-
dead ("*Bras-Coupé 'n pas oulé 'oir zombis*"). At the sight
of her he prostrates himself on the ground and refuses to
budge until she has left. When she temporarily delays his
marriage, he obeys for the moment but threatens to call
down his voodoo god's wrath if he finds that the *dotchians*
have deceived him.

He does not wait long. At the wedding supper he drinks
too much and strikes his master—a crime punishable by
death under the *Code Noir*. More than that offense, he calls
down a voodoo malediction on the master, using strange

signs and uttering dire-sounding words in his African language. The stock response, revealing the whites' basic fear of black men, is reflected in the first words spoken after the curse, "Look to your wives and daughters." Bras-Coupé escapes into a swamp and hides out there until the following winter when he returns for Palmyre. When refused again, even the sight of the pale white *zombi* fails to prevent his invoking a curse of death on all male members of the household. In time the slaveowner falls ill. Shortly thereafter, Bras-Coupé is captured at a voodoo celebration. Clemency from the death sentence for striking his master is granted, but as a fugitive slave he is punished in the customary way: his ears are cut off; the *fleur de lys* is branded on his shoulders; he is hamstrung and whipped. During his punishment, no sound is heard from the "mutilated but unconquered African." The noble savage can endure the pain but he cannot endure the humiliation of public flogging. Near death, he magnanimously lifts the curse from the slaveowner's newly born son.

A character whose portrait contains traits of both the noble savage and the atavist is Picquilo in William Wells Brown's *Clotel; or, The President's Daughter*. His name is as foreign-sounding as the name Daggoo. This is how he looks:

> He was a large, tall full-blooded negro, with a stern and savage countenance; the marks on his face showed that he was from one of the barbarous tribes in Africa, and claimed that country as his native land; his only covering was a girdle around his loins, made of the skins of wild beasts which he had killed.[84]

He is a runaway slave hiding out in the Dismal Swamp of Virginia. He is not alone.

> He had met a negro woman who was also a runaway; and after the fashion of his native land, has gone through the process of oiling her as the marriage ceremony. They had built a cave in a rising mound in the swamp; this was their home.[85]

He has a sword which he made for himself from a scythe he had stolen on a foray into a plantation bordering the swamp. Brown depicts him in action using stealth and tactics learned in Africa.

> He moved about with the activity of a cat, and neither the thickness of the trees, nor the depth of the water could stop him. He was a bold, turbulent spirit; and from revenge imbrued his hands in the blood of all the whites he could meet. Hunger, thirst, fatigue, and loss of sleep he seemed made to endure as if by peculiarity of constitution. . . Such was the character of one of the leaders in the Southhampton insurrection.[86]

Two characters who revert to primitivism after contacts with Western civilization are widely spaced in time, and their delineations as artistic portraits are by no means equal. They are Cudjo in *Cudjo's Cave* (1863) by J. T. Trowbridge, and Brutus Jones in *The Emperor Jones* (1921) by Eugene O'Neill. Cudjo's African name conforms to the primitive pattern. In appearance, he departs from it. Ugly, with a body "like a frog's," "immensely long arms," and "short bow legs," he gibbers, grimaces, and delights in mischief. Cudjo is a fugitive slave hiding in the Tennessee hills with Pomp, an idealized stock character whom we met earlier. In spite of Pomp's influence, Cudjo reverts to idolatrous fire-worshipping. The tendency to regard fire animistically is reawakened when he tries to cook an evening meal.

> . . . Crouched before the fire, . . . he poked and scolded with malicious energy, . . . "Burn, ye devil! Krrr! sputter! snap! get mad, why don't ye?" Then throwing himself back upon a heap of skins, with his heels at the fire, and his long arms swinging over his head, in a savage and picturesque attitude, he burst into a shout, like the cry of a wild beast.[87]

Later, during a forest fire, he performs a primitive rite and extends the meaning of the fire.

> . . . a wild human figure making fantastic gestures, and prostrating itself toward the burning forests. . . . folding his arms above his head, spread them forth towards the fire, bowing himself again and again, until his forehead

touched the stone. . . . "My God . . . me mos' forgit him; now me 'members! Him comin' fur burn up de white folks, and set de brack man free."[88]

The other character, Emperor Brutus Jones, does not willingly revert to primitivism; instead, in a prolonged hallucination, he finds himself regressing into his own ancestral past. His name is a paradoxical combination of elements. The last name is the commonest of English-American names, like John Doe, or simply Joe or Mac, all identifying no one person in particular but any ordinary American male. Adding Brutus to it recalls the sardonic complexity of slave-naming, along with associative attitudes and fears about black people. To precede Brutus Jones with the title, Emperor, is to skew its total effect with an uneasy feeling that something is wrong. Is it the incongruity of tall-tale humor? Does it echo the tyrranous injustice of misrule by inferiors? His opening lines in the play, threatening to "frayle" the hides of blacks whom he rules, indicates that his power is absolute.

In appearance he is like Daggoo and Bras-Coupé: "tall, powerfully-built, full-blooded Negro," radiating "strength of will" and "self-reliant confidence." Here the resemblance ends. His behavior is "shrewd, suspicious, and evasive." He wears a Panama hat, patent leather shoes, and a brightly colored uniform reminiscent of lavishly ornamented lodge regalia.

While working as a Pullman porter back in the States, he killed a black man and was sentenced to the chain gang. He killed a second time when a white prison guard beat him. With ingenuity and a bit of luck he escaped to an island in the Caribbean where, inside of two years, he rose from hunted fugitive to Emperor using what Smithers, a Cockney trader, calls "Yankee bluff" to insinuate himself into the islanders' lives by learning their language and pretending to share their cultural values.

In the States, he was a member of the Baptist church; on the island, he works hand in hand with voodoo witch doctors, not in the least disturbed by conscientious feeling about his duplicity. All he is after is "de coin" and, for the moment, he hides his "Jesus on de shelf." He attributes his rise to what he learned, when he was a Pullman porter, from those he considers "white quality," specifically those whites who specialize in grand instead of petit larceny. His successful evasion of punishment in the States and his comparatively easy rise to power on the island lure him into the hubristic belief that he is superhuman, that he can "out guess, out fight an' out play" the "ign'rant bush niggers" he rules, "who ain't got brains enough to know deir own names."

When the islanders revolt, he boldly invents the legend that his life is charmed, that only a silver bullet can kill him. Like some other mythmakers, he starts believing in the occult magic that he has given the bullet. Learning of a scheme to assassinate him, he prepares an escape route through the jungle. Frightened but refusing to show it, he again finds confidence in his Baptist faith and silver bullet, which become, in his mind, supportive fetish symbols.

As tom-toms vibrate ominously in the forest, he leaves the palace by the front portico, refusing to sneak away like a coward, and enters the forest a few hours before sunset. Six scenes later, at dawn the next morning, his body, pierced by a silver bullet, is brought back to the entrance. During his night journey, he explores his own unconscious, finds and destroys himself.

A jolt to his self-pride and confidence sets the events in motion. He, who is so sure of his ability to handle any situation, is unable to find the food he has previously hidden along the escape route. As he begins to doubt his senses, he is confronted with Little Formless Fears, symbolic of free-floating anxieties, waiting to attach themselves to his real anxiety or fear. As they move toward him, his fear of them becomes greater than his fear of revealing his position to the natives. He wastes one of his lead bullets on apparitions arising from his disturbed emotional state. From this point on, he periodically loses contact with reality as he wanders back through time and place to the jungle from which his ancestors were captured as slaves. The first hallucination begins with the sound of rolling dice. Turning toward the sound, he sees the black man he killed in a dice game, mechanically going through the motions of the game. Relieved to think that the man is still alive, he speaks, but the apparition does not respond. Brutus threatens, wastes another bullet, and giving away his position again, he dashes into the woods. By this time he has lost his Panama hat, torn his uniform, and scratched his face scrambling through thickets, Deciding that he can travel faster if he gets rid of unessential things, he discards the "fripperty Emperor Trappings," admitting wryly "dis Emperor job is sho' hard to shake." He tries also to rid his mind of superstitious fears by recalling his Baptist training against belief in such things as ghosts and "ha'nts."

In the next hallucination he is on a chain gang. A white guard cracks a whip and motions Brutus, in pantomime, to work. He obeys subserviently. Suppressed hatred wells up inside of him as he tries to kill the prison guard again. In the two hallucinations that follow, Brutus regresses far into black history. His clothes and shoes by this time have been reduced to rags. He finds himself being auctioned at a slave mart. Again initial terror gives way to hatred. Glaring at the auctioneer and his purchaser, he fires the gun, using his last two lead bullets. The terror of this illusion carries over to the next in which he finds himself in the hold of a slave ship. Nothing remains of his elegant uniform except a tattered rag that serves as a breechcloth. The cries of the slaves follow the rhythm of tom-toms. Jones, against his will, joins their lamentations, his cry mounting in anguish above the others' cries. In his final illusion, he stands before a jungle altar near a river. Like a sleepwalker "in obedience to some obscure impulse," Brutus kneels. A witch doctor enters and performs rites of propitiation as a crocodile god rises from the river demanding human sacrifice. In pantomime the witch doctor indicates that Jones must sacrifice himself. Propelled by a force more powerful than himself, Jones moves toward the river, praying, "Lawd, save me! Lawd Jesus, heah my prayer!" As if in answer, he remembers the silver bullet and uses it to kill the crocodile. Presumably the crocodile represents his own evil nature. Only by killing the animal can he come to terms with himself.

Brutus Jones is any man whose destruction is due to his own ruthless obsessions. He personifies the old argument of man's dual nature, against the evil part of which he must constantly struggle.

More common than Brutus Jones, in modern literature, are black sensualists who ignore cultural taboos. Inherited jungle rhythms beating in their "black" blood form a primary motif in literary portraits—a motif emphasized by Vachel Lindsay in "The Congo" (1914):

> Fat black bucks in a wine barrel room
> Barrel house kings, with feet unstable,
> Sagged and reeled and pounded on the table, . . .
>
> Wild crap-shooters with a whoop and a call
> Danced the juba in a gambling hall
> And laughed fit to kill, and shook the town. . . .[89]

Buried in the personality of this archetype is the haunting racial memory of voodooism ("Mumbo-Jumbo will hoo-doo you.") and the beating of jungle drums ("Boomlay, boomlay, boomlay, BOOM,"). Uninhibited gratification of the senses is a supporting motif that is stressed by Sherwood Anderson in *Dark Laughter* (1925):

> A brown woman having thirteen children—a different man for every child—going to church too, singing, dancing, broad shoulders, broad hips, soft eyes, a soft laughing voice—getting God on Sunday night—getting—what —on Wednesday night? . . .[90]
>
> On Sundays—when they go to church, or to a bayou baptizing, the brown girls sure do cut loose with the colors—gaudy nigger colors on nigger women making the streets flame—deep purple, reds, yellows, green like young corn-shoots coming up. . . .[91]
>
> Niggers like good things. Good big sweet words, flesh, corn, cane.[92]

DuBose Heyward's *Porgy* (1923) contains some memorable delineations of carnal sensualists. An interesting precedent to Heyward's use of the name Porgy occurs in *The Forayers* (1855) by William Gilmore Simms. The Loyalist father of the hero, Willie Sinclair, an American partisan during the Revolution, reveals the cultural attitude toward it:

> Is it possible . . . that your miserable service requires you to associate with persons having such detestable

names? Why, sir, among gentlemen, even the fish of that
name is only held fit for Negroes.[93]

With this background, assignment of the name to the main
character of the novel classifies him as inferior. From the
description of his face, the reader learns that although strong
character lines are present, the lips are full and sensuous
More convincing evidence is given later when Maria over-
hears his "deep, aboriginal, lustful" laugh as he strangles
Crown. Bess and Crown, however, are completely primitive.
Crown, a stevedore, has "the body of a gladiator and a bad
name" in Catfish Row. He drinks corn liquor and sniffs cocaine
for the happy feelings they give him. When first seen, he is
gambling. A throw of the dice erupts into a fight between
him and Robbins, depicting an image of primitive violence
with the two men regressing, "down, down, down" the centuries, until they become animals exuding "a heady, bestial
stench."

After killing Robbins, Crown escapes to nearby Kittiwar
Island leaving his woman Bess behind. She is a sorry figure
with a scarred face and lines of "bitter desperation" around
her lips. With the amoral freedom of the archetype, she
shares Porgy's bed, and for a time they find happiness together; but Bess is weak. When Sportin' Life, an evil octoroon, offers her cocaine, she is powerless to resist the pleasure it will give her. Later, Serena's prediction, that she needs
a killer like Crown to control her, comes true when Bess goes
to Kittiwar with a group of picknickers. While in the woods
gathering palmetto leaves, Bess feels his animal presence before she sees him. The animal in her responds to that in him:
her body stiffens; her eyes become "dark and knowing; her
face flushes." Violence begets violent passion among the
carnal sensualists. She laughs wildly when he grabs her. That
night he sends her back to Porgy, promising to come for her
in the fall. Porgy suspects that she has been with Crown but
waits patiently before demanding clarification of their relationship. Bess's honest answer shows how decisions are pre-
determined by the nature of the archetype. She admits that
when Crown returns and puts his hand on her, she will have
to go with him. Predictably, Crown's return precipitates the

final tragedies: his murder, Bess's return to degradation in the North, and Porgy's imprisonment and personal defeat at the loss of Bess.

Carl Van Vechten poses a dilemma for his hero in *Nigger Heaven* (1926). The young man, Byron Kasson, comes to New York City to find success as a writer. Coming from an upper-middle-class background and not having had close contact with lower-class primitives, he is torn between his expressed desire for intellectual success and his natural inclinations to explore the pleasures and vices of Harlem night life. The women in his life personify the horns of his dilemma. Mary Love, a librarian, offers intellectual encouragement and the tepid pleasure of blind adoration; Lasca Sartoris, whose first name could well be a shortened form of lascivious, offers him wild nights of dances, brawls, and sensual gratification. Goaded by newly aroused sensations, he succumbs to Lasca, centering all of his drive and ambition toward entering into a permanent relationship with her. She, however, cannot remain content for long with any one man. She seeks thrills that only a variety of men can provide. After a three-day orgy, she discards Byron as abruptly as she has discarded others before him. Blind with rage and vengeance, he shoots his successor after the latter already has been fatally wounded by another enemy.

Van Vechten glamorizes his main characters, making them exotic mulattoes who possess perfectly formed, golden brown bodies, which they clothe in flamboyant colors. In contrast, Julia Peterkin's characters are pure-blooded Gullahs with "tall straight bodies, and heads filled with sense." They look with disdain on Guinea Negroes with their "thick lips and wide noses and low ways," and with equal condescension on the Dinkas with their "squatty skulls and grey-tinged skins betraying their mean blood."[94] For all their hauteur, the Gullahs have their share of primitive sensualists too. Prime examples are Mary and her husband July in *Scarlet Sister Mary* (1928).

Heaven's Gate Church is a controlling element in the town; its elders withhold membership in the church from persons who disobey its strict moral code, threatening damnation and hell fire for sinners. Sinning, as defined by local cus-

tom, consists of crap-shooting, poker-playing, dancing, singing reels (almost any kind of tune that is not a hymn), and
playing wicked tunes so that other sinners can engage in
sensuous forms of dancing.

July never receives the blessing of baptism or acceptance
by the best people of the community. He not only commits
all of the sins listed but sings songs with bad words in them
that encourage lewdness in others. Everyone considers him
an unfit husband for Sister Mary, who has been accepted into
the church. What the community does not know is that she
is expecting his child when they are married. Had he been
faithful to her, she might not have become notorious as the
Scarlet Sister Mary of the town. July is not a man who can
withstand for long the lure of new places and new women.
Soon after their son is born, he deserts her, and she is ex-
pelled from the church for giving birth to a fully developed
baby so soon after marriage. During the next twenty years
she bears eight illegitimate children, all with different fathers. Never in all that time does she repent. Brazenly, she
glories in her freedom and in the children which exemplify
that independence. Nor is she worried about having been cast
out of the church: "When I git ol' an' tired seeing pleasure,
I'm gwine to seek and pray an' be a member again. . . ."[95]
She remains unregenerate until her daughter bears a child
out of wedlock and her eldest son dies. The death ululation
of the town's women almost drives her insane. She begins to
ask questions.

> God knew he was the only heart-child she had. The
> others were the fruit of eye-love, the children of her flesh,
> yet they were strong and healthy, and her joy-child, her
> first-born, her jewel, July's son, was gone.[96]

She concludes finally that God has plagued her enough and
that she will pray until she finds peace and answers to her
questions. In a vision, she sees her son, who shows her a
white cloth with ten scarlet stripes running across it, one for
each of the nine children that were born in sin. The tenth
stripe is for her daughter's illegitimate child. She prays fer-
vently until each stripe vanishes. A few days later she relates
the experience to the church deacons and is welcomed back
into the fold.

The superego forces constricting the lives of Julia Peterkin's Gullahs exert no similar influence on Claude McKay's
sensualists in *Home to Harlem* (1928). What influences
them is the magnetism of Harlem, which is symbolic of black
identity and ethos, of

> Ancient black life rooted upon its base with all its fas-
> cinating new layers of brown, low-brown, high-brown,
> nut-brown, lemon, maroon, olive, mauve, gold. Yellow
> balancing between black and white. Black reaching out
> beyond yellow. Almost-white on the brink of change.
> Sucked back down into the current of black by the ter-
> ribly sweet rhythm of black blood. . . .[97]

Jake Brown, the main character, is a big black longshore-
man who enlists in the army, when World War I is declared,
expecting to fight for his country. Once again for blacks, reality fails to approximate expectations; for, instead of fighting Germans, he and the other black soldiers are used as
construction workers and have to fight white American prejudice at army bases and in foreign towns. When stationed in
France he deserts to Le Havre where he joins the crew of an
English tugboat hard pressed to fill berths in wartime. In
London, he obtains work as a docker, makes friends, finds a
compatible white woman, is content with his life until the
Armistice, a race riot, and the lure of Harlem's sensual blackness pull him back to America. Denied work as a deck hand
because of his color, he works as a stoker aboard a stinking
freighter, determined to endure any indignity just so long as
he can get back to Harlem.

Among the forces pulling him and others like him to Harlem are its girls—black, brown, yellow—especially one "little
maroon brown" named Felice, whom he meets, sleeps with,
but is separated from, within twenty-four hours after his
freighter is docked. The remainder of the novel describes his
search for her, the perfect mate for him. According to the
author, the Harlem woman is an easy, casual "pickup" who,
if sufficiently excited by a man, will make him her "sweet,"
or kept, man for as long as he remains faithful to her and
keeps her interested in him. In addition, the Harlem woman
must have a man, cannot remain long without one. She will
take any acceptable man as a makeshift lover when she is

separated from the one she prefers; but without a single qualm of conscience, she will leave the temporary substitute when her "Daddy" returns to her. Such mating habits provide causes for some of the violent crimes in Harlem. Jake is too independent to become any woman's "sweet," but he agrees with Zeddy, his war buddy, that there is no sweetness in any woman comparable to that which comes from "our own belonging-to-us honeycomb." Harlem's night life exerts an equally forceful attraction, consisting of strolls down the avenues, of buffet gambling flats, of private rendezvous apartments, of night clubs where dancers "breast" each other in frenetic rhythmic joy or in primitive voluptuous abandonment. One club, The Congo, is a "throbbing little Africa," frequented by "the unwashed of the Black Belt," to which whites are denied admission. Another attraction, at a more visceral level, is the rich and delicious food of Harlem, its "down-home" cooking. Despite all of the gaiety and sensual delights, residents' feelings are not always what they appear to be. Indicating severe emotional disturbance, moans and sobs often lie just beneath the surface laughter. At one moment, lovers may appear enthralled by each other; at the next, one may have murdered the other.

More than a repository of joys of the flesh, Harlem is symbolic of a magnetic force pulling Jake back to a richer ethnic awareness of himself as a black man in danger of losing his identity in a predominantly white culture, as well as a force pulling him back to brotherhood with other black people. By black people McKay means not only those literally having his black skin but all of those who are symbolically black because McKay, like Langston Hughes in the poem "Harlem Sweeties," celebrates the whole diverse spectrum of Negro skin colors ranging from ebony to pink. So strong is the sense of black identity in Jake that he is able to make responsible decisions. When he finds himself becoming slavishly attached to the Harlem rhythm of black life, he sets out to break its hold and to broaden his experiences. He takes a job as a railroad cook, suffering no loss of sensual experience but, more importantly, gaining increased knowledge of his black heritage. During his free hours he takes advantage of every opportunity to talk with a waiter named Ray, a displaced Haitian intellectual whose conversation reveals a seriously disturbed ambivalence, about L'Ouverture and Dessalines, or Prempeh of Ashanti, Cetewayo of Zululand, and Menelik of Abyssinia, among other black historical figures.

Jake is not yet ready to make decisions on a broader level than the personal, but he demonstrates awareness of the black social situation. He and Zeddy resent the prejudices of whites that prevented them from fighting in the war; that made them unwelcome at the YMCA house for soldiers at Brest; that caused an American white soldier to kill a black one, that caused union leaders to discriminate against blacks by not admitting them to certain unions, or, if admitted, by reserving the better jobs for white members. Their understated resentment, considered along with the irrational street fighting that erupts periodically for no apparent reason, foreshadows the more intense anger and hostility that is to come.

The novel's primary focus, nonetheless, is on primitive sensualists and contains unusual portraits of a pair of West Indian women who fight over a man. One is an older woman, a laundress, who has come from Colon bringing her "sweet" man with her. The other, a young country girl from Jamaica, has been receiving more attention from the man than the laundress, who challenges the Jamaican girl to physical combat, the winner presumably getting the man. Their encounter takes place in a backyard between tall apartment buildings on adjacent streets. In line with ancient tribal custom, transported from Africa to Harlem by way of the West Indies according to the author, the women remove their clothing and fight naked, as spectators watch from rear-view apartment windows. At first it seems that the older, heavier woman has an advantage over the younger, frailer girl; but the latter proves to be a vicious combatant, using a technique popular in the islands. Holding the laundress firmly by the shoulder and neck, the Jamaican vanquishes her opponent by repeatedly and savagely butting her on the forehead.

Thomas Wolfe's portrait of Ella Corpening (*Look Homeward, Angel*, 1929) is a prime example of the carnalist. As her name suggests, she is all "body," and is described as "a handsome woman of Amazonian proportions with smooth tawny skin." Fourteen-year-old Eugene Gant, attracted to her,

sets the scene in motion when he partly begs, partly commands her to take off her clothes and to dance naked in
front of him. She begins to moan as she dances erotically.
So overcome by her passion, she catches him to her and rocks
him back and forth in her arms. Straining from her grasp,
he runs away, leaving her moaning "in a wailing minor key."

Carnalists and other sensualists persist in our literature
in Langston Hughes's portraits of Sister Laura, Sister Essie,
and Buddy in *Tambourines to Glory* (1958). Free and uninhibited blacks, never deterred by cultural dictates, are mani-
fest in Robert Gover's Kitten in *one hundred dollar misunderstanding* (1961) and in William Melvin Kelley's flamboyant
Glora in *dem* (1964).

Essie Belle Johnson is a fat, contemplative woman, who
goes into self-hypnotic states when circumstances force her
to face a perplexing situation. Feeling that any solution
comes from God, she repeats ecstatically, "Thank you God!
Thank you God! Thank God! Thank God!" In this way she
experiences erotic pleasure and release from tension. In contrast, Sister Laura is an alert, vigorously amoral woman.
She obtains money from older men to pay for the pleasure
that younger men can give her. An opportunist, she persuades Essie to start a street-corner "church," mainly as another way of obtaining money for her pleasures. She does
not delude herself about her motives.

Together, with Sister Essie supplying the mystical aspects
of religious experience and with Sister Laura supplying carefully contrived appeals to the purses of the congregation, the
two are more successful financially than either would have
believed possible. They begin on a street corner with a tam-
tourine, a Bible, and a camp stool; later they move into an
apartment decorated to look like a church; and finally they
progress to a large theater, renamed the "Garden of Eden
Temple" with their names blazoned on the marquee.

Trouble comes when Sister Laura meets Buddy, more
than sixteen years younger than she. Virile and primitively
erotic, he insinuates himself into her life as lover and as
assistant in fleecing money from her gullible congregation. But
Buddy soon tires of Sister Laura. When she confronts him
with evidences of his infidelity and threatens to break off

their relationship, she finds that he has no intention of giving up his easy life with her. His reaction is cruel and menacing, callously letting her know that a woman her age should expect to pay for attentions from a younger man and that he has no intention of releasing her from a relationship so satisfyingly remunerative to him.

She resorts to violence, killing him with a knife belonging to Essie, who is falsely accused of the stabbing and imprisoned. Laura is not completely depraved. She confesses and exonerates Essie. Essie forgives her and hires a lawyer to defend her.

In *one hundred dollar misunderstanding*, the ordinary adolescent frustrations of the protagonist are intensified when the nineteen-year-old sophomore reacts to the taunt of a fraternity brother that he can never consider himself "much of anything" so long as he has not "miscegenated." Suggestive of a cultural *rite de passage*, the taunt and the idea behind it exemplify a cultural taboo that retards the improvement of black-white relationships. As a first step in proving himself, he goes to the Black'n Tan Bar. From there he is directed to the Paradise, where he is appropriated by fourteen-year-old, but very knowledgeable, Kitten in competition with older, more experienced prostitutes. She has big eyes, a childish face, and the gamy speech of a hardened streetwalker.

Her personality is a mixture of the sensualist and the mercenary, with a bit of the buffoon included. Her ambition is to retire at age eighteen. It is made obvious that she enjoys her work, and equally obvious that she gets at least as much pleasure from the sight of a large amount of money as she gets from other forms of sensual gratification. Enraptured by the size of the protagonist's "wad," she decides to take him home with her, in spite of his being "so far out dum" and "dum's dum kin be," as her long-sought weekend "invessment," explained in terms of a mutually satisfying relationship involving the functional interdependence of "giving" and "getting." The apartment is expensive and elaborate; and as her investment, she expects him to pay one hundred dollars, the going rate, for a weekend. Too inexperienced to know how such affairs are handled, he egotistically thinks that her favors are due to her fondness for him. The consequence is hilarious confusion. Kitten, not really evil, does not hesitate, however, to drug his coffee in order to obtain what she firmly believes is rightfully hers: proper remuneration for services rendered. Other novels have been written about these two characters. Each grows older. The protagonist shows some slight increase in awareness of prevailing social deceits and inequities. Kitten's name changes. Neither undergoes drastic personality change.

Glora, another minor character in *dem,* is typical of some other sensualists in appearance. She is copper-colored, has lavender lips, gold teeth, wears a red wig, bright pink slacks, and a yellow blouse, on top of light green and lemon yellow underwear. This is how she looks when she meets the white protagonist, Mitchell, who is being helped by a black character named Carlyle to find the father of his wife's black baby. What makes her portrait noteworthy is its hint of militant separatism and its definite component of ethnic clannishness. As part of their search, the black man takes the white one to a house rent party in a black neighborhood. It is agreed that the white will be passed off as a white-skinned Negro. In preparation, Carlyle advises Mitchell not to dance, as his style of dancing is a dead giveaway of his race, and alerts him to customary procedures at such parties, saying that he should "lay something on" the hostess "for the Jew," meaning that he should inconspicuously make a contribution so that they can pay the landlord.

Glora, after warmly greeting Carlyle, looks suspiciously, and not entirely without hostility, at Mitchell and then accusingly back at Carlyle, her face demanding an explanation for his bringing a white guest to her party. Carlyle quickly introduces Mitchell as his Canadian cousin, whose fugitive slave ancestors settled in an all white town and, as a result, was forced to integrate "to keep the [black] blood moving." Only then does she welcome him as warmly as she does Carlyle. Other guests are, initially, as hostile to him as Glora. When she insists upon his dancing with her and discovers how tense he is, she derisively suggests that he has lived too long among "dem," or whites, to be able to relax and enjoy himself without the help of liquor. Later, in a more intimate situation, she laughs more derisively when he attributes his impotence to an old war wound.

Alter-Ego Symbols

One group of characters remains to be analyzed in this category of archetypes. Their portraits contain characteristics of stock Negroes as well as those of Negro individuals as defined earlier. None of these traits is evident to a degree that warrants including the characters in either of those categories, because it is upon these aspects of characterization that the writers have built extended meanings. The group includes Melville's Pip (*Moby Dick*, 1851) and Babo ("Benito Cereno," *Piazza Tales,* 1856), Stephen Crane's Henry Johnson (*The Monster*, 1899), and, sixty years later, Elizabeth Spencer's ghostlike figure ("First Dark," 1959) that shows the literary persistence of this archetypal figure.

Of the three orders of men aboard the *Pequod*—"mongrel renegades, and castaways, and cannibals"—little Pip is "another lonely castaway" and the most insignificant "though the loftiest and brightest" of them all. His real name is never given. He is "Pippin by nickname" and "Pip by abbreviation," a naming that indicates potentiality, like a tadpole's, for maturity and, in Pip's case, self-realization. Within him there is no "insular Tahiti, full of peace and joy" or strong self-concept to protect him from traumatic experience in an ocean that symbolizes "all the horrors of the half-known life." In consequence, his body can be rescued but his mind is forever lost. Like some obversely paradoxical cave allegory, one who has seen the light and has been returned to share it with others is an idiot, similar in some respects to a Shakespearean Fool.

Up to the point at which Pip jumps into the ocean the second time, his function aboard ship is similar to Fleece's. He is merely an instrument, a tambourine beater for the crew's excitement. When, at one point, his tambourine cannot be located, the French sailor orders him to beat his belly and wag his ears. The Chinese sailor commands him to rattle his teeth in rhythmic accompaniment to their jigs and dances. These commands reflect the cultural belief that Negroes are natural instruments of pleasure—an image that has been shown to predominate among stock Negroes.

> Pip, though over tender-hearted, was at bottom very bright, with that pleasant, genial, jolly brightness peculiar to his tribe; a tribe, which ever enjoy all holidays and festivities with finer, freer relish than any other race.[98]

Pip's cultural status is evident in Stubb's playful warning: "A whale would sell for thirty times what you would Pip, in Alabama."

To his credit, Melville rises above these stock aspects of black characterization. In the extended meaning of the novel, Pip is destined to play a more important role than, for example, the ones assigned to Fleece and Daggoo. An early clue is supplied by Melville's oxymoron describing his tambourine's sound in the forecastle: "so gloomy-jolly." Another is Melville's manipulation of Pip's appearance. His blackness takes on a glowing radiance, "for even blackness has its brilliancy." His brilliance is dimmed temporarily when he is lost in the ocean. Later the black's madness, like the artificial illumination of the diamond in Melville's analogy, has the power to accentuate white or colorless objects counterposed against its dark background:

> Then come out those fiery effulgences, infernally superb; then the evil-blazing diamond, once the divinest symbol of the crystal skies, look like some crown-jewel stolen from the King of Hell.[99]

Pip's transition from entertainer to perceptive (though mindless) commentator on events abroad the *Pequod* is forecast by the paradox. At this point, he becomes similar in some ways to one of Shakespeare's Fools, those quick-witted professional jesters whose speech is often wild and humorous but whose perception is clearer than that exhibited by the protagonist who is contrasted with him. Pip is different from them, however, because he is truly mad.

In the chapter titled "The Doubloon," Ahab and members of the crew study the gold coin nailed to the mast. To each it reveals something of themselves: in the three Andean peaks engraved upon the coin, Starbuck finds the Trinity; Stubb, the sign of the Zodiac; Flask, the cigars that the coin will buy. It is Pip who sees the effect of the coin on the men, revealed in his "crazy-witty" declension, "I look, you look, he looks. . . ." All look but none really sees. His metaphor comparing them to bats is obvious. Himself, he makes a crow, the comic symbol for Negroes in nineteenth-century fables.[100] As a crow perched on the pine mast, he can see the meaning of the doubloon. It is the navel of the ship, the symbol of Ahab's obsession which motivates the crew, for the most part, to help achieve his retaliatory vengeance against a force of nature or nature itself. Only Pip, in his madness, sees the futility of such obsession and motivation. He asks, "They are all on fire to unscrew it. But unscrew your navel, and what's the consequence?"[101] In his further rantings, he implies another question: what good will retaliation do when all have died? Man's feeble efforts will have no effect upon omnipotent, impersonal Nature. "God goes 'mong the worlds blackberrying."[102]

The effect on Ahab of the little Fool's insanity, which is "heaven's sense," explains Pip's function in the novel. Ahab sees something divine and sacred in Pip's unreflecting eyes. He commands the Manxman, "Hands off from that holiness!" He reveals also how much he is affected by the mindless lad, "Thou touchest my inmost centre boy; thou art tied to me by cords woven of my heart strings." He takes Pip's hand. This gesture—the act of one helpless person reaching out to another who is as helpless, and joining hands in mutual need and support—causes the boy to say,

> Ah, now, had poor Pip but felt so kind a thing as this, perhaps he had ne'er been lost! This seems to me, sir, as a man-rope; something that weak souls may hold by. Oh, sir, let old Perth now come and rivet those two hands together; the black one with the white, for I will not let this go."[103]

The two are joined—the black and the white; and, as the old Manxman summarizes, "one daft with strength, the other daft with weakness,"[104] each becoming in a sense the alter ego of the other. So affected is Ahab by their relationship that he finds it difficult to maintain his obsessive zeal when the boy is with him.

> There is that in thee, poor lad, which I feel too curing to my malady. Like cures like, and for this hunt, my malady becomes my most desired health.[105]

In order to accomplish his purpose, he forces the boy to remain in his cabin, promising Pip that he can sit in the captain's chair and pretend to be the captain. Pip wants only to be with him.

> No, no, no! Ye have not a whole body, sir; do ye but use poor me for your one lost leg; only tread upon me, sir; I ask no more, so I remain a part of ye.[106]

Among many other ideas in *Moby Dick*, Melville is insisting, with his manipulation of the various characters and symbols, that blacks and whites are inextricably bound together, as are Levin's "union of opposites,"[107] for good or evil, in mutual recognition and brotherhood. He seems also to be saying something similar in "Benito Cereno" (*Piazza Tales*, 1856), but his approach is different. The black and the white only appear to be joined in brotherhood.

Babo, the rebel slave, is not attached to Don Benito; and if it were not for the way in which Don Benito is attached to him, Babo could be classified as an early example of the Negro as individual in our literature. His story is revealed through the consciousness of a New England sea captain, Amasa Delano, whose ship lies at anchor in a Chilean port taking on a supply of fresh water. One gray morning he sees a ship, showing no colors, in distress off the coast. Goodheartedly he goes to her aid and discovers that she is a Spanish slaver, the *San Dominick*, presumably under the command of Don Benito Cereno, who is obviously a sick and ineffectual man. The slave, Babo, appears to be taking care of him.

> By his side stood a black of small stature, in whose rude face, as occasionally, like a shepherd's dog, he mutely turned it up into the Spaniard's, sorrow and affection were equally blended.[108]

Babo seems a selfless person, tenderly concerned for his master's welfare. Captain Delano tries to be helpful but lacks perceptiveness to appraise the situation adequately. Clues to what is actually happening on the *San Dominick* are either ignored by him or are explained away. Actually, Benito is being held hostage by the slaves who have taken over the ship, massacred its crew and the slave dealer, tied the latter's crudely bundled skeleton to the ship's prow, and inscribed beneath the corpse the sentence: "Follow your leader," as a threat of similar treatment to the whites on board if they do not help the slaves in their desperate effort to be free and to return to Africa. As leader of the insurrectionists, it is Babo who has master-minded the plot. His seeming devotion to Don Benito is his way of camouflaging the control he exercises over the behavior and speech of his hostage. Moreover, he takes sadistic pleasure in tormenting Don Benito.

> Setting down his basin, the negro searched among the razors, as for the sharpest, and having found it, gave it an additional edge by expertly stropping it on the firm, smooth, oily skin of his open palm; he then made a gesture as if to begin, but midway stood suspended for an instant, one hand elevating the razor, the other professionally dabbling among the bubbling suds on the Spaniard's lank neck. . . . Don Benito nervously shuddered; . . .[109]

In Babo's slapstick gesticulations and Benito's terror, basic elements of the grotesque are combined. Momentarily Delano is affected by the scene: ". . . in the black he saw a headsman, and in the white a man on the block." But he quickly explains away what he sees as an "antic conceit" from which "the best regulated mind is not always free."

Delano's life is spared many times aboard the *San Dominick* by such ability to allay his suspicions with rational explanations. In contrast, Benito, sensitively aware of the larger implications of human slavery, is destroyed. It is as if he recognizes, when applied to slaves, the contradiction of terms contained in the incident aboard the *Town-Ho:* denial of "that common decency of human recognition which is the meanest slave's right."[110] What right can a salable commodity have? To be a slave means automatically and irrevocably to be denied recognition as a human being. It is against this misuse of a human being that Babo rebels; but, like some other human beings when power over others is acquired, Babo becomes sadistic. His behavior can be understood as compensation for the cruelties and indignities heaped upon blacks by slavers. Moreover, these are all desperate men struggling, in hostile territory, to regain the freedom they have lost. Though finally rescued and avenged, Benito cannot free himself from the goadings of his conscience. Babo's function as superego figure becomes clear in Benito's final words to Captain Delano. When asked, "What has cast such a shadow upon you?" Benito answers, "The negro."[111] The Negro referred to is not simply Babo, but his complex symbolic referent: the whole spectrum of black symbolism that Melville explores in contrast with white symbols in *Moby Dick*. Included in his meaning are the nature of good and evil, the function of conscience, as well as the implications of human slavery.

Henry Johnson in *The Monster* (1899) functions as a sounding board for Crane's criticism of human behavior in a Northern community that he calls Whilomville. Henry Johnson takes personal pride in his job as coachman for Dr. Trescott and his family. Being in the employ of a prominent person gives him an important position in the Negro community. More than that, he is fond of the doctor and his wife and especially of their young son Jimmie. He takes personal pride in himself also. Being something of a dandy, he spends much time grooming himself for a social evening in Watermelon Alley with Miss Bella Farragut and her family. Although he favors lavender trousers and bright silk hatbands, there is nothing of the stereotyped "cake-walking" menial in his behavior:

> He was simply a quiet, well-bred gentleman of position, wealth, and other necessary achievements out for an evening stroll, and he had never washed a wagon in his life.[112]

He bears the ridicule of the community's whites with good-natured equanimity as he walks down the street. The German barber, his customers, and the street loafers in front of the shop remark, "Wow!" "You ought to see the coon that's coming!" "He's the biggest dude in town. . . ." Ain't he a taisy?" "Hello, Henry! Going to walk for a cake tonight?" In reply, he laughs with them—his laugh expressing "underground complacency of superior metal."[113]

Returning one evening he sees his employer's house ablaze and learns that little Jimmie is trapped in a second-floor bedroom. "Blue with horror" he plunges into the house, wraps the boy in a blanket, and starts out only to find his way of escape blocked by flames. For a moment he falters, almost giving up the desire to escape, "submitting because of his fathers, bending his mind in a most perfect slavery to this conflagration."[114] Then as he remembers another exit through the doctor's laboratory, the thought of submitting to the fire is abandoned. With the possibility of escape before him, he again becomes terrified but manages to make his way to the laboratory which has become a rainbow of colors from the burning chemicals and combustible fluids. Stumbling through the room, he falls on his back, releasing the blanket-wrapped body of the child, which rolls away from him to comparative safety. But Henry's head lies near a desk on which beakers are exploding. The chemicals, when ignited, shear the flesh from his face and sear his body. When the two are rescued the boy is severely burned, but Henry has been reduced to a monstrous thing, more dead than alive.

Newspapers prematurely announce his death, and he becomes a hero in the eyes of the whites and blacks of Whilomville. To the little boys who taunted him earlier with the jingle, "Nigger, Nigger, never die/ black face and shiny eye," he becomes a saint; they try to hide the fact that they once belittled him. Proudly Bella Farragut announces that she was engaged to marry him. When it is discovered that he is alive and that he is a face-less imbecile, their attitudes change. His being a Negro renders him the more grotesque. People become hysterical at sight of him. He represents an unholy thing to all except his grateful employer, who continues to take care of him despite personal loss of prestige and the rising animosity of the community which holds him responsible for its terror.

Crane's delineation of Henry's effect upon the community

raises a nice moral issue against which individual behavior is tested. The Negroes whom Dr. Trescott hires to care for him do not conceal their revulsion but are not above using Henry's condition to extort additional money from the doctor. An eminent judge, a wealthy businessman, and others of lower social position advise the doctor either to let Henry die or to put him in an institution. Young boys, with the cruelty of childhood, make a game of seeing which has courage enough to approach or touch him. Bella Farragut shudders, wails, and falls crawling away when the befuddled creature visits her.

The situation at Whilomville contains many implications, not all of which are racially oriented; but the reader might possibly wonder why Crane chose to intensify the moral issue by making Henry a Negro. Remembering Constance Rourke's analysis of American humor and character, one might conclude that Crane's use of skin color was a deliberate attempt to heighten the grotesqueness of his monster image against which community charity and ethic might be tested.

If Pip is the alter ego of a white, Babo the goader of consciences, and Henry the test of ethical behavior, then the shadowy figure in "First Dark" (1959) by Elizabeth Spencer is the modern aggregate of these archetypal figures. The scene of "First Dark" is Richton, a small town in Mississippi, which offers nothing but memory and hidebound tradition to young men and women after World War II. The townsfolk believe that the only hope of keeping their young at home lies in using Richton's one remaining antebellum mansion as a museum, like the ones in Natchez, to which tradition-minded Southerners can make pilgrimages. Tom Beavers is not one of those who never returns. He visits Richton each weekend, presumably to visit his aunt but more probably to find self-identity in past tradition. There he renews his childhood acquaintance with Frances Harvey, who is a descendant of Southern gentry and lives in the mansion. Tom's ancestors were gentle folk but not of the aristocracy. She is more attached to tradition than he because she has not escaped it to the extent that he has. Except for one trip to Europe, she has always lived in the mansion with her invalid mother, who, along with the mansion, represents the Old South.

One weekend, just at "first dark" or twilight, Tom sees a strange, elderly Negro standing in a ditch at the intersection of an old dirt road and the new one leading to Richton. Frances, driving home from Jackson, sees the shadowy figure on the same evening, and the two are drawn together by this unusual experience, as the Negro is part of Richton legend.

The author's delineation of the Negro removes him, the road intersection, and his effect on Frances from the realm of literal meaning and realistic story-writing. He is symbolic of all American Negroes; the road intersection, of the contemporary social situation; and the Negro's effect on Frances, of conscientious feeling among whites about that situation. In appearance, he is a mulatto, neither white nor black, but sometimes so white that it is difficult to tell whether or not he is Negro. Wraithlike and looking as if he were growing out of the weeds in the ditch, he looms "taller than any mortal could be." Townsfolk, not all of whom are known to be heavy drinkers, have seen him periodically, but only in crepuscular shadows and always at the intersection of the old and new roads. When seen, he signals to drivers passing by but disappears when they stop their cars. Legend said that the only people he ever spoke to were the workmen when they were building the new road. One evening he materialized out of the shadows and asked the men to move a bulldozer that was blocking his access to the new road. He explained that a sick girl was in his wagon farther down the dirt road and that he wanted to take her to the doctor in town. The men removed the bulldozer; but when they looked for him, he had disappeared.

Frances is more disturbed by seeing the Negro than Tom. This man is strange and different from those she has known: Sammie, the family cook, and Jerry, Sammie's "son, or husband, or something." Both Frances and Tom are Southerners in transition from old to new ideals. For her, the transition is the more drastic alteration of experience.

Her mother and the mansion are symbols of magnolia-laden Southern life, reaching out to manacle the younger woman firmly in tradition. Both mother and mansion are overwhelmingly feminine. It is as if all virility has been vitiated by that femininity. The house overflows with relics of the past: old clothing, jewels, furniture. Tom represents an avenue by which Frances can be freed from the past; but Mrs. Harvey does not want Frances to escape. She prefers to reach out and bring Tom, who represents an infusion of new blood, into the confines of the mansion and thereby to insure perpetuation of tradition as well as marital fulfillment for her daughter. She is not vicious, just tenacious. Frances realizes that so long as her mother lives she cannot leave her or the mansion, nor can she and Tom live together in that house. In some unsaid way, her feeling is communicated to the mother who, unknown to Frances, takes an overdose of sleeping pills, believing that after her death, the two can marry and live happily in the mansion.

Mrs. Harvey's death solves only one of Frances's problems. Unconscious guilt about Negroes continues to disturb her. The problem comes to a head late one afternoon when she sees the ghostly figure again after she has placed some wreaths on her mother's grave. He signals to her and explains that her parked automobile obstructs his passage from the dirt road to the new one and that he must take the sick girl to the doctor. Frances apologizes and drives away. Later she is conscience-stricken for not having offered to drive the girl to town. "No wonder they talk about us up North. A mile to town in a wagon! She might have been having a baby." After a tense, rest-broken night, she drives back to the intersection early the next morning, hoping to see the man and to apologize for her lack of compassion the night before. He is there as if waiting for her.

"She going to be all right now." Then he smiled at her. He did not say thank you, or anything more. Frances turned and walked back to the road and the car. And exactly as though the recovery of the Negro girl in the wagon had been her own recovery, she felt the return of a quiet breath and a steady pulse, and sensed the blessed stirring of a morning breeze.[115]

Tension in Frances is lowered by the man's reassurance and by her act of compassion for him and his effort to enter the new road that represents changing social currents and the ultimate rectification of evils. She now finds it possible to leave Richton, to relinquish the mansion and tradition, and to enter her own symbolic "new road" of social attitudes toward blacks.

The sample of archetypes examined reveals relatively few clear-cut shifts in cultural attitudes. Aesthetic symbols of culture—names and physical descriptions—are of less help in understanding archetypes than they are with stock characters. Most archetypes are assigned ordinary English-American names. Exceptions are noteworthy among mammies, mulattoes, and primitives: mammies go by many names, some of which reflect the ironic pattern of slave-naming and some others which are nicknames or shortened forms of ordinary names. Often their names are prefaced by familistic tags like mammy, maum, mom, or aunt. Among mulattoes and primitives, some names are exotic, foreign, or descriptive. No significant trend in naming is evident in the small sample of alter-ego symbols examined. Physical descriptions tend to construct characters in keeping with the dominant idea of the archetypal configuration, e.g., some protest symbols, mammies, and early primitives tend to be idealized; sensualists are generally glamorized as prime physical specimens; aspects of skin color permeate portraits of protest and alter-ego symbols. Depictions of archetypes in modern literature tend toward more realistic descriptions. Insofar as skin color is concerned, characters range throughout the spectrum of Negro skin colors, from tan to glossy black, with the exceptions of mulattoes, who range from white to brown, and the apparition in "First Dark," who cannot be identified at times as a Negro.

Of considerably more help in categorizing archetypes than either names or descriptions are aesthetic symbols of fictional "personality" that identify dominant cultural ideas influencing the depictions. Protest and alter-ego symbols are embodiments of environmental determinism against which authors protest and plead, in varying degrees, for universal brotherhood. Mammies, mulattoes, and primitives are embodiments of cultural attitudes toward and beliefs about certain blacks. Mammies generally identify with their special white "families" and exclude their own black families. Although they are quaintly authoritarian in prescribed relations with whites, they recognize their own inferiority and do not enter into social reciprocity with them. Mulattoes, sharing the general cultural attitude, look upon the "fatal black drop" as the mark of shame and cultural inferiority; hence they reject themselves and prefer that which is supposedly pure. Primitives and sensualists consider themselves superior to other people, man-made laws, or civilized customs. Shifts toward self-knowledge in reciprocal relations with others is evident among later portraits of mammies, mulattoes, and primitives. This is not to indicate that a groundswell exists, only that changes, though few, are significant. Noteworthy shifts have been documented among mammies in Dilsey (Faulkner), Nannie (Katherine Anne Porter), Berenice (Carson McCullers), and Aunt Harry (Henry Van Dyke); among mulattoes in Willis Featherstone (Joel Chandler Harris), Gracie (T. S. Stribling), Allbright (Hamilton Basso), and Alton Scales (Lorraine Hansberry); among primitives in Jake Brown (Claude McKay) and Sister Laura (Langston Hughes). Protest and alter-ego symbols reflect no essential change, with the exception of Jack Jefferson (Howard Sackler). Characters like Berenice, Nannie, Willis Featherstone, Sister Laura, Alton Scales, and Jack Jefferson could have been included in the next category but are retained here to dramatize the small trend toward individualism among archetypes.

Notes

1. R. Hildreth, *The White Slave, Another Picture of Life in America* (London, n.d.), p. 6.
2. *Ibid.*, p. 7.
3. *Ibid.*, p. 207.
4. For a fuller analysis of this resemblance, see Charles Nichols, "The Origins of Uncle Tom's Cabin," *Phylon* XIX, 3 (Third Quarter, 1958): 328–334.
5. William Wells Brown, *Clotel; or, The President's Daughter* (New York, 1969), p. xvii.
6. *Ibid.*, p. 55.
7. *Ibid.*, pp. 59ff.

8. *Ibid.*, pp. 217ff.
9. J. T. Trowbridge, *Neighbor Jackwood* (Boston and New York, 1884), p. 109.
10. Dion Boucicault, *The Octoroon; or, Life in Louisiana, A Play in Four Acts* (London, n.d.), p. 22.
11. Albion W. Tourgée, *A Royal Gentleman and Zouri's Christmas* (New York, 1874), p. 448.
12. George Washington Cable, "Madame Delphine," *Creoles and Cajuns* (Garden City, N.Y., 1959), p. 193.
13. Charles Waddell Chesnutt, "Her Virginia Mammy," *The Wife of His Youth and Other Stories of the Color Line* (Boston and New York, 1899), pp. 54ff.
14. Joel Chandler Harris, "Where's Duncan?" *Balaam and His Master and Other Sketches and Stories* (Boston and New York, 1891), p. 157.
15. *Ibid.*, pp. 157ff.
16. William Dean Howells, *An Imperative Duty* (New York, 1891), pp. 132ff.
17. Kate Chopin, "Desirée's Baby," *Bayou Folk* (Boston and New York, 1894), p. 156.
18. Charles Waddell Chesnutt, *The House Behind the Cedars* (Boston and New York, 1900), p. 78.
19. *Ibid.*
20. Thomas Dixon, *The Leopard's Spots* (New York, 1902), p. 391.
21. *Ibid.*, pp. 393ff.
22. James Weldon Johnson, *The Autobiography of An Ex-Coloured Man* (New York and London, 1912), p. 187.
23. *Ibid.*, p. 190.
24. *Ibid.*
25. Jean Toomer, "Blood-Burning Moon," *Cane* (New York, 1967), p. 51. Reprinted by permission of Liveright Publishing Corporation.
26. *Ibid.*, p. 52.
27. *Ibid.*
28. T. S. Stribling, *The Forge* (New York, 1931), p. 259. Reprinted by permission of Mrs. T. S. Stribling.
29. T. S. Stribling, *Unfinished Cathedral* (New York, 1934), p. 180. Reprinted by permission of Mrs. T. S. Stribling.
30. Lillian Smith, *Strange Fruit* (New York, 1944), p. 3.
31. Hamilton Basso, *The Light Infantry Ball* (Garden City, N.Y., 1959), p. 294. Reprinted by permission of Doubleday and Company, Inc. and Collins Publishers.
32. Lorraine Hansberry, *The Sign in Sidney Brustein's Window* (New York, 1966).
33. Harriet Beecher Stowe, *Uncle Tom's Cabin* (Boston, 1897), p. lx.
34. *Ibid.*, p. 26.
35. *Ibid.*, p. 47.
36. *Ibid.*, p. 115.

37. *Ibid.*, p. 239.
38. *Ibid.*, p. 356.
39. *Ibid.*, p. 254.
40. *Ibid.*, p. 413.
41. *Ibid.*, p. 489.
42. J. C. Furnas, *Goodbye to Uncle Tom* (New York, 1956).
43. William Faulkner, "A Justice," *The Portable Faulkner,* Malcolm Cowley, ed. (New York, 1946), pp. 27ff.
44. William Faulkner, "The Bear," *Six Great Modern Short Novels* (New York, 1954), p. 395.
45. *Ibid.*, p. 347.
46. Paul Green, *Lonesome Road: Six Plays for the Negro Theatre* (New York, 1926), p. xix. © 1926 by Paul Green. Used by permission of Crown Publishers, Inc.
47. T. S. Stribling, *Birthright* (New York, 1922), p. 98.
48. *Ibid.*
49. *Ibid.*, p. 136. Reprinted by permission of Mrs. T. S. Stribling.
50. *Ibid.*, p. 145.
51. Both of these plays are parts of a longer drama published under the title of the first one, *In Abraham's Bosom.* See Barret H. Clark's Introduction, *Lonesome Road: Six Plays for the Negro Theatre* by Paul Green (New York, 1926), p. xv.
52. Paul Green, *op. cit.*, p. 178.
53. John Steinbeck, *Of Mice and Men* (New York, 1958), pp. 88ff. Reprinted by permission of The Viking Press, Inc. and McIntosh and Otis, Inc.
54. Richard Wright, *Native Son* (New York, 1940), p. 18.
55. *Ibid.*, p. 393.
56. Ann Petry, *The Street* (Boston, 1946), p. 2. Reprinted by permission of Houghton Mifflin Company.
57. William Melvin Kelley, *dem* (Garden City, N.Y., 1969), pp. 136ff. Reprinted by permission of Doubleday and Company, Inc.
58. See John Henrik Clarke, ed., *William Styron's Nat Turner: Ten Black Writers Respond* (Boston, 1968).
59. William Wells Brown, *op. cit.*, p. 212.
60. "To Mammy . . . who gave to my family a fidelity without stint or calculation of recompense and to my childhood an immeasurable devotion and love."
61. Stephen Vincent Benét, *John Brown's Body* (New York, 1928), p. 138. Reprinted by permission of Brandt & Brandt.
62. Harriet Beecher Stowe, *Uncle Tom's Cabin* (Boston, 1897), p. 193.
63. Mary H. Eastman, *Aunt Phillis's Cabin; or, Southern Life as It Is* (Philadelphia, 1852), pp. 102, 253.
64. Thomas Nelson Page, *Red Rock, A Chronicle of Reconstruction* (New York, 1945), p. 23.
65. *Ibid.*
66. *Ibid.*, pp. 91ff.

67. *Ibid.*, p. 92.
68. *Ibid.*, p. 128.
69. Joel Chandler Harris: "Mom Bi: Her Friends and Her Enemies," *op. cit.*, pp. 172ff.
70. *Ibid.*, p. 176.
71. *Ibid.*, p. 185.
72. *Ibid.*, pp. 189ff.
73. Cf. Krenda in *Red Rock* (1898) and Mammy in *Gone With the Wind* (1936) by Margaret Mitchell.
74. Katherine Anne Porter, "The Old Order," *The Leaning Tower and Other Stories* (New York, 1940), p. 35. Reprinted by permission of Harcourt, Brace & World.
75. Katherine Anne Porter, "The Last Leaf," *op. cit.*, p. 61. Reprinted by permission of Harcourt, Brace & World.
76. J. C. Furnas, *op. cit.*, p. 17.
77. Carson McCullers, *The Member of the Wedding* (New York, 1958), p. 3. Reprinted by permission of Houghton Mifflin Company.
78. *Ibid.*, p. 91.
79. Henry Van Dyke, *Ladies of the Rachmaninoff Eyes* (New York, 1966), pp. 136ff. Reprinted by permission of Farrar, Straus & Giroux, Inc. and The Bodley Head, Ltd.
80. *Ibid.*, p. 126.
81. *Ibid.*, p. 133.
82. See Arlin Turner, ed., *Creoles and Cajuns, Stories of Old Louisiana by George Washington Cable* (New York, 1959), p. 20.
83. *Ibid.*, p. 179. (Freely translated: "Oh Palmyre, Palmyre, my little bird, I love you—I love you, I love you.)
84. William Wells Brown, *op. cit.*, p. 212.
85. *Ibid.*, p. 213.
86. *Ibid.*
87. J. T. Trowbridge, *Cudjo's Cave* (Boston, 1895), p. 116.
88. *Ibid.*, pp. 256ff.
89. Vachel Lindsay, "The Congo, A Study of the Negro Race," *Oxford Anthology of American Literature*, William Rose Benet and Norman Holmes Pearson, eds., II (New York, 1939), pp. 1150ff.
90. Sherwood Anderson, *Dark Laughter* (New York, 1925), p. 75. Reprinted by permission of Boni and Liveright, Inc.
91. *Ibid.*, p. 77.
92. *Ibid.*, p. 80.
93. William Gilmore Simms, *The Forayers, or the Raid of the Dog-Days* (New York, 1864), p. 175.
94. Julia Peterkin, *Scarlet Sister Mary* (New York, 1928), p. 11. The Bobbs-Merrill Company, Inc. R. 1956, reprinted by permission of the publisher.
95. *Ibid.*, p. 252.
96. *Ibid.*, p. 326.

97. Claude McKay, *Home to Harlem* (New York, 1928), pp. 57ff. Reprinted by permission of Harper & Row, Publishers.
98. Herman Melville, *Moby-Dick or, the Whale* (New York, 1958), p. 410.
99. *Ibid.*
100. See Constance Rourke, *American Humor: A Study of the National Character* (New York, 1931), p. 75.
101. Melville, *op. cit.*, p. 432.
102. *Ibid.*
103. *Ibid.*, p. 513.
104. *Ibid.*, p. 514.
105. *Ibid.*, p. 524.
106. *Ibid.*
107. Harry Levin, *The Power of Blackness* (New York, 1958), pp. xi ff.
108. Herman Melville, "Benito Cereno," *Selected Tales and Poems by Herman Melville*, Richard Chase, ed. (New York, 1959), pp. 8ff.
109. *Ibid.*, pp. 50ff.
110. Melville, *Moby-Dick*, p. 244.
111. Melville, "Benito Cereno," p. 90.
112. Stephen Crane, "The Monster," *The Red Badge of Courage and Four Great Stories by Stephen Crane* (New York, 1960), p. 244.
113. *Ibid.*, pp. 245ff.
114. *Ibid.*, p. 257.
115. Elizabeth Spencer, "First Dark," *The New Yorker*, XXXV, 18 (June 20, 1959): 39. From *Ship Island and Other Stories*. Copyright © 1968 by Elizabeth Spencer. Used with permission of McGraw-Hill Book Company, and *The New Yorker*.

CHAPTER

4

BLACK INDIVIDUALS

In the preceding chapters, changes in cultural attitudes toward blacks have been evidenced in shifting modes of fictional characterization. Although changes have occurred, some portraits still carry strong overtones of earlier cultural attitudes within the various categories. Among the characters analyzed in this chapter can be found dramatic changes from portraits that contain traces of earlier attitudes to those that depict blacks who have become or are in the process of becoming individuals, each possessing a strong sense of identity, independent responsibility, and reciprocal relatedness with whites. Those portraits containing evidence of earlier cultural attitudes toward blacks are classified here as individuals in transition from subservience to self-assertion.

Early and Transitional Figures

Abraham, in *Swallow Barn* (1832) by John Pendleton Kennedy, is an early example of a black character who is an individual in our literature. In physical appearance, personality, and behavior he is made atypical of other early, home-grown, garden-variety Negroes, with furtive animal eyes and squat, crazily constructed bodies. Almost as if grudgingly, he is "well-knit" and "of uncommonly symmetrical proportions for the race to which he belonged." His face has neither "the flat nose" nor "the broad lips of his tribe . . . but . . . moulded with the prevailing characteristics of the Negroes of the West Indies." In temperament, he is "noted for his spirit," and given to "occasional bursts of passion."[1] Trained to work as a blacksmith, he gives useful services when he has a mind to work; but that kind of work evidently neither interests nor challenges him sufficiently to make him a steady worker. Most of his time is spent with irresponsible companions harassing people on neighboring plantations. He gives his owners and his doting mother, Mammy Lucy, many troublesome moments. Out of deference to her, their old nurse, the owners do not whip or sell him; but they are determined to be rid of him and his pranks. They send him to sea on a Chesapeake Bay pilot boat. The roving life of a sailor excites him in ways that his job at the anvil did not; and, in time, he finds his place in life and redeems himself in the eyes of those who know him.

One night during a storm, when all pilot boats are safely anchored ashore, a distress signal comes from a brig foundering off Hampton Roads. None of the other seamen dares put out into the rough water to help her. Older, more experienced sailors urge him not to go, pointing out how foolhardy the venture is. Abe's answer to their good sense shows compassion: "You wouldn't say so . . . if you were one of the crew of the brig yourself. . . . And no man is going to die till his time comes. I don't set up for more spirit than other people, but I never was afeared of the sea."[2] This is, of course, youthful daring speaking. His boat is never seen again after it passes Old Point Comfort. Some time later, his body is washed ashore. The only survivor of the distressed ship reports that Abe's pilot boat reached the brig before it sank but was prevented from assisting her because of high winds and heavy seas.

As portrayed, Abe seems to belie Kennedy's overgeneralized comments that we noted in the chapter on stock characters. He makes Abe a heroic character who is capable of decisive and independent action. In the overall structure of the novel, however, Abe's story is a mere incident in the fuller delineation of Mammy Lucy to whom Kennedy pays sentimental tribute. It is as if Kennedy believed that any child of a beloved mammy could not have been all bad and that he must redeem Abe for her sake. Or it may be that, as earnest apologist of Southern feudalism, Kennedy tries to be fair to his Negro characters but succeeds only in revealing more clearly his myopic view of them. One can readily agree with Kennedy when he writes, "What the Negro is finally capable of in the way of civilization, I am not philosopher enough to determine."[3] Whatever the answer, Abe stands out as an early example of a black man portrayed as an individual in literature.

Another minor character possessing traits of an individual appears in John William DeForest's *Miss Ravenel's Conversion from Secession to Loyalty* (1867). The character, "Major" Scott, is a realistic blend of heroism and human fallibility. Just after emancipation, Dr. Ravenel, father of the novel's heroine, begins an experiment in Louisiana to help freedmen become self-supporting, responsible citizens. He leases a deserted plantation from the federal government, gathers together a few black families from the provost-marshal, and tries to inspire them to work not for him, as if he were their master, but for their individual and collective welfare. For services performed, the colonel pays them wages. In addition, his daughter Lillie teaches them the rudiments of literacy. That the doctor's experiment is slow getting under way is understandable. Because slave culture has denied them the opportunity to shoulder the responsibilities of free men in a competitive society, they cannot see beyond the fact that they are legally free, and they often misconceive what freedom means. DeForest does not balk at displaying their inadequacies, nor does he idealize them with platitudes.

"Major" Scott, the leader of the slave group, possesses all of these drawbacks but also a virtue that makes him an individual. He is a man in transition, emerging from emasculating slave dependence toward mature independence. His name is not the one he had while a slave, nor is it one of his own choosing. It was given him, probably in jest, by a member of the provost-marshal's staff in recognition of Scott's ability to lead other blacks. When first seen in the novel, he is more like a slave driver than a responsible leader of his people. As if the other blacks were cattle, he orders them about with little concern for their well-being. Worse yet, he tries to curry favor from the doctor by depreciating another black man named Jim, declaring, "Mighty poor mean nigger he is I specs. Sort o' no 'count nigger."[4] Instead of setting a good example for the others, he is as shiftless as they and more dishonest; and for personal defections from responsibility, he blames other people.

Trying to impress Dr. Ravenel, he sanctimoniously intersperses pious-sounding phrases throughout his speech: "That's the way Abraham an' Isaac an' Jacob went at it." "They was God's 'ticlar child'n an' lightened by his holy spirit." When the doctor discovers that his livestock is increasing more rapidly than could happen normally, he suspects that the former slaves have been stealing from his neighbor's stocks. "Major" Scott, who probably has assisted in the thefts, responds with hypocritical piety: "Specs it mebbe an anser to prayer."

Dr. Ravenel is not deceived by appearances, although Scott looks the part of a spiritual leader.

> In pious conversation, venerable air, grand physique, superb bass voice, musical ear, perfection of teeth and shining white of the eyes he was a counterpart of Mrs. Stowe's immortal idealism, Uncle Tom.[5]

But Scott is not an idealized black in fiction:

> [He] had not yet arrived at the ability to keep the whole Decalogue. He sometimes got a fall in his wrestlings with the sin of lying, and in regard to the Seventh Commandment he was even more liable to overthrow than King David.[6]

In this matter, Scott thinks that the Emancipation Proclamation frees him from everything including his slave marriage. Dr. Ravenel arranges for another ceremony and threatens to send Scott back to active duty in the army if he ever again defaults from his vows. Weeping copiously, the sinner promises to remain faithful to his wife.

When the plantation is attacked by a band of Texas Rangers, he becomes a man in the real sense of the word.

Dr. Ravenel sends the Negroes to a fort where they will be safe. Scott refuses to go. Although he is afraid, he is not a coward. He possesses a strong sense of independent responsibility and a wholesome sense of gratitude for those who have tried to help him. "I wants to fight for my liberty an' for Mars Ravenel an' for Miss Lillie." "I'se not gwine for ter be cotched alive."[7] This is Scott's moment of heroism during the skirmish:

> . . . wild with a sudden madness of conflict, [he] shouted like a lion, bounded beyond the angle of the house, planting himself on two feet set wide apart, his mad black face set toward the enemy and his gun aimed. Both fired at the same instant and both fell together. . . .[8]

Unlike Abe and "Major" Scott, both of whom are minor figures in fiction, Nigger Jim in *The Adventures of Huckleberry Finn* (1884) is the full-length portrait of a slave who has been given some characteristics of an individual. On the surface Jim conforms closely to the end-man comedians, like Jim Crow and Bone Squash, in minstrel shows. The comic image is projected in expressions he uses, in his simpleminded gullibility, and in his homespun beliefs.

He is first seen stretching his neck and listening suspiciously for repetition of a sound that has alarmed him. When he can stand the suspense no longer, he calls, "Who dah?"—an expression followed fairly close with, "Dog my cats." Later his supplication in the face of impending disaster is, "Oh, my, lordy, lordy!" Humorous word coinages used by him are the onomatopoetic "blim blammin'" and the magnificent superlative, "dad-fetchedes." Gullibility shines forth as he relates his venture in financial speculation. With the relish of a born storyteller, he reaches the climax of his tale (the low point of his finances) relating how he lost his last dime to a known "chuckle-head" called "Balum's Ass for short." Balum deposited the coin in the church collection plate, literally believing the preacher's promise that whatever is given to the poor will be returned to the donor a hundredfold.

End-man humor comes through most clearly in Jim's two arguments with Huck about the wisdom of Solomon and the "blame' ridic'lous way" that Frenchmen talk. Regarding Solomon's wisdom, Jim retorts, with mind closed, that he "doan' take no stock in dat." He argues that all those wives and children must have made the harem, a kind of boarding-house to Jim, a "rackety" place; and if a man were wise, why would he want to live "in de mids' er sich blim blammin' all de time?" When Huck tries to show Jim that he has missed the whole point of the story, Jim accuses Huck of not seeing the real point "down deeper" in the story. According to Jim, Solomon himself had missed the point, or he would not have proposed cutting the baby in half in the first place. With this rhythmic tongue-twisting argument, he once and for all disposes of Solomon and his wisdom:

> De 'spute warn't 'bout a half a chile, de 'spute was 'bout a whole child; en de man dat think he kin settle a 'spute 'bout a whole child wid a half a chile, doan know enough to come in out'n de rain. Doan talk to me 'bout Sollermun, Huck, I knows him by de back.[9]

Then Jim goes on to teach Huck the real point which "lays in de way Sollermun was raised." According to him, polygamy makes a man callous. Jim's indignation mounts superbly in comic intensity.

> You take a man dat's got o'ny one er two chillen; is dat man gwyne to be waseful o' chillen? No, he ain't; he can't 'ford it. He know how to value 'em. But you take a man dat's got 'bout five million chillen runnin' roun' de house, en it's diffunt. He as soon chop a chile in two as a cat. Dey's plenty mo'. A chile er two, mo' er less, warn't no consekens to Sollermun, dad fetch him![10]

Recognizing the futility of continuing this discussion, Huck shifts the conversation to the French language and people, but he is as unsuccessful with this topic. Jim remains adamant, thinking French a "blame' ridic'lous way" for a man to talk; "dey ain't no sense in it." Using an analogy to a cat and a cow, Huck argues that since it is natural and right for a cat and a cow to speak different "languages" and for both animals to speak differently from man, then it is also natural and right for Frenchmen to speak a different language from the one spoken by Huck and Jim. To this argument, Jim retaliates,

> "Is a cat a man, Huck?"
> "No."
> "Well, den, dey ain't no sense in a cat talkin' like a man. Is a cow a man?—er is a cow a cat?"
> "No, she ain't either of them."
> "Well, den she ain't got no business to talk like either one er the yuther of 'em. Is a Frenchman a man?"
> "Yes."
> "*Well*, den! Dad blame it, why doan he *talk* like a man? You answer me dat!"[11]

Huck is squelched; "Mr. Bones" has topped his adversary once more.

At the end of the novel, Mark Twain assigns Jim a role that is woefully reminiscent of the submissive slave prototype, the kind of character who patiently endures any indignity. This transformation occurs during his imprisonment at the Phelps plantation. Huck, after the famous soul-searching episode, conceives a simple plan to free him. Then Tom Sawyer arrives on the scene. Tom's offer to help complicates the problem, for he insists that a game be made of the escape and that it be carried out according to romantic, story-book formula, similar to Monte-Cristo's escape from Château d'If. To make matters worse, Tom knows that the escape is unnecessary as the Widow Watson has died and freed Jim in her will. Jim, with only nominal disagreement and hesitancy, submits to the ridiculous ritual. Furthermore, accommodative submissiveness to Tom is complete; he calls him "Mars Tom," refuses to escape when Tom is wounded, endangering the probability of freedom for himself and his family.

Because the "Evasion" episodes come last in the novel and the author chose to give them ten chapters (approximately one fourth of the total number) of prominent space, this impression of Jim creates a disturbingly contradictory image when one remembers some of his saving graces in earlier parts of the novel. Just after Jim's escape from his owner, he was a man capable of assuming responsibility for his welfare and that of his family. Learning that Miss Watson planned to sell him, he "lit out mighty quick" rather than submit to that indignity. He carefully planned his escape into free territory where he hoped to find work, save all of his money, and either buy the freedom of his family or hire an abolitionist to steal them from their owner. Such concern for his own family and recognition of alternatives in making decisions are atypical of traditional slave behavior in literature.

Added to these is the fact that he is a warm and loving parent, quick to admit his shortsightedness with regard to his little daughter Elizabeth. Unknown to Jim she has been maimed by scarlet fever. Outwardly she appears to have recovered from the illness; but at the same time, she seems to have become strangely disobedient and unruly. On one occasion when she does not respond to a command, he slaps her so hard that she falls sprawling on the floor.

> My but I *wuz* mad, I was agwyne for de chile, but jis' den—it was a do' dat open innerds—jis' den, 'long came de wind en slam it to, behine de child, ker-*blam!*— en my lan', de chile never move'! My breff mos' hop outer me; en I feel so—so—I doan' know *how* I feel. I crope out, all a-tremblin', . . . en open de do' easy an slow, en poke my head in behind de chile, sof' en still, en all uv a sudden, I says *pow!* jis' as loud as I could yell: *She never budge!* Oh, Huck, I bust out a-cryin' en grab her up in my arms, en say, "Oh, de po' little thing! de Lord God Amighty fogive po' ole Jim, kaze he never gwyne to fogive hisself as long's he live!" Oh, she was plumb deef en dumb . . . en I'd ben a-treat'n her so.[12]

In this early relationship with Huck, Jim is not only a warm individual but one who demands that the relationship between them be mutually respectful and reciprocal. This can be seen most clearly in the episode that takes place after he and Huck have been separated by fog and strong river currents, Huck in the canoe and Jim on the raft. After calling Huck and getting no response, Jim assumes that the boy has been drowned in the turbulent water. Grief-stricken, he mourns until exhausted and falls asleep. When Huck returns to the raft, he decides to play a trick on Jim by pretending that the two have not been separated. On awakening and finding Huck safe beside him, Jim is at first overjoyed and then confused when he is told that he has dreamed the events of the previous night. Prior to this incident, Jim somewhat pompously claimed the powers of a seer in interpreting the hidden meanings of natural signs, events, and dreams. At Huck's sarcastic urgings, he goes to work divining the warnings supposedly sent to him in his "dream." Huck, relishing his advantage and wanting to keep the joke in motion, asks him to interpret the meaning of the debris that accumulated on the raft during the bad weather, thereby calling attention to evidence that proves Jim has not dreamed the events. Jim looks from Huck to the debris and back to Huck.

> What do dey stan' for? I'se gwyne to tell you. When I got all wore out wid work, en wid callin' for you, en went to sleep, my heart wuz mos' broke bekase you wuz los', en I didn' k'yer no mo' what become er me en de raf'. En when I wake up en fine you back agin', all safe en soun', de tears come en I could a got down on my knees en kiss' yo' foot I's so thankful. En all you wuz thinkin' 'bout wuz how you could make a fool uv ole Jim wid a lie. Dat truck dah is *trash*; en trash is what people is dat puts dirt on de head er dey fren's en makes 'em ashamed.[13]

Huck's joke momentarily threatens the transactional nature of a relationship enjoyable to both. Jim's reaction, revealing self-pride, shames Huck and prevents deterioration of the relationship.

> Then he [Jim] got up slow, and walked to the wigwam, and went in there, without saying anything but that. But that was enough. It made me feel so mean I could almost *kissed his* foot. . . .
>
> It was fifteen minutes before I could work myself up to go and humble myself to a nigger—but I done it, and I warn't ever sorry for it afterwards, neither. I didn't do him no more mean tricks, and I wouldn't done that one if I'd a knowed it would make him feel that way.[14]

Mark Twain is an early, major novelist to give qualities of an individual to a Negro in our literature; but because he gives him characteristics of the submissive slave and end-man comedian also, Jim's is a transitional image of a Negro as an individual. The trend was definitely established, however, by 1884 when *The Adventures of Huckleberry Finn* was first published in England. Since then, other more fully realized images of slaves who are also individuals have appeared in literature. Two characters created by Stephen Vincent Benét are good examples. They are Spade in *John Brown's Body* (1927) and Cue in "Freedom's a Hard Bought Thing" (1940).

Spade and Cue are so similar in bodily configuration and self-interest that they might be the same character. Each is big and strong. Cue is "black as night," and Spade is "black as a pine at night." Cue is a younger version of what Spade must have been. The son of Cuffee, the grandson of Shango the Corromantee–"a bold and free people"—Cue has inherited his grandfather's untamable spirit which bypassed Cue's father, Cuffee, who accepted enslavement passively. Slowly, Cue becomes aware of himself as a person; and as awareness grows, determination to be free becomes a sickness within him. With youthful impetuousness he runs away, is captured and whipped; but he reaffirms his determination when he tells Aunt Rachel and her granddaughter Sukey, "I been whipped, but I ain't beaten." Aided by the two women, he prepares himself for the next attempt to escape, fully recognizing the alternatives involved: if he tries again and is caught, his punishment will be more severe, and he will probably be sold to a worse master; if he relinquishes his desire for freedom, he will not expose himself to danger as a runaway slave and can remain on the plantation in relative security with Sukey as his wife.

When Cue's second chance comes, he discovers that there is space enough in the abolitionist's boat for either Sukey or him. He shoves her into the boat "before he can think too hard." Recaptured, he is punished and sold several times; but from then on, everything that he does and learns is directed toward that moment when he reaches Canada and can freely assert his individuality. This is his poetic song of self-identity and freedom:

My name's Cue—John H. Cue. I got a strong back and strong arms. I got freedom in my heart. I got a first name and a last name and a middle name. I never had them all before. . . . I got a name and a tale to tell. I got a hammer to swing. I got a tale to tell my people. I got recollection.[15]

When Spade is first identified by name in *John Brown's Body* (1927), he has the clipped ear, the limp, and the scarred back that testify to repeated failures and the intense desire to be free. He dreams of walking down the white man's street up north and being spoken to with respectful deference: "Good mawnin', Mr. Spade." He too profits from earlier abortive attempts to escape. For over a year he pretends that he is content with being a slave in order to allay his master's suspicions, while inside him the "freedom sickness" rages stronger than ever before. When the signs are right, he steals away, endures fear and hardship, and reaches free land only to discover that the reality of freedom bears little resemblance to his dream. He is impressed into service on a road gang and later into the Union Army. After being wounded in the Battle of the Crater, he is separated from the army and returns north, a pitiful "ragamuffin something," but free. He finds employment on Jake Diefer's farm, and it is enough for him that he has a job. He now sees himself and freedom realistically. When Jake hesitates to hire him and says, "I ain't payin' a hired man much," he answers simply, "Dey calls me Spade."[16] Both slaves, in contrast with Nigger Jim, are consistently self-determining, allowing nothing to interfere with their search for freedom and self-identity in freedom.

Shortly after the turn of the twentieth century, Paul Lawrence Dunbar skillfully delineated the fictional image of a black man who is influential in the life of his community. The character is Robinson Asbury in "The Scapegoat" (1904). Asbury lives in Cadgers, a growing town with a fifty percent Negro population that tended to "colonize" in one section of the town, a "tendency encouraged and in fact compelled, by circumstances." Asbury is an enterprising man, one undaunted by segregation, beginning his career as a bootblack, advancing to porter-messenger of a barber

shop where he learns the trade, later rents a chair, and
eventually progresses to ownership of the Equal Rights
Barbershop, which becomes the popular meeting place of
men in the black community. In addition to barbering
services and a friendly atmosphere, he provides little extras,
such as copies of the black press, race-course information,
and policy results.

His popularity and growing prestige in the community
do not long go unnoticed by local politicians who give him
money, power, and patronage. In return, he delivers the
black vote. Still not content to rest on gains achieved he reads
law at night and eventually applies for admission to the bar.
Most people, especially white political figures, advise him
against the move, expressing fear that as a lawyer he will
not have the broad and frequent social contacts with the
people that he has as their friendly barber. One man, influential old Judge Davis, initially goes along with the majority but is persuaded to change his mind by something, not
revealed to the reader, that Asbury whispers in his ear. The
judge's laughing response only hints at Asbury's skill in
manipulating others for his own purposes.

> Asbury, . . . you are—you are—well, you ought to be
> white, that's all. When we find a black man like you we
> send him to State's prison. If you were white, you'd go
> to the Senate.[17]

Later, he opens a law office next door to the barber shop.
His success now at its peak, he settles down to work for
black people.

His downfall is due to the jealousy of the entrenched
black political figures and the heads of the town's rival black
law firm who infiltrate Asbury's activities in search of evidence that can be used to discredit him in the community.
With the rise of a political reform movement, party leaders
look among vulnerable and expendable members for a scapegoat. Asbury is accused of fraud, tried before Judge Davis,
and convicted on evidence supplied by the infiltrators, in
spite of the judge's lenient charge to the jury. Before passing
sentence, the judge allows him to speak to the court. In no
way the cliché of a dewy-eyed political idealist, he tells "a

tale of rottenness and corruption in high places," bringing
about the downfall of others, naming all involved along with
him except one, Judge Davis. In the minds of the community,
Asbury the scapegoat slowly changes into Asbury the martyr.
After serving his sentence, he returns to the community,
patiently awaits the right moment to discredit his enemies
and regain his former status in the community.

Another transitional figure is Gertrude Stein's Melanctha
(*Three Lives*, 1909). Her name suggests mournfulness of
spirit, but she is never comforted in her search for identity
and fulfillment. Her portrait just misses being an image of
an individual as defined here.

Melanctha is a bright mulatto, "pale yellow and mysterious and a little like her mother." From her "robust and pleasant and very unendurable black father," she inherits primitive instinct and "Negro power." Her relationship with both
parents is strained, although she is drawn a bit closer to the
father than to the mother because the latter rejects her. As a
result, she cannot identify with either parent and is cursed
with personality conflicts. One part of her wants only "peace,
gentleness, and goodness"; the other demands "earth-born,
boundless joy" and "simple, promiscuous immorality." Such
conflicting duality causes her always to be at odds with herself and with her associates. All she seems able to do is "find
new ways to be in trouble."

In adolescence, she becomes reckless and begins to wander about the streets of Bridgeport in search of exciting experiences. This roaming, according to Miss Stein, is attributable to animal desires inherited from her father.

> . . . when the darkness covered everything all over, she
> would begin to learn this man or that. She would ad-
> vance, they would respond, and then she would withdraw
> a little, dimly, and always she did not know what it was
> that really held her. Sometimes she would almost go over,
> and then the strength in her of not really knowing, would
> stop the average man in his endeavor.[18]

For all her recklessness and desire, she is bewildered by these
experiences. She goes to an older and more experienced
woman, Jane Harden, to understand herself better in male-

female relationships. Jane, a white-skinned Negro, has animal desires also; but, according to the author, her white blood makes her know how to use her Negro power. She teaches Melanctha "how to go the ways that lead to wisdom," or, more precisely, what she knows about men. Melanctha learns all that Jane has to teach. Thus armed, Melanctha enters a life of promiscuity with the white and black men of the town.

Her first serious attachment occurs when she meets Jeff Campbell, a young Negro doctor. Jeff is a thinker and, though attracted to Melanctha, cannot overlook the way she lives. In his opinion, her promiscuity is a bad way of life for any human being and especially for Negroes, who should try to attain social respect and higher economic status in the culture. To him there are two ways of loving—one good, the other bad.

> One kind of loving seems to me, is like one has a good quiet feeling in a family when one does his work, and is always living good and being regular, and then the other way of loving is just having it like any animal that's low in the streets together and that don't seem to me very good.[19]

With Melanctha, the instinctualist, this philosophy does not sit well.

> You certainly are just too scared Dr. Campbell to really feel things way down in you. All you are wanting . . . , is just to talk about being good, and to play with people just to have a good time, and yet always to certainly keep yourself out of trouble. It don't seem to me . . . that I admire that way to do things very much. It certainly ain't really to me being very good.[20]

He cannot be what she calls "strong in love"; she cannot promise to be what he calls "regular"; hence, neither can find satisfaction in their relationship. The tension created by reason in one and primitive instinct in the other frustrates both.

At this point, Gertrude Stein shows the precariousness of timing in interpersonal relationships. In the beginning,

Melanctha's feeling for Jeff is stronger than his for her. By the time that his love for her becomes "a real religion" to him, she has begun to seek more varied experiences. When they part, nevertheless, it is he who can relinquish the relationship without regret. She can never forget him.

She continues to wander. Because she still cannot find happiness, she turns to another woman, Rose Johnson, for advice. Rose is a black-skinned woman who was reared by whites. They showed her how to use her black power to get and hold a man. To Melanctha, Rose's life exemplifies the effectiveness of their training. She enjoys the pleasures her animal instincts demand, and is, at the same time, decently married. She advises Melanctha to refrain from promiscuous wanderings with men and to conform to approved social behavior by becoming properly engaged before permitting intimacies.

Then Melanctha meets a gambler, Jem Richards, whose instinctive nature matches hers. Remembering Rose's advice, Melanctha is soon engaged to marry Jem. At first, his love is the stronger. This situation continues as long as his luck in gambling holds good. As her love grows, his diminishes in proportion to his gambling losses. Her failure to understand his problem drives him away from her. Pressed too hard to set the marriage date, he finally tells her, "I just don't give a damn now for you any more." Her story ends on a note of dramatic irony. She obtains a job, lives respectably, and dies of tuberculosis as if she were a heroine in a sentimental novel.

Melanctha gives the appearance of being an individual in fiction, because her motivation is directed toward finding a pattern of life that is suitable for her. Her wandering through the dark streets of Bridgeport is a search for self-understanding in relationships with other people. In neither is she successful. Her confused overdependence on Jane and Rose, her failures with Jeff and Jem, are symptomatic of her inability to understand and come to terms with herself in interpersonal relationships. Her inadequacy in such matters is more a testimony of human fallibility than lack of individuality. Yet cultural determinism, reflected in two archetypal character patterns, causes her to be less than individualistic as defined here. The dominant overtone in her portrait harks back to the power of inherited white or black "blood" to control the personality of a tragic mulatto, within whom the two strains are in constant conflict. A minor tone of the carnal sensualists makes her reminiscent of characters whose only aim in life is sensual gratification. Melanctha is, therefore, a complex portrait of a Negro in transition from cultural determinism to individualistic self-assertion.

Another youthful female seeker for identity and fulfillment, more fully realized as an individual than Melanctha, is Zora Neale Hurston's Janie (*Their Eyes Were Watching God*, 1937). Her adolescence is channeled into constricting social conformity by her grandmother Nannie, who, during slavery, gave birth to the octoroon daughter of her master. The daughter, in turn, bore Janie out of wedlock with a Negro. Nannie is determined that Janie will not be so misused by either white or black men. When she sees a boy "lacerating her Janie with a kiss" beneath the pollinated air of a pear tree, she arranges a marriage for Janie with middle-aged, prosperous Logan Killicks. But Janie is searching for her own pattern of life and demanding answers to important questions: does "marriage end the cosmic loneliness of the unmated" and "does marriage compel love like the sun the day?" Obviously Nannie is removed too far from youthful urgencies to understand precisely what the child wants to know. Janie begins to realize that she will have to find her own answers. She waits patiently through "a bloom time, a green time, and an orange time" and then she knows that the answer to both questions is negative. When the pear tree is again in bloom, she begins waiting at the gate for something to happen. Along comes Jody Starks, a vibrant go-getter, with whom she thinks she might find fulfillment.

They elope to an all Negro town where he becomes storekeeper-mayor and prominent citizen. He finds his place in life, but Janie chafes under the restrictions that social prominence imposes upon them. He demands that she act the part of a respected matron by binding her beautiful hair with the head cloths customarily worn by the elderly women of the town. Her life with him is as constricted as it was with Nannie. Janie complains that it was not for the bowing and scraping of other people that she ran off with him; but, by that time, Jody has become insensitive to anything except his authoritative position, and there is no basis for communication between them. He dies when she is forty years old. Although she stops wearing head cloths and allows her braids to hang free, she resigns herself to an unfulfilled old age.

Janie comes to that decision before she meets Tea Cake. Twelve years her junior, a man of easy, engaging ways, he brings into her life the joy and companionship she has ceased hoping to find. At first, she is disturbed by the difference in their ages and suspicious of his motives. When she is sure that it is she and not Jody's prestige or money that he wants, she goes off with him to the Florida Everglades where they work together as harvest pickers. She works beside him because it gives her pleasure to be with him. Two years later Tea Cake is bitten by a rabid dog during a hurricane. No one realizes that he has been infected with the disease until some weeks later. When he goes mad, Janie is forced to kill him after he attacks her for refusing to give him water. Exonerated of willful intent to kill, she returns to a life of retrospection. But she can proudly declare, "Ah been a delegate to de big 'ssociation of life."

During the 1930's and continuing into the 1940's, many excellently drawn portraits of males who can be called self-asserting individuals appeared in literature. Five of these, two from the early 1930's and three from the 1940's, are included in the sample because each is different from the others and relatively free from dominant, if not recessive, stock and archetypal overtones. They are Sandy Rogers in Langston Hughes's *Not without Laughter* (1930), Sam Lucas in Countee Cullen's *One Way to Heaven* (1932), Joe Mott in Eugene O'Neill's *The Iceman Cometh* (1946), Lucas Beauchamp in William Faulkner's *Intruder in the Dust* (1948), and Eric Gardner in Bucklin Moon's *Without Magnolias* (1949).

Young Sandy Rogers is the grandson of Aunt Hager Williams, a washerwoman who is the mainstay of her black family in Kansas before World War I. Her name is reminiscent of the biblical concubine and suggestive of the outsider theme in literature. Although she is called "Aunt," wears a dust cap and apron, and, as a result, bears some resemblance to archetypal mammies, her personality designates her an emancipated black mother, emotionally attached only to her family of three daughters and Sandy. His parents are her middle daughter, black-skinned Annjee, and her yellow-skinned husband, a long, tall, sweet-talking, banjo-playing wanderer named Jimboy. Hager openly disapproves of him, casts doubt on his identity ("Who ever heard of a nigger named Jimboy?") and his motives for marrying her Annjee ("Never seen a yaller dude yet that meant a dark woman no good."). Annjee is not a bad mother. She loves Sandy but adores Jimboy, feels desolate without her husband and compelled to be wherever he is. For this reason Hager has to assume the responsibility of rearing her grandchild. Her one remaining ambition is to see that he is educated. Her eldest daughter Tempy is the only one of her children who finished school. Harriet, the youngest, considers her mother an old fogy and rejects the mother's way of life. The conflict between them becomes nearly irreparable when she denounces Christianity, Hager's principal emotional support, as hypocritical in its "lip-support" of brotherhood in the face of its denial of it to blacks. Further, she rejects Hager's rigid Baptist constriction of people's lives, forbidding such behavior as laughter on Sundays, dancing at any time, and sensual pleasure eternally.

Hager's death, before she can achieve her goal for Sandy, releases him from such rigid indoctrination only to expose him to another sort of rigidity at his Aunt Tempy's house. Tempy and her husband are members of a pretentious black middle class, really "whitewashed" Negroes, who are disdainful of black Negroes and any unrestrained behavior or speech that they term "niggerish." Long before Hager died, they, too, rejected her Baptist church on the grounds that the church had too many low-class, shouting niggers as members. They joined the Episcopal church, the one that the "best people" attended. Sandy stays with them until Annjee—once again lonely for Jimboy, who is overseas as a World War I volunteer—allows him to come live with her in Chicago. There, his job as elevator operator interferes with his education, a situation that does not disturb Annjee, who feels that earning money is more important than school learning.

At this point, Sandy asserts himself and makes an important decision about himself and his future. He decides that although he loves his father, he is not a wanderer and that constant wandering would become as monotonous to him as his job as elevator operator has become. Furthermore, although he has enjoyed the comfortable life his Aunt Tempy and her husband provided for him, he wants no part of her social relationships, limited to those she calls the best people. On the positive side, he decides that he will continue his education, with generous financial assistance offered by Harriet, so that he can be forever free from dependence on the economic "mercies of white people," and that, like Harriet, he must live his life free from the cultural rigidities that dominated Hager's life.

Sandy's story ends on a high note of hope for the future. When first seen, Sam Lucas, in contrast, is a pitiable creature, "striding through the raw, mordant December night" and feeling apprehensive that he has, after so many years, finally reached "the big time," Harlem—still Mecca for Southern blacks in the 1930's. New York is colder, the people less friendly than those in the South. In appearance, he is gaunt, one-armed, jet-black, with elongated head, high cheekbones, sunken jaws—the right one slashed by a tan scar, the result of a knife wound. "Deep electric brown" eyes look out of his finely shaped, intelligent face. He is inordinately proud of his black skin. The facial scar and dangling left coat sleeve are essential properties for his "act."

Sam loses no time in getting to Mount Hebron African Methodist Episcopal Church where he plans to put on his well-practiced hoax. Toward the end of the service, the guest evangelist, the Reverend Johnson, invites sinners to come to the mourners' bench and to kneel there as a sign of repentance, of acceptance of Christ's teachings, of spiritual rebirth, and of firm commitment, thereafter to lead sinless, exemplary lives. Hardly anyone moves in the direction of the pulpit until Sam, with tear-filled eyes and left coat sleeve hanging limply, rises and walks down the aisle. Just before kneeling, he takes a pack of cards, symbolic among churchgoers as "the devil's own tools," and an "evil-shining" razor from his pocket and throws them to the floor with studied histrionics as testimony of his salvation. Nine other converts, inspired by Sam's performance, come also to the mourners' bench, including Mattie, a black girl who is so moved by Sam's "conversion" that she, who has been a skeptic, instantaneously believes in all of the church's teachings.

Members of the congregation congratulate him and indicate their approval by pressing money into his hand as they shake it in fellowship, at which time Sam's face takes on just the right proportions of reproach and gratitude, indicating—as he pockets the gifts—reluctance to accept material profit from spiritual gain as well as unwillingness to hurt the donor's feelings by rejection of his gift. Only the Reverend Johnson is unhappy. He has been a victim once before of Sam's hypocrisy. At that time, in Memphis, Sam's deceit inspired twenty-three conversions. While he finds Sam's behavior despicable, he is chagrined by Sam's success, as compared with his own meager achievements, in bringing sinners to Christ. He satisfies himself with the rationalization that quite possibly Sam is an "unwitting instrument" of God's unfathomable grace.

Amoral Sam feels not the slightest qualm about what he has done or about his subsequent marriage to Mattie based on deception. To his credit, however, he never deludes himself about his behavior, even when he tries to make himself hate her so that parting from her will be made easier. They are temporarily reconciled when she becomes pregnant; for he is intrigued by the idea of having a child so black he can boast that there is not a single drop of white blood between its parents. When she miscarries, he leaves in disgust, refusing to remain in a house where there is so much religion and so little vitality.

He becomes ill. Mattie, with genuine Christian charity, brings him home to die. Her only worry is that Sam's sinfulness may prevent their being together in heaven with their child. She confesses this fear to her aunt, who tries to comfort her by telling her that sometimes people on the verge of death are granted certain indicators of salvation, such as visions of shining lights and sounds of angelic choirs singing. Overhearing their conversation, Sam, though very near death, exerts himself to put on one final act for her peace of mind, performing so well that Mattie is convinced, once more, of his salvation and of their reunion.

Joe Mott provides a sharp contrast to Sam Lucas. Sam has no illusions about himself; but for Joe, existence is completely encased in illusions. He is depicted as a deteriorating, comical show-off. His clothing, faded and falling apart, supports that image. He wears a ragged tan suit, pointed shoes, a faded pink shirt, and a brightly colored tie. On his "mildly Negroid face," "a scar from a knife slash runs from his left cheekbone to jaw." His expression is one of "good nature and lazy humor." This stock picture has the effect of pointing up the tragic results of caste on the character's personality.

Joe was once the owner of a Negro gambling house and believes that one day he will win enough money to set himself up in business again, despite the fact that he barely survives from day to day on Harry Hope's charity and never has enough money to pay for his next drink much less gamble for high stakes. Paradoxically, he thinks of himself as white, even though he knows that his skin is black. This belief is dramatic testimony of culturally conditioned self-rejection, common among Negroes who believe the only worthwhile people are whites. They hate themselves and try to become "white" by behaving as they think whites behave. Joe's belief is supported by compliments from other derelicts and by things that happened during his affluent period when he was the only Negro permitted to gamble in white establishments. To him this concession was his baptism as a white man. When he obtained a license to open his own establishment, with Harry Hope's backing, an inspector substantiated the black man's "whiteness" when he called Joe a "black-son-of-a-bitch" and threatened, "Harry says you're white and you better be white." Only in this way could a black man obtain a license to open a gambling parlor at that time. To Joe, being white means operating an illegal business, prompt payment of graft, and behaving generously but foolishly toward one's friends. To this end he promises the other derelicts that when he reopens his establishment, he will give them money to gamble with if they are broke, overlook any losses, and let them keep their winnings.

In *The Iceman Cometh,* O'Neill seems to be saying that

although man is deluded by futile illusions, he cannot survive without them. Joe's special illusions expose his personality defects as poignantly as do those held by the other characters, all of whom have taken refuge from reality in Harry Hope's stronghold of illusion, the Last Chance Saloon. None of the derelicts deprecates himself overtly until Hickey arrives on the scene. Joe, stripped of his illusion, becomes angry and aggressively hypersensitive. But Hickey's coming is only a troublesome interlude for all except two of the dreamers. The rest, including Joe, bounce back to illusionary concepts of themselves and to the reciprocal relationship they formerly enjoyed with each other. Within the context of the drama, it seems safe to say that Joe, like the others, represents an individual who is doomed to half-life in illusion because reality is totally unendurable.

In contrast, Lucas Beauchamp holds few illusions about himself. He is a down-to-earth realist. More than that, he is the black-skinned embodiment of man's aspiration for dignity and personal freedom; but most important, he possesses the personal courage and integrity to rise above cultural belief about him. These are attributes that make Lucas an individual.

Faulkner substantiates Lucas's differentness from other Negroes in descriptions of his appearance and personality. His town clothes are not those usually worn by Negroes, or poor whites for that matter, on their Saturday shopping trips. Lucas goes to town on weekdays and wears a neat black broadcloth suit, much worn and well brushed, a heavy gold watchchain looped across his vest, and an ancient handmade beaver hat that reminds young Charles Mallison of his grandfather. Also, Lucas is never without his gold toothpick. When Lucas rescues Charles Mallison, the nephew of lawyer Gavin Stevens, from the icy water of a creek near his cabin, the boy is shocked by what he sees on the old man's face. Unlike most Negroes, Lucas does not smile. He is calm and watchful, unemotional and objective.

As his appearance differs from what whites think Negroes ought to look like, so does his behavior. In their minds, he takes unfair advantage of them by not adhering to the role white society has assigned to him. But to get the whole picture of Lucas's deviant behavior, the reader has to go to Faulkner's earlier stories. In "The Bear" we learn how Lucas alters his name in a way that suits and predicts his behavior in *Intruder in the Dust*. In the fourth part of "The Bear" Ike McCaslin comes to the last page of his father's and uncle's yellowed journals and realizes that Lucas's name ought to be written there, as he is the last of old Carothers McCaslin's mulatto heirs. But Ike realizes also that, if it were there, the name would not be the one given Lucas at birth. In accord with the practices of naming slaves, he should have been entered in the journal as Lucius Quintus; for Lucas is the illegitimate great-grandson of Carothers McCaslin, white progenitor of the McCaslin family of Yoknapatawpha County, Mississippi, whose first two names were also Lucius Quintus, and for whom Lucius may have been named. More than that, as Ike also realizes, Carothers was not only Lucas's great-grandfather, but also his grandfather, a relationship resulting from Carothers's lust for his own slave daughter, Tomasina (Tomy), who was Lucas's grandmother. The offspring of that incestuous union was Terrel (Turl), Lucas's father. Like Ike, Lucas realizes the true nature of the relationship and the significance of the name; but he does not want the name. He spurns it, renaming himself Lucas, and in a sense creating for himself his own identity. Also recorded in "The Bear" is the manner in which, on his twenty-first birthday, Lucas receives his part of the legacy left by Carothers for his illegitimate offspring. Abruptly, he comes to Ike's door and without preamble demands that Old Carothers's money left to Turl be turned over to him, emphasizing that he wants all that remains of it.

About three years later, when Lucas is twenty-four, a much more serious encounter, clearly revealing pride and assertion of black manhood, is recorded in a flashback in "The Fire and the Hearth," involving Lucas's wife Mollie and Zack Edmonds, also a descendant of old Carothers, but white and three generations removed by way of the female line; whereas Lucas is only one generation removed and by way of the male, though slave, line. The two men grew up together and were married at approximately the same time. Mollie gives birth before Zack's wife and is therefore able to assist at the white mother's delivery. Complications arise; Zack's wife dies, and Mollie stays on as nurse to her own and the white mother's child, leaving Lucas at home alone. He broods. He begins to suspect that the old system of concubinage is being reestablished with his wife. When he can bear his thoughts no longer, he goes to Zack and demands the return of his wife. Mollie immediately returns with both children, but Lucas's suspicions are not allayed. With murderous rage, he goes to Zack's house late that night to kill him but is stopped by the fact of their relatedness, both descendants of the same flesh and blood. The two men fight as equals. Lucas, obtaining the advantage over Zack, presses the trigger of a gun which misfires, saving both of their lives, Zack from a bullet and Lucas from a lynch mob.

That is the background of the seventy-two-year-old character whom the reader meets in *Intruder in the Dust*. After rescuing young Charles Mallison from the creek, Lucas takes the reluctant lad to his cabin, dries his clothes, and feeds him. Charles, behaving according to the dictates of his caste position, offers the old man money for these services because a white cannot be humiliated by indebtedness to a Negro. When Lucas fails to react in any way, neither accepting nor rejecting the money, Charles, true to his Southern upbringing, drops the coins to the floor and orders Lucas to pick them up. Still no response from Lucas; the silence and stillness become unbearable. Charles, unable to control the situation as a white boy should, waits, blushes, pales until Lucas finally releases him by telling Aleck Sander, the white boy's black playmate, to get the coins and return them to Charles, and, only then, shooing them both out of the house with a warning not to fall into the creek again.

Lucas's relationships with whites are always transactional; he "gets under the skin" of white adults who are as frustrated as Charles by the man's refusal to perform caste ritual in a spirit befitting that position. He is notorious in their minds as the Negro who addresses whites with "ma'm" and "sir" and "mister," but they could tell that the words implied no customary recognition of himself as inferior. Moreover, Lucas is not above flaunting "old family" rank in front of poor whites and red-necked newcomers, even though he is the illegitimate descendant of the aristocratic McCaslins and Beauchamps. One Saturday when he goes into the crossroads store, his aloofness infuriates the whites assembled there. One assails him verbally, calling him a "biggity stiffnecked stinking burrheaded Edmonds" among some other salty expressions. Compared to the McCaslins, the Edmondses are newcomers and related to the McCaslins only on the distaff side of the family. Slowly, unruffled, Lucas informs them that he is a McCaslin, a member of one of the first families of the County. At this effrontery a white threatens to make crowbait of him. Lucas pauses, looking intently at the man, retorts that he has been told that on other occasions and that the people who have threatened him "ain't even Edmondses." Only the quick restraint by two of the man's companions prevents Lucas from being lynched on the spot. The consensus among whites is that if Lucas would only act like a nigger just once, then they might be willing to accept him as he insists on being accepted.

Their chance to get even comes when Lucas is discovered standing over the dead body of Vinson Gowrie, a lumberman in business with his brother Crawford and their mother's uncle Mr. Workitt in Beat Four, the roughest section of Yoknapatawpha County. Evidence seems to point to his guilt because, when apprehended, his Grandfather McCaslin's pistol could be seen protruding suspiciously from his pocket. Lucas hires Gavin Stevens to defend him. Knowing that Stevens believes him guilty, Lucas cues Charles Mallison, Stevens's nephew, to exhume Vinson's body to prove that it had not been shot with a bullet from Lucas's gun.

In his intractable way, Lucas does not tell either Gavin or Charles exactly what happened before he was arrested. Some time earlier, Lucas learned that Crawford was swindling his partners and informed Crawford that he knew. The white man tried to bribe him. Lucas refused to be bribed, telling Crawford that he had decided to inform Mr. Workitt that his nephews have been stealing from him, unless Crawford makes proper restitution within a specified time limit, a dangerous decision made doubly dangerous by threatening the thief. Crawford, in retaliation, killed Vinson and implicated Lucas, making it look as if the latter were the culprit.

Evidence proving Lucas innocent is obtained by Charles and an elderly, courageous white woman. Afterwards, Lucas presents himself at Gavin's law office, ostensibly to pay his bill but more to gloat over Gavin's having been wrong in assuming Lucas guilty. He enters blithely, twitting young Charles. "You ain't fell in no more creeks lately, have you?" Then he turns to Gavin. They shadow-box about the amount Lucas should pay for services that Gavin has not rendered until it is mutually agreed that Lucas should pay two dollars for Gavin's expenses.

It is evident that Lucas possesses the integrity of a mature individual who makes important decisions in his culture and is satisfied with nothing less than transactional relationships with whites. Both of these behaviors stem from firm knowledge of himself as an individual and his sense of independent responsibility.

Eric Gardner in Bucklin Moon's *Without Magnolias* (1949), is as individualistic as Lucas Beauchamp; but he does not engage the reader's emotions quite so much. Eric is a Northern-bred, almost white mulatto, who goes south to teach at a Negro college. His family reminds the reader of the "Society of Blue Veins," met earlier among archetypal figures. They isolate themselves from darker Negroes, believing themselves superior because of their white skins. Eric does not share their prejudice. In the South he marries a ginger-colored girl, not in defiance of his parents' beliefs but because he loves her. He knows that they will disapprove his choice. Eric is not ashamed of being a Negro, nor does he unconsciously hate himself because he is so classified by American definition.

Eric is different in more than skin color from the other teachers at Bayerton College. He prefers casual clothing in contrast to the plain blue serge and starched white shirt that is their academic uniform. What is more, he enjoys the "blues," a form of music that the others consider embarrassingly representative of uneducated Negroes and that must, because of that association, be avoided.

Deliberately and calmly, like Lucas Beauchamp, he violates Southern ritual, fully realizing the alternatives involved, the most frightening being the possibility of arousing latent and violent conflicts between the two groups. As active agent in the culture, he organizes a boycott of a drugstore that refuses service to Negroes; he encourages his students to question the validity of cultural attitudes toward them, so that they might be freed from the stultifying psychological effects of prejudice; and he goads the town's newspaper editor about ineffectual duplicity in race matters. For example, at the same time that the editor bows to local convention, he takes pride in liberal views in trivial things, such as shaking hands with Negroes and capitalizing the letter "N" in "Negro" whenever he uses the word in his columns. Eric, having antagonized whites and having refused to go along with his employer's middle-of-the-road policies, is fired from his job; but because he is a mature individual, he is not defeated as are protagonists in other sociological novels analyzed earlier.

Youthful Males in Search of Self

In the 1950's, the trend toward individualization reaches a peak in portraits of youthful blacks in search of identity and fulfillment, such as the nameless protagonist of *Invisible Man* (1952) by Ralph Ellison; Cross Damon in *The Outsider* (1953) by Richard Wright; John Grimes in *Go Tell It on the Mountain* (1953) by James Baldwin; Spencer Scott in *Take a Giant Step* (1954) by Louis Peterson; and Walter Lee Younger in *Raisin in the Sun* (1959) by Lorraine Hansberry.

Invisible Man is the story of a Negro youth's peculiar conditioning in a society that denies him recognition as an individual. His first shock comes in early childhood from his grandfather, who, when on his deathbed, advised him to continue the fight, begun during Reconstruction just after blacks lay down their guns, to conquer whites by undermining them with grinning faces, by agreeing with all they think and say, and by overpowering them with accommodativeness until the whites are destroyed. Neither he nor his father can accept this as his role in life. The youth envisions himself a potential Booker T. Washington and studies hard to fit himself for that role until the second shock, his obscene *rites de passage,* introduces him to his role in society.

After graduation from high school, at which he delivers

the commencement oration, he is invited to repeat his speech at a gathering of prominent whites in the community. The event turns out to be a men's smoker, and the boys have been invited mainly to provide entertainment. Their initiation takes four forms. First is the symbolic castration ritual of black men: a naked white woman performs a sensuous dance; while whites chase and manhandle her, the black boys are required to remain spectators. Next comes the Battle Royal: blindfolded, the youths are incited, by promise of rewards, to fight each other, the idea being to keep blacks fighting among themselves without purpose or knowledge of whom they are fighting. After that comes the double-cross: instead of rewards going to winners, all are allowed to scramble for coins that have been placed on an electrified rug; as a result, all are stunned and none is rewarded. Finally, the protagonist, swallowing his own blood drawn in the Battle Royal, is made to deliver the commencement oration that ironically urges blacks to be humble in order to insure social advancement for the group. The lad no longer believes what he is saying. For this performance he is rewarded with a shiny new briefcase. That night he dreams that the briefcase contains a sheet of paper on which these words are written: "To Whom It May Concern: Keep this Nigger-Boy Running." Awakening, he imagines that he hears his grandfather's sardonic laughter ringing in his ears.

Thus psychologically emasculated and thoroughly bewildered, the youth enters a Negro college hoping that he can earn a name for himself and learn what useful function exists for a black man in American society. It is from an educated man, Dr. Bledsoe, president of the college and "coal black daddy" of the students who fear him, that the protagonist receives the third shock when he violates the ritual of race relations required by black leaders. Unwittingly, he allows Mr. Norton, Northern benefactor of the college, to see an earthy side of black life, thereby destroying the white man's image of blacks as simple, devout people and endangering continuation of the Northerner's contributions to the college. As in a nightmare of misadventure, the boy introduces Mr. Norton to Trueblood, a man guilty of incest. The Northerner becomes emotionally disturbed as he listens to Trueblood's sanguine recount of the details of his daughter's seduction. When Mr. Norton can stand to hear no more, he hastily gives Trueblood some money and orders the protagonist to take him to a saloon for a drink. The youth naïvely takes the white man to a tavern-brothel, euphemistically named The Golden Day, to which emotionally disturbed black inmates of a veterans' hospital are brought periodically. This happens to be the day of their visit. The boy tries to protect Mr. Norton from the patients but is refused permission to take a drink out of the tavern for off-premises consumption. The white man is obliged to go into The Golden Day where he is abused verbally and physically. For committing these sins, Dr. Bledsoe suspends the youth from college, intimating, however, that he will be allowed to return later. With feigned helpfulness, the president gives the boy several sealed letters, presumably of introduction and recommendation, to altruistic Northern whites. Actually, the letters contain a message similar to the one the boy dreamed was in the briefcase: keep this nigger running; we do not want him to return to the college.

After a futile round of delivering the letters and being rebuffed by prospective employers, the protagonist learns the content of the letters from a compassionate white man. Only then does he realize that he can depend only on himself if he is ever to earn a name and control his destiny. With new-found self-reliance he gets a job in a paint factory, at which the main product is Optic White, a paint used on national shrines and monuments. His job is to stir ten drops of black fluid into the basic formula until the paint becomes a glossy white. By mistake he stirs ten drops of a concentrated color remover into the formula, turning it crystal clear and rendering it useless. Fired by a white supervisor from that job, he goes to work under a black one in the boiler room at the factory. In this job he is supposed to watch pressure gauges. During an altercation with the supervisor, the boilers explode injuring them both. When he awakes in the hospital, he has lost his memory. Symbolically he has died and is about to be reborn.

This is his birth. On leaving the hospital he finds temporary asylum with an elderly woman named Mary who takes care of him as a mother would. One day, while wandering aimlessly through the streets of Harlem, he becomes emotionally involved with an old man and his wife who have been evicted from their apartment. He makes an impassioned speech in their behalf and attracts the attention of the Brotherhood, a Communist organization headed by Brother Jack, a one-eyed man who views the world only partially and delusively. The Brotherhood is not really interested in the elderly couple, but it is interested in recruiting the boy. He joins the group, believing that in it he can make a name for himself and help his people at the same time. He is sent to Hambro (brother of Ham) for instruction and brainwashing; but the boy's attachment to Mary and the party's disregard for the aged make him doubt the validity of the Brotherhood's doctrines. He questions its right to control men's minds and to negate individuality by demanding absolute obedience to its creed. Counterpoised with the Brotherhood is a group advocating black supremacy. Its similarity to the Marcus Garvey movement or the Black Muslims is obvious. Headed by Ras the Destroyer, the group demands strict obedience to a doctrine as absolute as the Brotherhood's: all blacks must hate all whites. Incurring the wrath of both groups and realizing that in no segment of society is there recognition of a black person as an individual, he descends underground to search within himself for his real identity. In his retreat, he begins to see clearly the absurdity of life aboveground.

Cross Damon in *The Outsider* (1953) by Richard Wright is similar to the nameless protagonist in *Invisible Man*. Both, like the mythological Sisyphus, are required by their society to perform meaningless rituals that negate individual freedom. Each comes to believe that only by performing an intensely willful act can he find self-identity. The rebellion of Ellison's protagonist takes the form of hibernation or gestation from which, it is predicted, he will be reborn to the splendor of conscious manhood. Cross Damon could be a portrait of what might happen to Ellison's character if the latter were faced with a similar set of motivations and circumstances on emerging from hibernation.

In *The Outsider* Wright explores the same subject that

Ellison explores, human consciousness; that is, how does a person know who and what he is. Merely to be born physically carries no guarantee that a person will know himself. One must also be intelligent and inquisitive if he is to free himself from the slavery of cultural totems and taboos that tend to stifle him. Cross's name suggests, among other things, that he is an American Negro. Because of his paradoxical position in society, according to Wright, he is blessed and cursed with "double vision" and can see social defects more clearly than can some other people. Because Cross is intelligent and inquisitive, he asks questions that some others might not ask.

The fact that he is black is less important than the fact that he is a human being, seeking self-identity and relatedness proper for him with other people. Although he wholeheartedly supports the racial struggle and would fight for any black caught in a racial conflict, he is not emotionally involved in the struggle. His non-attachment, very close to Hindu Yoga, is due to his upbringing. Like a good many other blacks, he was protected in early life, by his mother and close associates, from the more barbaric forms of white racism. Further, his mother instilled in him almost Puritan habits of acute conscientious reflection on the rightness or wrongness of personal behavior. Hers is a "dark" gift to her son. As he watches her, he notices the similarity between them and asks a question that cannot be answered simply. "Why were some people fated, like Job, to live a never ending debate between themselves and their sense of what they believed life should be?" This mental exercise is the only way in which the two are similar. Her purpose in training him to examine each thought and act was to help him sublimate instinctive drives, such as sex, so that he might conform to the dictates of American culture. Actually her insistence accomplished just the opposite: it stirred up such drives, made him more inquisitive to explore them, and made life difficult for him in the society in which he lives. As one of his friends estimates the situation, his four A's are his downfall: "alcohol, abortions, automobiles, and alimony."

When the story opens, Cross has come to the conclusion that his life is absurd and that he is a fool to go on living it.

He is trapped in a dull, routine clerk's job at the Chicago Post Office in order to support his children and wife from whom he is separated. His wife is greedy and punitive, believing he must pay eternally for marital infidelities. To make matters worse, he is involved with a young girl who has deliberately gotten herself pregnant in order to compel Cross to marry her. What she does not realize is that his wife will never grant him an uncontested divorce and would rather cause him to be fired from his job on a charge of moral turpitude. What is worse yet, the girl has lied about her age and he can be charged with statutory rape. Caught between the women's determinations and his mother's goadings, he is squeezed into nothingness and non-identity. Moreover, there is no one with whom he can discuss his predicament freely. None of his acquaintances dares question time-honored customs. One question he asks concerns laws regulating relationships between men and women: Why does man persist in trying to regulate, by statute, human conditions as unstable and uncontrollable as the emotions? Cross is so overwhelmed by this thought that he is unable to go on with it. His awe is close to religious fervor and marks the beginning of iconoclastic commitment. At the same time, he feels more urgently the need to discuss his radical ideas with people who are as rebellious as he and as desirous of cutting through cultural illusions to discover who and what he and they really are as individuals.

A subway accident frees him from past constrictions and catapults him into a new life in which he believes he can test good and evil through his own acts. During the confusion following the accident, he transfers his coat and articles of identification to a corpse that is mutilated beyond recognition. In deciding to remain "dead," he fully realizes the alternatives. His family will be taken care of with his insurance money. He will be freed from the domination of his mother and the unscrupulousness of his wife and mistress. He realizes regretfully that his escape will separate him from his sons, but he concludes that anyone would be a fool not to seize the chance to shape his life according to his own assumptions. Later, he knows the awful consequence of his deception when he kills a friend in order to safeguard the new life. He knows also the isolation of one who has placed himself outside the cushioning support of culture; for he must now independently, relying solely on his lonely will, set the course for the remainder of his life. Terror seizes him as he begins to comprehend the nature of the task ahead of him and how ill-prepared he is to cope with it. Such thoughts sober his initial elation; and for some time after he arrives in New York he wanders in a meaningless limbo that is as lacking in knowledge of self-identity as his life in Chicago was. His dream is static. He seems powerless to do anything about it until he decides that in order to become human, he must mingle with people. The first thing he has to do is establish a new identity. To do that he must have a name. He appropriates one from a cemetery grave-marker and obtains a birth certificate in the name of the dead man by pretending to be a simple-minded, servile Negro—a type of behavior that convinces white clerks he is who he pretends to be. With some amusement, Cross thinks, "Maybe some day I could rule this nation with means like this." Later, without compunction he commits burglary and arson to obtain a draft card in the dead man's name.

Emboldened in his new identity, he sets about meeting people so that he can find out what his purpose in life ought to be. He observes the way that Communists stifle individuality and personal freedom among adherents of the party and, as a result, feels compelled to infiltrate the party to destroy its stultifying influence on human personality. On a larger scale, he sees the party as the same kind of threat to humanity as the friend whom he killed had been to him personally in Chicago. As he killed the friend to protect his freedom, so for the good of humanity, not in anger or hate, he plans to kill the "little gods" who run the party. For him, this is the challenge and responsibility of his new life.

In deciding to join the party, he is aware of how unethical his decision is when measured by usual cultural standards. It is an act of bad faith, but he is convinced that bad faith is part and parcel of everyday pretensions and illusions about life and of man's function in life. Nevertheless, he feels compelled to wipe out bad faith as practiced by the Communists and Fascists. His commitment is selfish rather than altruistic. He is moved to act by an intense desire "to feel and weigh the worth of himself," that is, to discover who he is and to prove to himself that he is worthy of existence. He deliberately kills a Fascist and two Communist agents. Initially reflecting on his acts, he smiles grimly, "I killed two little gods." Then the horror of the deed strikes fear in him. The horror is not in the least connected with the fact that he has committed murder. It is caused by the realization that he also has behaved hubristically, as if he were "a little god," by presuming to punish them for disagreeing with his principles.

Cross's sense of guilt is part of his emerging concept of himself that began when he joined the party. He has tried to overcome his separateness from other people by assuming power over them. Discovering this relationship unworthy, he tries to unite himself with one other human being—a woman who, in his need for relatedness and for the first time in his life, represents more than "woman as body of woman." Here again he is unsuccessful. In order to enjoy free and open reciprocity with her, he must tell her the truth about himself; but knowledge that he is a wife-deserter and murderer destroys her. Witnessing the effect of that knowledge upon her makes him vulnerable to his enemies and leads to his death.

The next two characters in this section are teen-aged boys. John Grimes (James Baldwin's *Go Tell It on the Mountain,* 1953) and Spencer Scott (Louis Peterson's *Take a Giant Step,* 1954) are not iconoclasts like Cross Damon, but their portraits represent a similar break with traditional stock and archetypal images of blacks in fiction. They, too, are searching for patterns of living that are compatible for them as maturing individuals. Each one's search is essentially a reaching out to find his separate and particular identity in proper relatedness with other people. Both are confronted with obstacles that tend to channel them and their lives in culturally prescribed ways. Spencer Scott moves toward adult maturity. Concerning John Grimes, the problem is more difficult, and the author offers no easy solution.

Grimes goes through a harrowing experience in an attempt to reconcile inner conflicts. His most serious problem is inability to relate satisfactorily to his stepfather Gabriel Grimes, who married John's mother knowing that she had borne the boy out of wedlock but promised to love John as if he were the boy's father. At the heart of Gabriel's generosity lies hidden guilt about his own sinful lusts in youth. Throughout their life together he holds her sin as a threat over her, consciously hating her son and unconsciously seeking to destroy him emotionally. Gabriel's feelings, though unspoken, are transmitted to the youngster. Guilt of both parents is transmitted also to John by the extreme emotionalism of their religious fervor and by the strictness of their public views on sex which postulates a rigid either-or proposition in which a misdemeanor is as damning as a felony, demanding physical death and eternal hell-fire. John's attitude toward Gabriel is a mixture of love and hate. To him, there are two Gabriels: Gabriel as superego ideal, whom he wants to love and from whom he wants to win love; and Gabriel as man, whom he hates. He sees Gabriel the man as an unworthy rival for the mother's affection, evidenced by the numerous pregnancies that seem to take her farther away from him, her eldest child. In John's mind, Gabriel the man is unworthy of such advantage because he mistreats the mother, sometimes striking her during arguments.

The adolescent's immediate and most urgent problem, however, is his inability to handle adequately the sex drive that is building within him. On the eve of his fourteenth birthday, he masturbates and afterwards feels dirty and disreputable. His anxiety about sex started much earlier, when his father, while bathing, asked the boy to wash his back. As his eyes wandered inquisitively over the father's body, John felt that he was a true son of Ham and was terrified by his boldness. He had learned his lessons well at the family's fundamentalist church, the Temple of the Fire Baptized.

Complicating both problems is the boy's burning desire for broader, more varied experiences than those provided in the house and church of his parents. For this reason he decides early in life that he will not let the pattern of his life be imitative of the life pattern of his parents, that he will raise himself above Gabriel, particularly, and by such attainment, finally win what he wants most, Gabriel's love. Up to this point, his is a portrait of any adolescent in whom individuality is emerging; but from this moment on, subsequent events impel him toward what seems like a grotesque solution to his problem, suggesting a retreat from reality and capitulation to cultural demands that are not primarily racial. Not yet a "saint," in the religious sense of having undergone the highly emotional union with God required by his sect, John is nudged toward some outward manifestation of inner spiritual salvation. The person who influences John most is a young man named Elisha who is three years older than he and already not only a saint but a preacher in the church. What impresses John most about Elisha is that he was once caught dallying with a girl, was publicly reprimanded, and ever since has been able to sublimate sex impulses successfully in mystical experiences. Another saint whose behavior impresses him is mournful Sister Price, a spinster who is considered specially blessed by the members of the church because she has never engaged in sex relations and can boast of her virginity in prayer meetings. As a result, John sees sublimation of sex in mystical experiences as the immediate solution to his more urgent problem, what Baldwin has called "the tyranny of the flesh," and also as a way of winning respect from Gabriel, who is a pillar of the church.

His ordeal of spiritual rebirth takes place, but the reader cannot be sure whether or not John believes in what is happening. At one point in the prolonged paroxysmal outburst, his rational mind urges him to stop writhing on the filthy floor, to get out of that place at once if he is not to be trapped in a life similar to that of "the other niggers." Afterwards, doubt about the efficacy of the highly emotional experience to solve either of his problems can be seen in his parting words to Brother Elisha to remember that, no matter what he may hear about John in the future, John once gave evidence in church of his salvation. Turning to Gabriel, John smiles but receives no smile in return from the stepfather. John knows that he has not won Gabriel's love. For Gabriel, it is a bitter pill that his real son, John's younger brother, is not the first member of the rising generation to achieve this mark of distinction in the family. Then John hears his mother calling to him and answers, "I'm on my way." But which way he is going is the question that the reader is left to ponder.

In contrast, the conflict with which Spencer Scott wrestles in *Take a Giant Step* (1954) is racially oriented. When the play opens, Spencer has been kicked out of high school for smoking a cigar in the men's washroom. The rebellion is caused by an incident in his history class. One student wanted to know why Negroes submitted so passively to enslavement, why they waited for Northern whites to free them. The teacher's explanation implies that they were too simple-minded to help themselves. Aroused, Spencer mentions Frederick Douglass, accuses her of not knowing her subject, and stalks out of the room into the toilet where he consoles himself by breaking school law.

The incident evokes submerged self-hatred when he cries out in pain that he hates his blackness and its cultural significance, that he hates "the hell out of it." In early childhood he and his white friends played together without incident caused by differences in race. Now that they are adolescents, a more crucial time of life, he notices a change in their attitudes toward him. He is no longer welcome at social events to which girls have been invited. In retaliation he tries to hurt them as they have hurt him but succeeds only in revealing his tortured feelings more clearly. Iggy, a Jewish boy, sensing how miserable Spencer is, makes a friendly overture to him; but Spencer, seeing only a white face, rebuffs him.

To complicate the problem, Spencer's mother does not understand the struggle that is raging within him. She nags, accusing him of ingratitude for his parents' efforts to provide a home for him in an integrated, therefore, in her mind "decent neighborhood"; of failure on his part to remember his place, specifically that he is a little Negro boy and, by implication, inferior; and that if he lived in the South, he would be lynched for "talking back" to a white woman. Although the mother is too myopic to realize that her son is approaching manhood, she is not totally dense. She observes that his friends no longer visit him as frequently as they once did, and she comes to the conclusion that Spencer's isolation from his companions is probably at the root of his difficulties. Trying to be useful, she arranges a party, inviting all of his white friends, much to Spencer's embarrassment. Her effort proves beneficial. Seeing all of them together helps Spencer to realize that they are not directly responsible for what has happened, that they are as constricted by cultural convention as he. He dismisses them from his life; but more significantly, he begins to see that Iggy is a different kind of white person from the others and makes a friendly overture to him. In learning to discriminate among individuals, he takes his "giant step" and moves toward maturity.

Similarly, Brother Younger (Walter Lee) in *A Raisin in the Sun* (1959) takes a big step when he learns to assess cultural values discriminatively. Transposition of name elements by which he is known in the family provides a symbolic clue to his personality. He is an immature younger brother among men, even though he is Mama's elder child, a married man in his middle thirties, and the father of a ten-year-old son. Unable to assume responsibility, he and his family live with Mama in her inadequate apartment. He dissipates his energy impractically dreaming of getting rich quick. Only in obtaining money, the great American ambition, does he place real value. When Mama asks why he talks so much about money, his answer is, "Because it is life, Mama!" Delay in becoming rich frustrates him.

He is different from the other members of his family who place higher values on love, family, and pride of race. Papa felt the same as they before he died; and it is for this quality that he is remembered and loved. Brother's bid for immortality is committed to material comforts that he can buy for the family. His motive is good. He wants a decent place for them to live, the pleasure of buying expensive gifts for his wife, and freedom from everlasting worry about money. In his zeal, however, he deemphasizes more human values. In his frustration be blames his family and the world for his failure: specifically, Mama, for hesitating to let him use Papa's insurance money in a liquor business; his sister, for being a potential threat to his getting the money because she wants to become a doctor; his wife, for failing to support his pleas to Mama; and all Negroes "Cause we all tied to a race of people who don't know how to do nothing but moan, and pray and have babies." This last is directed to his wife who is carrying their second child.

Out of compassion, Mama relents and gives him the major portion of Papa's money, having used part of it for a down payment on a house in a white neighborhood. Brother proves how justifiable the family's disapproval of his business venture is when he promptly loses the money to his unscrupulous partner. In desperation he decides to degrade himself by accepting a proposal from whites living in the neighborhood to which they plan to move. The whites offer to give the Youngers more money than Mama has left as security for the house, in order to keep blacks out of the community. The other members of his family are shocked by his proposed capitulation to racial segregation just for the sake of money. He thinks they are impractical and foolish not to take the money, that in the competitive world in which they live, the smartest operators are always those who grab all they can, whenever they can, without concern for principles or ideals. When the moment of actual taking or grabbing comes and the eyes of his family—particularly those of his young son—are staring at him, love of family and pride of race win. Looking the representative of the white group "absolutely in the eyes," he rejects the bribe, telling him that his family has decided to occupy the house in question and to try to live as good neighbors to the other members of the community. His rejection shows him in the process of becoming a mature human being, shedding the ignobility of a confused younger brother.

One of the most unusual of youthful black individuals in fiction of the 1960's is seventeen-year-old Oliver Eugene, nephew of Harriet Gibbs, whom we met in the archetypal mammy pattern. Oliver is narrator-protagonist of Henry Van Dyke's *Ladies of the Rachmaninoff Eyes* (1965) and *Blood of Strawberries* (1968) in which he undergoes two identity crises—in the earlier novel with regard to sexuality, and in the latter with regard to his blackness. When first encountered, he is the product of an overprotected existence with his only living relative, Aunt Harry, and her Jewish employer, Etta Klein, in beautiful, symbolically innocent-green, rural

Michigan. Described with a twinge of jealousy by Jerome, Etta's married son, as her "toy" to ease the pain of her favorite son Sargeant's suicide some years earlier in New York, Oliver is a substitute for him and the pampered "son" of the two indulgent women sharing responsibility for his upbringing as they earlier shared the rearing of Sargeant. Etta supplies the luxuries—the English tweeds, the first editions of the classics, the tutors—and has made provision for his college education at Cornell. Aunt Harry supplies training in what she considers proper behavior, advising him, for example, always to wear clean underwear so that if he is, perchance, in an accident and has to be taken to a hospital, she will not be mortified "within an inch" of her life, because hospital attendants will have seen him in dirty linen.

As narrator, his personality is revealed partly by comments he makes about himself and partly by comments of other characters, as recorded by him. We learn from him that he enjoys studying the classics, listening to classical records, and reading aloud to Etta and to another white woman of dubious morals, named Belle. His favorite author is Baudelaire; his favorite book *Fleurs du Mal*. The opinions of others about Oliver are another matter. Jerome calls him "priss-foot"; Jerome's wife Patricia Jo denigrates him as "too impossibly precious," a designation that really rankles. Della, the maid, a prime specimen of the contemporary black sensualist, ridicules his "prissy airs" and condemns him for thinking and acting like a white boy. His Aunt Harry condemns him for hypocritically "sucking up" to Etta as if the white woman were his blood relative instead of Harriet, and also for letting Etta make a white boy of him.

And that is exactly what has been done. He has no black friends his own age; nor does he have any strong, black, masculine image with which he can identify; hence his effeminacy. As a consequence, he is overwhelmed and frightened by Della's rough-and-ready sex play and good-humored attempts to rape him, doing all that he can never to be alone with her. He prefers Belle's equally obvious but, to him, more subtle and provocative seductiveness which, inexperienced as he is, he misinterprets as an overture to intimacy. She rebuffs him. His reaction is typical. He thinks her refusal is due, first, to his youth. When she denies that reason, he assumes her refusal is due to the love affairs that he thinks she is having with Jerome. She confesses, finally, that she has never "bestowed her favors on a colored man," and that she has to get used to the idea before she can accomplish the deed. Her reason does not disturb him. He has not lived in a vacuum where newspapers do not exist; and, as he comments, he has had to "skirt around tricky situations at school dances [and] in the drama club." Actually, he has never thought of himself as any particular color, simply as Oliver Eugene, as yet an unknown element, because he has never discovered who he is.

When the mystery surrounding Sargeant's suicide is disclosed by Aunt Harry as a consequence of his homosexuality, Oliver is spurred on to discover his own identity, what kind of person he is. But he does not know where to begin. Aunt Harry is dead and Etta Klein is dying. Always sensitive to the link in Etta's mind between himself and Sargeant, whose secret was concealed so long by Etta and Aunt Harry, he decides to begin his search by learning more about Sargeant, specifically by searching among his few remaining possessions stored in the attic. He finds, of course, nothing that positively identifies him to himself, but he does find a clue to what he does not want to become. Quickly reading some of Sargeant's letters, he comes across a love letter, the explicitness of which makes him dash out of the attic and into the empty room once occupied by Della, wishing she were back in it, hoping for at least a whiff of her cheap Turkish Kiss Kologne, but most of all regretting that he had not been nicer to her.

Events in *Blood of Strawberries* take place four years later when Oliver is nearly twenty-one and a rising senior at Cornell. He is still being handsomely taken care of by surrogate parents, Etta's elderly sister Tanja and the latter's octogenarian husband Max Rhode. Oliver now wants to become a writer and has developed an affinity for Scarlatti and Hegelian discourse, and a passion for the writings of Gertrude Stein. Admiration for Stein has been sparked by his acquaintance with Max, who actually knew Stein and Toklas in Paris. Oliver plans to write his senior paper on Stein's literary indebtedness to Baudelaire, his favorite writer in the earlier novel.

Oliver's masculinity is no longer in doubt, but he continues unaware of his lack of black identity. Unawareness still indicates no loss of contact with reality. He knows what he is not: that he is not white, but still has no firm grasp on what he is. When he thinks of himself, he thinks of other things, still not of any particular color, and certainly not in terms of the American black-white syndrome. For instance, one big problem, revealing the contemporary rootlessness of not only Oliver and his roommate Karl but also of other undergraduates, is religious affiliation. Oliver, having been reared in a Jewish household by a Baptist aunt, and Karl, in a Swedish Lutheran home, reject both atheism and agnosticism as "cop-outs" and devise their own ceremony that passes for "a religion of sorts," in which quantities of Pernod and a recording of *Four Saints in Three Acts* become essential ingredients of a new liturgical communion. By this time it is obvious to the reader that Oliver is black only in skin color, which he accepts as a fact of no great significance. In his thinking, his motivation, his life-style, he is white because he has never come in contact with any dominant blacks with whom to identify. Except for Aunt Harry, his contacts with blacks have been of the most superficial sort. Even his sexual initiation rite, occurring in the summer following his freshman year, is accomplished with a white girl, "aggressive-bosomed, green-eyed" Rita Schwartz, smelling of patchouli and rose, who, after the initiation, begins calling herself Desdemona while candidly admitting that he, by no stretch of the imagination, can be called Othello. Furthermore, Oliver discovers to his everlasting chagrin that she, paradoxically, is "blacker" than he.

Moreover, it is only after face-to-face, menacing confrontation with three black children in Harlem that Oliver even begins to recognize the existence of any problem connected with his identity. Accompanied by Desdemona on an errand for Max, he travels from Greenwich Village, where they live, uptown to Harlem to give Willa, their maid, her wages. Willa, supposedly ill, is not at home when they arrive. Her sister Willette volunteers to keep the money for her; Oliver, distrusting her, decides against this proposal. While waiting for Willa, he experiences firsthand, and probably for the first time, the sights, sounds, and smells of ghetto life.

Quietly and unnoticed by Oliver and Desdemona, the door to the room in which they are sitting is closed and locked. There is no response to their cries for Willette. When the door is opened, three youths, under fifteen years of age, enter, order him to sit, immobilize him with a switchblade, all the while indicating their hatred of a "goddam white nigger." He gives them his wallet, appealing to them to take the money and let him retain the other things contained in it. When their "signifying" is recognized by Desdemona as lewd preamble to threats of rape, and somehow communicated also to Oliver, he courageously moves to intervene, "knife or no knife." He is stopped by "one hellish bray" from Desdemona, followed by an outpouring of argot, so precise in its pithy expressions and so skillfully used that communication between her and them is instantaneous, clear, and equally as menacing as theirs. They quickly disperse in fear.

On their way back downtown to safety, it is Desdemona who defines his inadequacy as a Negro and suggests, not completely without scornful derision, that the "precious, effete, intellectualizing" life he leads is a false kind of life sapping his vigor and virility. Her evaluation of him, though helpful, still does not move him toward precise comprehension of what being black means. For further guidance, he goes to Willa asking an unanswerable question: "What's it like—I mean, how do you become a Negro?" Willa, with simple wisdom, advises him to "worry first 'bout life," adding that it is terribly difficult "to get through it alive."

His experiences with Max, Tanja, and their elderly friends, the summer before he achieves his legal majority, teach him some important lessons about life and death, about loneliness that leads the aged to desperate actions just to prove to themselves and to other people that they are still alive—actions they find imperative in a culture that places an inordinately high value on youth. He learns something important also about the need for compassion, patience, and understanding in interpersonal relationships. Up to this time he has been able to take refuge in the acquisition of knowledge and could remain half submerged in a veneer of supercilious detachment from a basic factor of his existence, his blackness. At the end of the novel he is on the verge of gaining knowledge of himself, of becoming a mature individual, and of learning to survive in the society in which he must live.

Token Blacks

Oliver is a youthful representative of many blacks in fiction who, for whatever devious reasons, are delineated as recipients of white recognition and beneficence and who may be classified as token blacks whose life sagas have been narrated in a group of popular novels published during the 1960's. Within portraits of these figures are sometimes contained undertones of stock black accommodativeness, culturally designated as Uncle Tomism, but never to any extent precluding the characters' responses as individuals to the situations confronting them. Notable among these are two politicians, Cullee Hamilton in Allen Drury's *A Shade of Difference* (1962) and Douglass Dilman in Irving Wallace's *The Man* (1964); one student of international law, David Champlin in Ann Fairbairn's *Five Smooth Stones* (1966); and an actor, Leo Proudhammer in James Baldwin's *Tell Me How Long the Train's Been Gone* (1968).

The action of *A Shade of Difference* takes place in the future after the United States and Russia have both achieved moon landings. Cullee Hamilton, an important character in the novel, is an intelligent, honorable, courageous Congressman from California, whose given name is paradoxically reminiscent of earlier devious naming patterns in our literature, recalling the seldom used *cully* and the archaic *cullion* denoting the inferiority of dupe and dastard respectively. The etymon of the latter recalls H. L. Mencken's observation in this connection, which is explained in the analysis of stock buffoons (see chapter 2). As Cullee's portrait contains none of these connotations, one wonders whether or not the author is deliberately manipulating traditional symbols of American attitudes toward blacks.

Born in South Carolina of a house-maid mother and field-hand father, Cullee is one of five children pushed toward social advancement by their mother, who plays the dominant role in the family after the death of her husband in a tractor accident. She taught them the "delicate art of being successfully black" in a white racist society, emphasizing virtues of neatness, thrift, diligence, and encouraging self-pride and respectability. She taught them also the rituals of black-white relations which were for her and generations preceding hers essential for survival. What had been *de rigueur* for her was not at all for him. He balked at performance of all "servile defensive mechanisms," living, as he was, at a time when discriminatory practices were being openly defied and the constitutionality of discriminatory statutes legally tested. Against her wishes he applies for and is denied admission to the University of South Carolina Law School. When she warns that he is "getting above" himself, that he will suffer a great fall, he reminds her that it was she who taught black pride to her children, that so far as he is concerned, nobody is better than he. Despite failure to integrate the state university, he takes pride in the fact that he has "let his little light shine" in defiance of segregative practices. His ulterior purpose was to promote closer approximation of at least one traditional American ideal, equality of educational opportunity.

Contentedly, he attends the Law School of Howard University, where he gains fame as an Olympic track star, where he meets Sue-Dan who becomes his wife, and where LeGage Shelby—impatient, intense, militant—is his roommate and later becomes head of a militant organization named DEFY. Upon graduation he receives the first practical token of social esteem: invitations to join seven law firms, three black and four white. Feeling that California offers superior opportunity for a political career, he accepts a job with a firm in Los Angeles and buys a house in an all-white San Fernando Valley community where he becomes the target of racist opposition in the form of protest meetings, of garbage dumped on his lawn, of threatening letters, and of self-righteously indignant press releases. LeGage Shelby, gleefully recognizing the propaganda values inherent in white racist discrimination against an outstanding black lawyer and athlete, offers the services of DEFY to help Cullee integrate the community by protests and pickets and condemnatory press releases. Cullee refuses, much to Sue-Dan's disgust, because he prefers approaches to the problem that appeal to the better natures of whites, that avoid potentially disastrous confrontations of violently angry blacks and whites, and that at the same time permit reasoned opposition to all forms of segregation and denigration of blacks. To LeGage, Sue-Dan, and others, white is synonymous with evil. Cullee, in contrast, has learned discrimination and refuses to castigate all whites because, as he says, he has known many "kind and decent white people." Successful, he and Sue-Dan and their neighbors learn to co-exist; and in time, he is equally successful in putting together a coalition of middle-class, conservative black and white voters who elect him their congressional Representative for three successive terms.

This is his second reward as "showcase" or token black, and he sees himself and his achievement as the symbolic manifestation of traditional cultural ideals. In gratitude, he is determined to represent all of his constituents, black and white, equitably. Moreover, when he uses the word *us,* he means not simply himself and someone else, or black people, or his black and white constituents, but all of the people of the United States. In relationships with other people, the cultural myth of respect and fair play for others who are different or who espouse different views has become a way of life for him, even to the point of honoring, as he opposes them, the opinions of a white racist like "Seab" Cooley, President Pro Tempore of the Senate. In addition, he feels obligated to remain loyal to his country for the opportunity it has given him and for its idealistic foundations which, if ever realized, offer the best hope for the future of all mankind.

As a supporter of gradualism, he sees himself as a kind of ambassadorial mediator of racial problems. He refuses to join more radical militants, confident that the best plan is to work within the system to effect desirable changes; but he insists that as a sign of good faith in promoting desirable change, definite evidence be observable pointing to that change. Empty promises are not sufficient to pacify him.

Decisions he makes, understandably, grow out of his convictions. He refuses, for example, to join Terence Ajkaje, the

M'Bulu of Mbuele, an African ruler, when the latter carries
a black child through a mob of screaming white women to
integrate an elementary school in South Carolina; for Cullee
knows that the M'Bulu's action is not simply motivated by a
desire to promote integration for his black American brothers.
Of greater importance to him is the opportunity to embarrass
the United States at its most vulnerable point and to mobilize
world opinion against United States racial practices which
persist uncriticized by Great Britain. As a consequence of
such newly raised criticism he hopes to force Britain into
granting his country its independence.

For the cowardice of allowing a foreigner to do what any
red-blooded black American ought to have done, Cullee loses
the respect and support of the black as well as some segments of the white communities. Accused of playing at being
white, or being "the white man's nigger," his "lap dog," he is
spurned as despicable by Sue-Dan, spat upon by the delegate
of Kenya to the United Nations, and savagely beaten by
angry militants. White Congressmen and Senators, with
whom interrelationships are reciprocal, do not agree. They
know that he is neither a carbon copy of whites nor a yes-
man of blacks. Based on experience with him, the Secretary
of State observes that Cullee is no man's stooge. Because he
is his own man and in spite of public vilification, he continues to do what he thinks is right within the scope of his
knowledge and experiences. To avert a motion of censure
against his country, he introduces a congressional resolution
designed to pacify the M'Bulu and counteract derogatory
world opinion.

In contrast with the fictional portrait of Cullee Hamilton,
which at times represents that of an exuberantly naïve All-
American black boy, the portrait of Douglass Dilman in *The
Man* is that of a mature individual in whom youthful idealism has been replaced by the realism of age and experience.
Intelligent, gentle, somewhat shy and deferential in relationships with blacks and whites, he is the product of centuries of black sensitization in an arrogant, white-dominated
society. The reader learns that he is "sensitive about his
color," actually afraid of his own blackness; that he is hypersensitive, in interracial relations, to white attitudes of "subtle

mockery and superiority," even when whites do not intend to be deliberately insulting. In order to avoid difficulties with whites, he observes scrupulously most of the inherited rules controlling interracial relations, such as never allowing himself to be alone with a white woman, having learned well how violently white men react to even the most casual of relationships between black men and white women. All along, however, he has tried to avoid overreacting, or becoming mean, paranoid, or servile, or a white nigger, wanting only to be what he is, a sensitive, warm, outgoing individual, to whom the Golden Rule still has great significance.

He is a fifty-year-old widower, stocky, black, with impressive facial features—a full, wide nose and heavy, protruding lips. He has two children. Mindy, his daughter, is white-skinned like his late wife Aldora and as unhappy about being classified as a Negro as her mother was. She has severed all ties to her black father and lives as a white girl in New York City. His son Julian is black like the father, but the relationship between them also is strained. Julian has been caught up in the new wave of militancy and has given so much time to it that he is in danger of suspension from college.

Dilman began his political career, like Cullee Hamilton, as a Congressman. With the sponsorship of a labor leader, he was four times elected Representative of a Michigan slum district. Upon the retirement of the senior Senator, the governor of the state, in order to strengthen his position among Michigan's blacks, appointed Dilman, the state's most prominent black, to complete the Senator's unexpired term. In his second elective term as Senator and following the death of the Vice President, he is appointed President Pro Tempore of the Senate, an office conferred on him, the nation's "showcase colored man," as a "political gesture" or "sop" to black constituencies. From this point on, not tokenism but chance takes charge of his career and, by a couple of fatal accidents to the President and to the Speaker of the House of Representatives, catapults him into the Presidency.

His reaction is one of modest amazement that somehow God has chosen him, the least of all others, to be President. Like Cullee, he is determined to serve the entire population and not only the Negro population, although he is in a quiet way intensely proud of his race and well aware of injustices done to blacks. He, too, is patriotic and vows to do all possible to preserve his country's security and well-being, at the same time not overlooking existing inequities. Being also a gradualist, he envisions interracial progress emerging as a consequence of "due process under law" with all wrongs, hopefully, being redressed and with equality eventually an actuality. Then, he dreams, "this country will be everyone's country." As subsequent events make clear, he too is also his own man and not the stooge of the Secretary of State or of others in government. At the first Cabinet meeting, he asserts his individuality as he calls for unity and the members' assistance in carrying out policies set in motion by his predecessor. He modifies a speech prepared by the Secretary of State for him to deliver at his first public appearance as President, because he refuses to speak specifically about things with which he is not personally knowledgeable.

His troubles begin immediately afterwards. He represents different things to different people. Some whites, possibly remembering—at something like an unconscious level—what has been done to blacks over the centuries, fear retaliation, the erosion of white power, black arrogation of it, and, horror of horrors, black minority rule. Some blacks rejoice in the fact that they now have one of their own in a powerful place who will compensate them for centuries of derogation by granting extralegal concessions and privileges. Dilman refuses to be manipulated by either. Overriding a new Tenure of Office and Succession Bill, hastily rammed through Congress to limit his power, he removes the Secretary of State from office for insubordination, thereby alienating whites. Similarly, he alienates blacks by vetoing a Minorities Rehabilitation Bill that allocates funds to repay minorities for centuries of cultural deprivation, his reason being that the bill is an obvious boondoggle because "one cannot substitute dollars for dignity and liberty." In its place he calls on Congress to enact legislation guaranteeing equality. Blacks call him an Uncle Tom, a white nigger, and his veto a betrayal of his own people.

Impeachment proceedings are instituted. Added to the charges is one accusing him of alleged immoral behavior, an accusation that capitalizes on the all too prevalent image of a Negro as "not martyr but satyr, not public official but public fool." Despite an impending impeachment trial, personal vilification, and widespread anti-black prejudice, he never loses his head, never acts in haste, and continues to be strictly legalistic in making decisions, refusing, for example, to commute the death sentence of a black militant in Texas because of the absence of impartial evidence, thereby reaffirming the necessity for law, that which "keeps us a civilized community" and prevents citizens from deteriorating into packs of "roving barbarians." In addition, he sends the Dragon Flies, a segregated white corps of elite counter-guerrilla fighters to a black country in order to prevent the spread of Communism in Africa. What matters more to him than personal problems is the integrity of his government's promise to come to another country's defense, whether it be a black or a white country. He will not compromise his or his country's cherished principles. Although he sends the troops to Africa, he refuses to panic and move the country from defensive to offensive strategy by putting the United States on wartime alert. He thus avoids confrontation with the Communists by a demonstration of determination and strength. The maneuver successful, he regains the support of a large part of the black community and of white liberals. Party politicians, ever alert to shifts in public feeling, find it expedient to vote against impeachment. But they try to make a deal with him, promising negative votes in return for his promise neither to seek reelection nor to allow himself to be drafted. Dilman refuses. The vote to impeach fails anyway, by a single vote; and the Senate is adjourned *sine die*. At the end he is a battered but still unbeaten man: his family is reunited, and he will continue to do what is best for his country.

With training in self-pride from his grandparents and singled out for special assistance by altruistic whites, David Champlin, in *Five Smooth Stones*, nearly succeeds in escaping the seemingly immovable obstacles preventing black youths from achieving full membership and the "good life" in American society. David, a child of the Great Depression of the 1930's, was reared by his paternal grandfather Li'l Joe Champlin and his step-grandmother Neva in New Orleans.

His father died before he was born and his mother died giving him birth. Li'l Joe's mother, familiarly known as Tant'Irene, took one look at him just after his birth and cried out the name David, the name of her husband who many years before had been tied to a pile of logs in a nearby state and burned alive. The memory of this cruel murder lived long in the French quarter where David is exposed to the customary sensitization to skin color values. He learns that the American dream, insofar as blacks are concerned, is more accurately described as the American nightmare with its denial of economic and social equality. He learns that all whites, except one, can never be trusted by blacks; that if one is black, the normal reaction of whites is to find pleasure in scorning, ridiculing, insulting, or inflicting physical injury on blacks. He learns also to be proud of his heritage, particularly Afro-Creole music, and to commit himself to the advancement of his people through activities of such groups as the moderate NAACP and the more militant ALEC, or the American League for Equal Citizenship.

The one white person whom he learns to trust is a Danish professor, Bjarne Knudsen, not long enough in the country to be contaminated by cultural attitudes toward blacks. Bjarne brings a bit of financial relief to their miserable economic situation when he pays Li'l Joe for banjo lessons in order to learn Afro-Creole music. The genuineness of his friendship with the Champlins earns their respect and makes him the only white with whom they want to be associated. When Bjarne learns how David's great-grandfather died, he makes himself responsible for the boy's education and after high school sends him to Pengard College in Ohio, which provides scholarships for Negro students of "marked intellectual promise." Bjarne's brother Karl, a professor at Pengard, helps David through the academic pitfalls as well as some others supplied by prejudiced whites; but as a faculty member, some areas of campus life are forbidden to him. When a situation occurs involving a Southern white student and a prejudiced dean, three white students, who have appropriated David as their black friend, in the best sense of the expression, bring every bit of pressure they can to the situation and see to it that he is exonerated.

At first his association with so many whites goes against

all that he had learned in the early sensitization process. He tortures himself imagining that his friends back home would call him a "white man's pet puppy," a "bootlicking, ass-kissing, Uncle Tom jr.," if they could see him at Pengard. But his experiences teach him discrimination. He learns from practical demonstration that all whites are not racists, that all white Southerners are not racists, and concludes that there are only two kinds of whites that he detests: those who love him and those who hate him simply because he is black. In another area, his sensitization to skin color prevents him from admitting that he loves a white girl, Sara. It is only just before graduation that he expresses his feeling to her and many years later before he considers the possibility of their marriage. Generally, however, the years at Pengard were filled with hope. Integration still seemed possible. David and his friends all look forward to school desegregation as the cure for social injustice and disunity.

After college and Harvard Law School, he receives further evidence of Bjarne's friendship. In his will he leaves David a legacy large enough to allow him to study international law at Oxford. While there, he receives an offer of an appointment, from the State Department, to become an adviser on constitutional and international law to the government of an African state on the brink of independence. Reunited, he and Sara are set to make a life for themselves away from prejudice in the United States. Meanwhile, in New Orleans, Li'l Joe is killed by white hoodlums who are hell bent to "get a nigger." Instead of escaping David settles down to carry on the fight for freedom and justice for his people. He is killed. Sara gives birth to their child and names him David, who may one day kill his particular Goliath.

Surmounting the frustrations of life in the slums, an actor whose name is Leo Proudhammer, in *Tell Me How Long the Train's Been Gone*, succeeds mainly by his own efforts in becoming America's token black in the theater. At age thirty-nine he is hospitalized by a heart attack, an experience that becomes for him "the door to . . . maturity." Recollections of the past, of how he rose to prominence and became the sort of man that he is, are interspersed throughout the novel with his recovery from illness. Son of a Barbadian farmer, exiled from warmth and beauty, and a lovely "banana-colored" mother from New Orleans, he is reared in New York's Harlem along with his older brother Caleb, whom he adored.

He remembers his father's inability to pay the rent, Mr. Rabinowitz's insults and threats of eviction. He remembers also the derogatory comments of policemen, storekeepers, pawnbrokers, welfare workers: how everyone and everything seemed bent on emasculating and debasing the father, the titular head of the black family. Leo, the child, knew that the father, a proud man, would never have permitted black men, or anyone with whom he was on an equal footing, to speak to him as these whites did. His mother was allowed by white merchants to handle difficult situations differently. When Mr. Shapiro, the grocer, reminded her of her long overdue bill, she coolly reminded him of the higher cost of food in her neighborhood than elsewhere in the city as she made partial payment before buying more food on credit. He remembers vividly the deprivations and activities connected with a slum childhood: the time when *beat* literally meant beaten, without hope, and *funky* meant a foul odor, the odor of abject poverty; his period of petty but selective thievery, never from stores at which the family traded; his brother Caleb's trips to a house of prostitution, once taking his little brother with him; and the time when Caleb was arrested and sent to prison. But more poignantly, and probably more importantly in his struggle to become a great actor, he remembers and reassesses the day-to-day events by which he was sensitized to the cultural significance of his blackness, of his being made to feel inferior, and of the constant necessity to prove his right to existence because of it.

His rise to fame also follows a fairly typical pattern; the only difference from the experiences of other young people, with similar ambition, is because he is black. In late adolescence he leaves home, moves in with some other young aspirants—among them Barbara King, a Kentucky white girl —and scrounges with them for survival in Greenwich Village. Later he and Barbara join the Art Students' League and participate in an experimental summer theater where he experiences hostility from rural whites over his close reciprocal relations with whites. A brief affair with an older white actress, ending in his arrest, indicates something of the harassment he has to endure. Seen leaving her apartment, he is charged with suspicion of burglary, but is soon released when he stands up to the police, demands his right to see a lawyer, and police officials discover that he has the full support of prominent whites connected with the experimental theater. That same summer he and Barbara face a crisis and make an important decision regarding their relationship. Though they love each other, they recognize the futility of any permanent liaison such as marriage. Each is ambitious and wants to become a successful stage performer. The social situation being what it is, an interracial marriage is an unnecessary obstacle to advancement in the theater. Another problem is Leo's bisexuality. The third is probably the most difficult of all for Leo. If, as he knows from bitter experience, he cannot protect Barbara from the insults and threats of incensed whites because she sleeps with a black man, the situation would be much worse for him if she were his wife. Instead of marriage, they decide to share each other's lives in as close and as permanent a relationship as possible considering all of the circumstances. Into this dyad they admit one other person, young militant black Christopher, and share him in a complicated relationship.

Success does not come easily. He becomes a singing waiter in a West Indian restaurant in the Village where, like David Champlin, he learns to resent those whites whose consciences "blackmail" them into doing things for him as much as he resents those who hate him. He recognizes the behavior of the former as merely prejudice in reverse and not at all a satisfactory basis for reciprocal relatedness. His first successful role comes from a Greek play director who is not blackmailed by Leo's blackness.

All of his life Leo is a moderate, a "middle grounder" who tries to work within the existing social situation to attain what for him is the good life: first, success in the theater, and, second, the reciprocal relatedness with whites that is denied his father and Caleb. When he finishes taking stock of himself, as a token black who has been allowed to succeed and to receive cultural rewards, and when he looks at the

socio-economic conditions of other black men, he realizes that because of defects in the system, no significant changes in the direction of equality and justice are likely to occur during his lifetime, nor has he done anything to promote change. His pessimistic conclusion, metaphorically stated, is that he has "conquered the city" only to find that the city is "stricken with the plague," that the crisis has reached epidemic proportions and will respond only to drastic curative methods, perhaps those of young militants like Christopher.

Black Avengers

The patterns of violence, explicit or implicit, in portraits of black avengers, in the next sub-category of individuals, reveal the explosive consequence of too long suppressed and internalized anger at society's denial of the ordinary self-assertive rights of manhood to black men. As one looks at these figures in the literature of the 1960's, he sees that violent eruptions do not always take the same form. A first step for some characters in the direction of self-assertion is severing physical ties to the past. For others, it is rejection by an act of violence of a philosophy that requires blacks, but not whites, to turn the other cheek and patiently await changes in the hearts of whites. Still others go straight to the core of the problem, the establishment of transactional relationships with whites, "an eye for an eye" as the only solution. Contained in the portraits is evidence of firm self-knowledge, of ability to make decisions and to take vigorous action in order to equalize differences and right wrongs. All are surprisingly idealistic, believing that a better world for all will emerge as a result of their violence.

Roots of the black avengers extend through Richard Wright's Bigger Thomas (*Native Son*, 1940) back to Sutton Griggs's Belton Piedmont and Bernard Belgrave (*Imperium in Imperio*, 1899) and possibly farther. Just before his execution, Bigger Thomas confesses that he was compelled to kill in order to know that he was really alive. His portrait is analyzed in the preceding chapter to demonstrate the persistence of archetypal sacrifice symbols in fiction. The slightly

fanciful names that Sutton Griggs assigns to his characters, along with their stilted speech, both reminiscent of Mrs. Sophia Little's counter-stereotypical figures (*Thrice Through the Furnace*, 1852), do not appreciably detract from their determination as self-assertive individuals to avenge the inequities and injustices imposed on blacks during Reconstruction, which resulted in the caste system, another form of slavery denying them the right to live in dignity as free men.

Griggs's characters symbolize "the new Negro, self-respecting, fearless, and determined in the assertion of his rights." An early instance of rebellion against segregation occurs while Belton is at college, at one of the highly regimented Southern "institutes" and "universities" founded for blacks after the Civil War by Northern philanthropy and staffed, for the most part, by whites. Negro teachers were hired as they became qualified to teach. At Belton's college the sole Negro teacher is not permitted to eat his meals at the table for white teachers in the dining room; he sits with the students. Belton mobilizes student opinion against the segregation of their black teacher and organizes a "sit-in" in the dining room. He sends a written bill of particulars to the president and demonstrates disapproval of segregation by refusing to leave the dining room when the president gives the customary signal indicating that the students may leave. After disobeying several signals, each student, no doubt influenced by Patrick Henry, raises a small sign which reads "Equality or Death." The students ignore another signal. Belton rises and reaffirms their determination to remain seated until the matter is settled satisfactorily. Gaining the concession that they want, the students joyously exit waving a black flag and singing "John Brown's Body."

Later in his career, Belton publishes a newspaper in which he speaks out editorially against frauds perpetrated by whites at the polls, in many underhanded ways, to nullify opposition votes and especially those of Negroes who oppose the party in power. He demands justice for blacks, but, more idealistically, appeals to whites to consider the "debauching" effect of what they are doing to "the flower of the Anglo-Saxon race."

Much later it is revealed that Belton has been a member,

since his college days, of an underground movement known as the Imperium, a separate black "authority" with its own constitution and representative government. Its headquarters are Thomas Jefferson College located some miles outside of Waco, Texas. The Imperium, organized by free Negroes around the time of the Revolution, seeks to obtain for itself "all the rights and privileges of man according to the teachings of Thomas Jefferson" and "to secure the freedom of enslaved Negroes the world over." After the Civil War, educated freedmen were invited to join, and chapters of the organization flourished at Negro colleges and as the final "degree" of Negro secret societies, lodges, and other Negro fraternal orders. Over the years the Imperium kept records of all injustices and encouraged blacks to work in any possible way toward achievement of its goals.

Belton influences his friend Bernard Belgrave to join. More fiery than Belton, he becomes charismatic president of the organization. His initial speech arouses the members to forgo their former passive tactics and take on more militant ones. An elderly member, obviously out of step with the prevailing mood, rises and advocates amalgamation or loss of identity in the general culture. A second advocates mass emigration to Africa. A third introduces a war resolution which catches the mood of the group but to which Belton offers a substitute resolution that the Imperium notify the country of its existence and of its members' preference, like Patrick Henry, of dying with honor rather than continuing to live in the disgrace of second-class citizenship; further, that if equality and justice are still denied after a set period of time, all seven and one-quarter million members of the Imperium will take residence in Texas, in this way creating a political majority, facilitating seizure of Texas, and achieving separation of blacks from the United States.

Bernard, more distrustful of whites and much more vengeful, goes along with Belton's plan for separation but not by peaceful means. He is convinced that any gains obtained from whites will come only by force. To that end, he proposes that the Imperium achieve its destiny by secretly isolating Texas from its contiguous states by buying all border lands and installing underground fortifications with "rapid fire disappearing guns" for protection against its enemy, the United States. He further proposes that it enter into secret negotiations with all foreign countries that are enemies of the United States for assistance, offering an adjacent state as a reward. These proposals constitute his substitute plan for achieving the glorious destiny of a separate black country on the North American continent. Belton cannot go along with Bernard and is killed by the Imperium, his last words revealing his idealism:

> Tell posterity . . . that I loved the race to which I belonged and the flag that floated over me; and being unable to see these objects of my love engage in mortal combat, I went to my God. . . .[21]

Although some members of the Imperium have come to hate the American flag, seeing it as a symbol of white racism, they shroud his body in it and bury him where they executed him.

Two outstanding portraits of violent avengers appearing in the early 1960's are Tucker Caliban in *A Different Drummer* (1962) by William Melvin Kelley and Walker Vessels in *The Slave* (1964) by LeRoi Jones. Local gossip whispered that there was something unusual in the blood of twenty-two-year-old Tucker Caliban because he is the great-grandson of an indomitable slave whose delineation in the novel is reminiscent of the legendary Bras Coupé (*The Grandissimes*, 1880). Two incidents attest to his differentness. At the funeral of his grandfather, who had worked all of his life for one of the first families of the state, no one could think of a thing to say except platitudes: that he had been a good man, a happy man who sacrificed himself for others, that he had been "good with horses." At this point in the burial ceremony, Tucker cries out that there ought to be something more that can be said of a man, that "sacrifice be damned," and walks out of the church. The other incident occurs when the local chapter of the National Society for Colored Affairs is conducting a membership drive. In spite of arguments from Bethrah, who becomes his wife, he refuses to join, maintaining that he will fight his own battles and secure his own civil rights. Bethrah comes to respect his individuality, to trust him, and to rely on him to help her develop comparable faith in herself. In all of his dealings, he does only that which, after careful deliberation, he decides is best.

One day, as blacks and whites watch, he deliberately ruins his land, bought from whites who had owned his ancestors, by sowing it with tons of rock salt. Neighbors comment: "He don't even look like he hates it." Next he leads his livestock out of the barn, gently strokes them one by one, then taking careful aim, shoots them. Afterwards he destroys the grandfather clock that had been brought to this country on the same ship that brought his great-great-grandfather. Both the African and the clock became the property of the same slaveowner. Years later, a descendant of the slaveowner gave the clock to a descendant of the African when the latter reached his seventy-fifth birthday, in appreciation for years of good service as slave and freedman. Still without anger, Tucker swings his ax, reducing the heirloom to "scrap metal and kindling." Using the same ax, he chops down a tree that another of the slaveholding family had particularly liked. Finally, looking at his home, he hesitates, looks a bit afraid. Encouraged by Bethrah, he sets it afire without further display of emotion. By these deeds he renounces every link to a heritage that perversely insists on denying black men their manhood. The flames redden the faces of the onlookers who are at first curious, then stunned by his calm, deliberate ruthlessness. He leaves without giving any explanation to the spectators. The only person to whom he speaks is a white boy, whose father, more enlightened than some other whites, tries to instill in his son a proper sense of relatedness with other human beings, black and white. A year earlier, Tucker had bought the boy a small gift, a bag of peanuts in a store window at which he had seen the youngster gazing longingly. At the same time he sent a message to the boy's father indicating his appreciation for what the father was trying to do. As Tucker and his family start off, the boy runs after them. Before sending him back, Tucker tries to tell the lad, the one white to whom it seems important to offer an explanation, why he has behaved as he has. Tucker explains that for years blacks have been physically free from bondage but not psychologically ready to break the emotional chains binding them to the past. But if blacks are ever really to be free, they must free themselves. No one else can do it for them. And that is what he has just done. Without symbols holding him to the past, he can seek a fresh start elsewhere.

Walker Vessels in *The Slave* frees himself even more ruthlessly from past connections than Tucker Caliban; but, in contrast with Tucker, he has nothing to which he can look forward, nor anything in the past on which he can look back with satisfaction. His marriage to Grace, a white woman, has ended before the play begins because of his increasingly militant racism which frightened and sickened her. The failure of their marriage was due to Walker's insensitivity to her feelings when he became a black racist as well as to her insecurity in an interracial marriage that prevented her from realizing that he no longer thought of her as white, that so far as he was concerned, she no longer had any particular color. She was simply the woman he loved, the mother of his children, and therefore totally excluded from his condemnation of other whites. He failed to take into consideration that she, a product of American cultural indoctrination, had been as sensitized to black-white color values as he had. When she left him, taking the children, he felt deserted; and when she married Easley, whom Walker accuses of "playing Iago to his second rate Othello," he was convinced of her treachery.

Incensed by these and other aspects of his experience as a black man, he, "single-handedly and with no other adviser" except his ego, incites blacks and whites to kill each other in a racial war that rages offstage throughout the play, knowing full well that, man's nature being what it is, a black victory will change nothing except "the complexion of tyranny." When the first-act curtain rises, he stands in the darkened living room of Grace and Easley, with gun in hand, awaiting their return so that he can kill them as he has killed his daughters offstage, in order to sever all personal ties to the past. For some reason, he cannot kill them immediately. Instead he plays a cat-and-mouse game. At times strange undercurrents seem to flow between him and Grace which hint at an earlier, pleasanter relationship but which are always instantly supplanted by bitter memories now separating them.

His vengeance has destroyed everything, including himself.

Walker is more than a black avenger, however. In the prologue and at the end of the play he is an "old field slave" who speaks about selfish man's lying and killing and self-destruction because of concepts that man himself creates. Jones seems to make him representative of all men who are slaves to their passions and self-imposed tyrannies, recalling Ishmael's rhetorical question, "Who ain't a slave?"

In a sense a character like John Williams's celebrated black writer, Max Reddick in *The Man Who Cried I Am* (1967), stands midway between characterizations of token blacks, or recipients of social rewards, and those of black avengers, with traits of both contained in his portrait. When first seen in the novel, Max is in Europe and dying, at age forty-nine, of cancer of the rectum, an illness that is a macabre symbol of cultural emasculation of black men. But as he thinks of his life and of his battle with pain, he is not sorry that he will soon die; his only regret is that his disease prevents him from just once more enjoying sexual intercourse with his Dutch wife Margrit or one of the other women who send out signals to him. He has given up the comparative comfort of a hospital bed in order to settle differences between himself and Margrit before he dies, particularly to tell her how much he regrets the failure of their marriage, a casualty of American disapproval of interracial marriage and punishment of both partners in such marriages.

On his way to Amsterdam he stops off in Paris to attend the funeral of an old friend and professional rival, Harry Ames, writer and "Dean" of expatriate black writers in Europe. There he learns that Harry has left some papers and a letter for him with Harry's French mistress at Leiden. Within twenty-four hours, Max sees Margrit, acts decisively on information contained in Harry's papers, and at the same time, in a series of skillfully executed flashbacks, recalls and takes stock of his life as token black writer. His portrait shows him to be a displaced lonely individual, only partly because he is a sensitive artist, mostly because he is an American Negro for whom there exists no "spiritual home" in America, Europe, or Africa which can serve as psychological refuge.

Recollection begins with the publication of his first novel

in 1939, the time when he meets Harry Ames and together
they evaluate mutual experiences as writers, specifically how
liberal whites, with what were probably the best intentions,
never allow blacks to forget the black-white problem. They
demand that blacks "be serious, even angry, twenty-four
hours a day," and if a black relaxes a moment they consider
him a traitor to his race. Similarly, black writers who yearn
"to soar, to sing golden arias" in their works are expected,
and paid well by certain minority group editors and publishers, to speak in tones of "unreasonable black fury," as if
those who control the flow of publication and are also sympathetic to black writers want the general public, for complex psychological reasons, constantly to be flagellated with
evidence of white injustice to blacks. Max recalls also his
being the recipient of two kinds of prejudice, both demoraliz-
ing to the ego. One sort was the anti-black variety which
meant being denied a job, scholarship, or award for which
one is qualified, solely because one was black. The other occurred when, after a long and difficult struggle, he was hired
as a reporter on a white newspaper and, as a result, was
awarded plaques, citations, and other honors for superior
reporting from both black and white organizations simply
because he was black. Yet, he thinks with some gratitude, the
job provided him a living; he was able to eat regularly.

The peculiar conditioning and sensitization that are integral to the black American experience are not limited to his
contacts with whites. Max remembers a black policeman in
Harlem who, also for complex psychological reasons, boasted
sadistically that he liked nothing better than "beatin' a bad
nigger's head." Also he remembers Big Ola Mae, who with
her "benignly-creased, motherly, . . . chocolate brown" face,
sarcastically assumed that he had begun chasing white
women when he became successful: "every big nigger gets
him a white girl." He thinks, further, about how other blacks
rejected him when success finally came to him. But the memory that seared most, that left the worst scar, was his tragic
love affair with Lillian, who was so afraid of economic insecurity that she dared not risk marriage with an impoverished but promising novelist although he was in every other
way desirable to her. For him, she was the perfect mate, the

black girl for whom he was willing to do anything except stagnate in a job that would interfere with his writing. She became pregnant, had an abortion, and died. Financial stability came too late.

By 1953, at the age of thirty-nine, Max is thoroughly disillusioned with life in the United States. He joins Harry and the other expatriates in Europe, not all of whom are disillusioned with America. Two members of the group, Alphonse Edwards—dilettante, tourist, connected, in some mysterious way, with American officialdom—and Roger Wilkinson, writer, are superpatriots or "red, white, and black" Americans. Most of the others exhibit mixed feelings about their country. They have taken residence abroad out of disgust for the country's inability to handle racial pluralism equitably and justly. Yet all are homesick, as if still tied to it by some psychological umbilicus. They remain intensely interested in all that goes on there, as in the case of the 1954 Supreme Court decision. All greet the news with skepticism, doubting that outlawing segregation in education would really effect any social change, and dismissing it as just another gimmick or "fake-out" because "Charlie" and "Miss Ann" would never allow white kids to sit next to black kids in school. Soon, however, they begin wondering about how the people back home are taking the news. They conclude that it is just possible that the decision might turn out to be something important in the struggle for equality. In that case, they argue, they might as well celebrate. Their struggle between hope and skepticism attests to countless promises broken and aspirations shattered.

Not all expatriates are pro-Africa either. Unlike those who hold romantic notions about Africa, Max, while there as magazine correspondent, was disturbed by the realities of longstanding intertribal animosities and disappointed by African rejection. They made it plain that they did not like American blacks, actually held them in contempt. As a result, he learns, African countries generally prefer to have white, rather than black, diplomats appointed to their countries. In this way, he discovers, they share white American prejudice against American black people. Once again it is Harry who states the case for most of the expatriates, baldly admitting that he has "nothing in common with Africa," but at the same time acknowledging the strange attraction that it has on him. When one is away from Africa, "something keeps pulling you back to it."

With regard to his relationship with Margrit, Max carefully weighs the alternatives before proposing marriage: whether or not it would be worse for him to live without her warmth and love or to face the disadvantages of having a white wife back in the States. The latter problem has great significance for him at this time, as he has been a presidential speech writer and is becoming increasingly involved in the civil rights movement of the late 1950's and early 1960's. He considers another matter carefully also. He was initially attracted to her because she looks, strangely, a lot like Lillian, albeit a "bleached" Lillian, and he wonders whether or not he has been unconsciously avoiding marriage since Lillian's death because he has been searching for a reasonable substitute. He worries if that connection might be his only reason for wanting to marry Margrit. In addition, he recalls an odd comment made by Harry many years earlier when he married his white wife Charlotte: "The day will come when a black man will not marry a woman he loves simply because she's white."

Unlike Harry, however, Max, in a sense, has been more accommodative, never really doing anything deliberately calculated to attack the status quo in race relations or "rock" the Ship of State. He has always followed the tradition, like other token blacks, of working within the system to effect desirable social change, never really losing belief in the perfectability of man by peaceful, evolutionary means. Further, the customary sensitization of black youths in regard to sexual relationships with white women made him believe the old myth that survival for blacks depends on anonymity in interracial affairs, with brief liaisons preferable, even *de rigueur* in certain circumstances as sub-cultural *rites de passage*, to the notoriety attending strictly taboo black-white marriages. This time something in him rebelled. They were married. It was as if cautious Max finally stood up, "reared back," and, like the voice from the burning bush, asserted his manhood, celebrated it, declaring for all to hear and know that he is who he is, a black man, free and independent, and that he will do as he pleases. It is as if he knows at last that any other course is self-denial or suicide. The decision made, he wonders why it takes so long for a man to grow up.

But tensions of life back in the States—stepped-up civil rights confrontations, marches, demonstrations, Max's increasing emotional involvement, the onset of his illness—all contribute to the failure of the marriage. Margrit, more concerned about him than the movement, suggests that they return to Amsterdam. Max refuses, saying that he would feel like a traitor if he deserted his people at that time. When medical tests reveal incurable cancer, he provokes one final, irrevocable argument, indicating that he no longer loves her, in order to release her from witnessing the horrible last stages of the illness and experiencing the social ostracism and economic reprisal that are the normal consequences of interracial marriage. As he comes closer to death, however, his conscience will not allow him to continue the deception; yet when they meet in Amsterdam, he hesitates, promising himself to tell her the next day when he returns from Leiden.

Harry's letter and papers contain evidence of a secret coalition of Western powers, called Alliance Blanc, to prevent the confederation of black states as more and more African countries become independent. The method used is provocation of intertribal and interregional conflicts. Its job is unwittingly facilitated by a few greedy, power-hungry blacks. Other, more honest leaders who are killed, deposed, or exiled are the first victims of the white conspiracy. More shocking than that, however, is evidence among Harry's papers of a sinister American plan, called King Alfred, to intern and, if necessary, exterminate all American Negroes in the event that a national or international crisis between blacks and whites arises resulting from a security leak about Alliance Blanc and its anti-black activities. The King Alfred plot spelled out, in great detail, the locations in the United States of proposed detention centers and identified the government agencies that would assist in carrying it out. It also pinpointed the black groups and the individuals, including whites sympathetic to blacks, who might constitute a threat to the government and who must be kept under constant surveillance.

Max learns further that two men have already been killed,

the African who originally obtained the documentary evidence and Harry Ames who fell heir to it. He knows that he is next on the hired assassins' list, that they are awaiting him on the road back to Amsterdam. Furthermore, he knows their identities, that they are the two "red, white, and black" superpatriots. For the last time, Max rebels now that he has, once again, something else evil to strike out against. He decides to "tear up that unreal tranquility that exists in the United States," that façade that lulls the majority of whites and blacks into a sense of false harmony, by doing precisely what his government has killed twice to prevent: the dissemination of knowledge about its anti-black activities which have resulted in the King Alfred plot of genocide. To that end, he places a transatlantic telephone call to Minister Q, leader of a black extremist group whose telephone is known to be monitored, and reads the evidence concerning Alliance Blanc and King Alfred over the wire while Minister Q tape-records it at the other end.

Max's arrival at a "point of no return" in his growing intolerance of American attitudes and behavior toward blacks foreshadows the emergence of the last group of characters, the avengers who have passed beyond continued endurance of broken promises, some more than a century old, and beyond passive tolerance of white prejudice of two varieties, that of the violent minority and that of the silent majority. Like Walker Vessels, none believes any longer that bloodless revolution is possible. Three novels reflecting this aspect of cultural conflict were published in 1969 and contain well-drawn portraits of black avengers: Dan Freeman in *The Spook Who Sat by the Door*, by Sam Greenlee, and Stanley Shawcross in *Siege* by Edwin Corley, both of whom actively foment revolutions; and Eugene Browning, in *Sons of Darkness, Sons of Light* by John A. Williams, who sets a revolution in motion when he takes steps to avenge a wrong.

Dan Freeman, the CIA infiltrator, is motivated to seek revenge earlier in life than the other two. Growing up in the Midwest with parents who, according to him, are refugees from the South, he soon sees the futility of patiently waiting at the back door with hat in hand for cultural handouts. Aided by "nigger pride," he concludes that he, and others like him, will "tolerate no more head whippings," actual or symbolic, that they must and will retaliate. But first they must acquire skill from whites, those most skillful in the art of subjugating and intimidating black people, in order to be successful. When the word goes out that the CIA is to be integrated he is one of the educated and intelligent blacks selected for training, the idea behind the experiment being to ease them all out of the training program, by a process of skillful elimination, as untrainable for service in the organization. The officials reckon without knowledge of their antagonist. He decides to become an undercover agent or spy, a job that, he observes, any Negro is well qualified for, because blacks have been forced by circumstances, historically, to mask their true feelings behind yesses and grins and pretensions to be the kind of people whites expected them to be. Any other behavior could have meant annihilation. He, alone, is successful because he becomes, like a chameleon, the stereotype of the nigger that whites expect him to be. The other candidates fail because they behave as what they are, middle-class Negroes or, as Dan sees it, "white niggers," those blacks who lead wasted lives straining to become superficial imitations of whites instead of pridefully being who they are.

Images of blacks held by whites, once again, are more important than information about him contained in the Agency's files. With skillful underplaying, he fakes an accent, a protective, subservient smile, an Uncle Tom sense of humor, wears ill-fitting clothes that are in "quiet bad taste," and even goes so far as to replace his plain toothcap, necessitated by a college sports accident, with one rimmed in gold. Above all, he is scrupulously careful, as "good nigger," to obey all rules and to meet all of the physical and educational requirements of the Agency. Away from the Agency he sheds his "cover," becoming himself, an urbane intellectual who dresses in modest good taste, without gold-rimmed toothcap, and who has sophisticated tastes in food, liquor, and the lively arts. His secret ambition is to acquire, from this "Olympus-on-the-Potomac," all of the skills and strategic knowledge that he will need to train black youth for the revolution that must surely come. His diligence and determination insure success in becoming the Agency's "spook beside the door." "Spook," a once popular, but somewhat derisive, in-group name for Negroes, as well as the popular name for CIA agent, provides not only double identification of the protagonist, but functions also in another way: he is never permitted to function fully as an agent; his job is to "sit by the door," on display as the Agency's token or showcase black.

After five years his patience with the condescending attitudes of whites nears the breaking point, causing him to endanger his future plans by revealing the side of himself never before seen at the Agency. He quietly resigns, sheds his CIA cover, and obtains a job with a social welfare agency back home in Chicago, where he proceeds to transform a South Side street gang, the Cobras, into an elite corps of underground freedom fighters. He gives them a sense of black pride which has less to do with skin color than with unity resulting from shared experiences, feelings, and aspirations that weld people together into cohesive groups. From a series of well-planned robberies, they obtain a sizable treasury and an arsenal of modern weapons for the coming fight, which is set in motion by the overreaction of a white policeman who, in panic, kills a fifteen-year-old black boy.

A series of incidents contributes to Marine Major General Stanley Shawcross's disillusionment with his country, beginning with a humiliating experience in his youth with white hoboes and including an accidental involvement in the Watts rebellion. Up to the time of the Watts experience, he is the "white nigger" that other Negroes call him, for he considers it better, in the long run, for his people to work within the system, according to the rules set down by the oppressor, in order to effect desirable social change. This "sit-tight," "do-nothing" behavior attracts the hostility of other blacks. Two events compel a change in him. When he sees that a higher percentage of black soldiers are dying in Southeast Asia than whites, in comparison with national population figures, he becomes disturbed and lashes out bitterly against a system that permits such discrepancies. Emotional disturbance turns to anger and revolution when his wife and small sons are brutally murdered for no apparent reason while he is away fighting for his country.

He joins in with another revolutionist, William Gray,

whose plan includes separation of blacks from whites in an all-black state and reparations from whites for past offenses against blacks. Under the guise of a business enterprise which they call the Uncle Tom Flour Company, and financially assisted by an African government with funds diverted from American foreign aid grants, the two men begin organizing and training the Afro-American Army of Liberation, at isolated installations throughout the country, to fight under the Marcus Garvey flag with its symbolic colors of red, black, and green. Their strategy is to occupy the island of Manhattan, isolate it from surrounding areas, and hold residents hostage in order to force the government to cede the State of New Jersey to blacks so that their new nation, Redemption, may be established there.

Unlike Shawcross, Eugene Browning, political scientist and fund raiser for the Institute for Racial Justice, opposes both separation and reparation as methods of avenging age-old wrongs. Also, he has never been a white nigger. One reason is that he is a true cultural as well as racial blend, neither Afrophile nor Europhile, although of the two paintings in his apartment, he wonders why an original Nigerian tempera of Ibadan is not quite so appealing to him as a Van Gogh print of the drawbridge at Arles, even though the colors of Ibadan are more brilliant and beautiful. Presently he sees himself as a black American dedicated to social change, but still believing problems must be solved within the social structure by establishing and maintaining truly transactional relationships between blacks and whites. Nor, at this point, is he willing, as are Shawcross and Freeman, to concede that total destruction of society is imperative in order to achieve the goals that all three seek. He recognizes one preeminently practical point, which is that there would be no chance of blacks', who are in the minority, winning a shooting war polarized along color lines.

When an Irish policeman—who has been culturally "programmed" in the belief that if a person is black he must necessarily be bad—kills a black youth, Browning feels compelled to give notice to others like the white policeman that the black community will no longer allow white violence against blacks to go unchallenged or unpunished. The method of retaliation that he advocates is reciprocal and transactional, "an eye for an eye"; in this case specifically, assassination of the white policeman. Not a murderer or an assassin himself, he must get someone better suited and trained for the job. He makes contact with a "connection" who, in turn, contacts an aging Mafia Don; the latter arranges for an Irgun fighter to kill the policeman. Browning pays for the Israeli's services with money he has obtained, as fund raiser, from a black businessman. The amount of money that he has, however, is insufficient for the job. The Mafia Don, in sympathy with what is being done, supplies the remainder needed. That job done, the Israeli, also sympathetic, decides to kill the white murderer of three black college students in the South without additional remuneration. These retaliatory acts, attributed to black militants, set off violent clashes between blacks and whites throughout the country, causing Browning anguish and guilt for having sparked the chain reaction in the first place. Browning and his family take refuge in their summer house at Sag Harbor.

One soon begins to wonder whether or not the author's title refers only to the conflict between blacks and whites that rages and increases in intensity by the end of the novel. An angry black mob kills another policeman; a white mob retaliates. Then one remembers the Mafia Don, the Irgun fighter, and Young Woody, the boy with whom Browning's older daughter keeps company and of whom her mother disapproves only because he is white. When Woody hears that a group of white toughs are organizing to "shoot up" black neighborhoods, he comes to the Brownings' cottage armed with guns and ammunition and prepared to fight with them in order to "make the whole thing a little more equal, if it happens." All whites do not line up on one side against all blacks on the other. Nor are traditional symbolic values of blackness and whiteness employed here. Williams's manipulation of them suggests, quite simply, that neither blacks nor whites have any "corner" or proprietary rights in virtue or evil.

Each avenger is idealistic in his goal of a better life, as he sees it, for his people. Each, as an active agent in society, recognizes the possibly dire consequences of his decisions and is willing to take whatever comes his way. None can find satisfactory alternatives for achieving the goal. Each course of action taken, in a sense, fails because none of the novels ends with a better life for blacks. In only one, *Siege*, is the revolution ended. In the others chain reactions have been set in motion that seem headed toward revolution. In the sense that blacks have scored a point and have made themselves visible as active participants in society, each novel ends at the onset of an emergent society in which blacks and whites are almost ready to enter into transactional relationships with neither arrogantly dominant or slavishly submissive to the other.

Only two portraits from the late 1960's, different from token blacks and avengers, remain to be analyzed. Each is a sensitive depiction of blacks in day-to-day interactions with other blacks, with some whites, and in situations forcing them to take critical looks at their lives.

Particularly noteworthy in this respect is Paule Marshall's battered Merle Kinbona in *The Chosen Place, the Timeless People* (1969). She is proprietor of a guest house at Bournehills, a place of "shabby woe-begotten hills and spent land" on a Caribbean island. The name of the community suggests its location at the end of the island and symbolizes the outer limit, the point beyond which there is no return to viable life for either land or inhabitants. Merle is such a one. With island grace and charm, the poorer people call her Mis-Merle. Behind her back, her friends, not altogether unkindly, call her Mad-Merle. At first glance she seems a gay, vibrant extrovert. She smokes constantly, her face indistinct in the haze. Noises made by numerous heavy silver bangles "lend a clangorous, unsettling" resonance to her movements that seems to carry over into her quieter moments. Always in motion, long silver earrings, replicas of elongated saints that decorate some European churches, hang from her ears. Add to these a compulsive stream of chatter, and one can understand why she is considered slightly daft. It is as if she is afraid to let herself be seen clearly in repose and without distracting sound, as if some secret may be revealed by stillness, unclouded vision, or silence, hence the need for a protective façade. Laughing,

she admits as much to Saul Amron, her Jewish house guest
and later her lover, when she confides to him that smoke is
an excellent fetish against *obeah* and that the racket of her
bangles provides protection against the devil himself.

She is ashamed of two memories, we learn, one from
early childhood and the other from young womanhood. Her
mother, an unmarried sixteen-year-old laborer in the cane
fields, was murdered in cold blood while Merle watched. Her
white father made no effort to find the murderer, a lack of
concern that she bitterly resents but not so shamefully as
her own inability to identify, or even remember, the face of
the murderer. People later told her that afterwards she was
found beside her mother's body, placidly sucking her thumb
as if nothing had happened. Some years later she sought
professional help to remember the face, with no success.
The other memory she tries to keep suppressed is the reason
for the dissolution of her marriage, while in England, to
African Ketu Kinbona and the loss of custody of her daughter. While destitute in London, she was helped by a wealthy
Englishwoman, a lesbian, and whose lover she became until,
confused and disgusted, she left to take stock of herself
as a woman after three years of not being sure of exactly
what she was. Ketu helped her without ever learning of the
three-year interlude. The Englishwoman, jealous and vindic-
tive, exposed their former relationship to Ketu, who de-
nounced her as unfit to be his wife and the mother of their
child and returned to Africa taking the child with him. He
considered her his one mistake while in England and simply
rejected the mistake and her, never answering her letters
or doing anything to acknowledge the fact of her existence.
These secrets are the source of her shame which, as violence
directed inside herself, is slowly destroying her.

The relationship with Saul, mutually comforting and
supportive, helps release her from the self-destructive consequences of shame. He, like Ketu, proves to her that she is
a woman. Neither deludes the other about the nature of the
relationship. She knows, as he does, that she is making use
of him to gain release from inner torment. She knows also
that she has never really known who she is, that she has
always depended on a lover for self-definition, and that,

possibly as a consequence, her relationship with lovers has always been deficient. This self-assessment is comparable to the cyclic self-cleansing of the sea at Bournehills, when seaweed is sloughed off onto the shore, "like so much dead skin," annually. By finally coming to terms with herself, she has taken the first important action in the direction of firm self-knowledge and vigorous self-determination.

Also noteworthy for penetrating depiction of survival rituals engaged in by ghetto blacks is Mr. Russell Parker, a character in *Ceremonies in Dark Old Men* (1969) by Lonne Elder III. He and his sons Theopolis and Bobby are primarily interested in "getting a piece of the action," that is, their share of cultural rewards doled out to the token few, often called Uncle Toms, but withheld from the unexceptional or common black man. The rituals in which he engages make life meaningful and help him maintain some semblance of dignity in relation to his children who think differently from him about most things.

In the script, his lines are always identified as those of Mr. Parker and those of his checker-playing crony as Mr. Jenkins, a naming practice that immediately alerts the reader to the first ceremony or ritual, that is, insistence on a respectful form of address by blacks, too often and for too long addressed as "you there," "boy," or "you people." The second is his pretense of being head of the household when actually he and the sons are supported by Adele, the daughter of the family, as they were supported by his wife and their mother before she worked herself to death. Mr. Parker, a former vaudeville dancer until his "legs got wobbly," is the unsuccessful proprietor of a dilapidated barber shop in Harlem, for which Adele has to pay rent because in seven years he "hasn't earned enough money to buy two hotdogs." Whatever problem arises, Mr. Parker always promises that he will take care of it immediately but never does, always using the same excuse: he needs time to "straighten things out." At age fifty-four, he is a pretentiously comical failure who has to sneak checker games with his friend Mr. Jenkins, because of the fear that if Adele catches him, she will bawl him out for loafing when he ought to be out seeking a job. When he does go downtown looking for a job, he still has no luck. Neither white nor black job interviewers find any reason to hire him. Further, he has never been able to win a game of checkers from Mr. Jenkins. Though ineffectual as father and provider, he is not insensitive or stupid. He agrees with Adele that she is being treated unfairly and that she should not have to support the men of the family. Finally, now that he is getting old, he is not unaware of the imminence of death and wants one more love affair.

The crisis in their lives is precipitated by the men's desire to be something more than subservient dependents of women. It is his son Theo who introduces him to a Harlem character, Blue Haven, who is another black man trying to avoid the peril of female domination. Blue is Prime Minister of the Harlem De-Colonization Association. His long-range scheme is to preserve Harlem for black men. The Association's immediate goal, however, is to make money by whatever means possible in order to regain the community from the whites who own it. They consider themselves revolutionary businessmen and, as such, never draw attention to themselves by demonstrating, picketing, rioting, or engaging in other activities that will draw attention to themselves and their "business" ventures, such as the Piano Brigade, an organization of store burglars working nights to ruin white businesses on 125th Street and to increase the wealth of the Association. Another venture is called Black Heaven, a new policy game with the built-in racial incentive of numbers paired with colors; only a number paired with black can win. In order to promote a "symbolic life force" in the community, there is the Red Square Circle Brigade, guaranteed to be a best seller, featuring dart boards on which faces of white racists have been painted. The Parker barber shop becomes district headquarters for one of their best ventures, the distillation of Black Lightning, or corn whiskey, with Theo as chief distiller. All are deadly earnest games at which they play in order to assert their manhood. Success brings only despair. Mr. Parker has deluded himself into believing that at his age he can be a successful lover to a young woman. His son Bobby becomes a member of the Piano Brigade, against his father's and his brother's wishes, and is killed. All that remains is the compassion that each human being must have for another. As a compassionate gesture, Mr. Jenkins, who has already learned about Bobby's death, permits Mr. Parker to win at checkers just before he is to be told the tragic news.

This survey of fictional symbols, representing black individuals as defined, reveals that names and physical descriptions, useful in previous sections, are of little value in classifying individuals. Of more value are aesthetic symbols of fictional personality: identity, decision-making ability, proper relatedness with other people, particularly whites. Each character analyzed has been classified an individual because he has, or comes to have, a pretty good idea of who he is and what his function in life is to be; or because he is searching for knowledge of self within a pattern of life that will be suitable for him. All of the characters make important decisions, at least about themselves, within the plot structure of the literary work. In making decisions, they examine alternatives and possible consequences. Of equal importance is their ability to enter into nothing less than transactional relationships with other people. Understandably, most of the characters are depicted in the process of becoming whatever kinds of fictional personalities they eventually will be. They are shown undergoing the same kinds of struggles, successes, and defeats that all human beings endure. Their goals are not always worthy ones; nor are characters always successful in realizing their goals; but each is humanly individualistic in his search for identity and fulfillment.

Abe's portrait is the earliest and least developed of all. "Major" Scott, Nigger Jim, Melanctha, Spade, Cue are obviously black portraits in transition from stock and archetypal configurations. Robinson Asbury's is the only well-developed one among the early figures analyzed. Belton Piedmont, Lucas Beauchamp, and Eric Gardner, though admirable, display certain rigidities tending, in varying degrees, to detract from their portraits as individuals. Life is never so simple that one can stand adamantly on inflexible principles; there are always doubts, frustrations, failures. These fictional symbols seldom doubt, are never frustrated, and can always find reasonable solutions to their dilemmas.

For these reasons, it is not always possible to believe in them as fictional representatives of individuals. In contrast, all of the youthful blacks searching for identity, self-determination, and fulfillment—Sandy Rogers, Janie, the protagonist of *Invisible Man,* John Grimes, Spencer Scott, and Oliver Eugene—are thoroughly believable. Insofar as human potential is concerned, Sam Lucas and Joe Mott are abject failures; but Sam, along with Janie, Sandy, and Cross Damon, achieves freedom from religion and other cultural constrictions. The portrait of Cross is a particularly good example of the individual who discovers himself by investigating his existence in terms of his desires and tensions.

Each recipient of token cultural rewards—Cullee Hamilton, Douglass Dilman, David Champlin, Leo Proudhammer —is depicted as having a firm sense of his black identity even though each is a "white nigger" in the eyes of some blacks. Each is committed to social change, however, but only by peaceful means within the existing social framework. Unfortunately, they are out of step with the times in which their narratives are set. As a result, they face apparently insuperable problems of relatedness with other blacks and with some whites as well. Only Leo comes to recognize militancy and revolution as probably the best workable solution to intergroup problems.

Similarly, each black avenger—Bernard Belgrave, Tucker Caliban, Walker Vessels, Dan Freeman, Stanley Shawcross, Eugene Browning—has a firm sense of his identity. Each is driven by despair, frustration, and anger to assert himself, to make his existence a matter of significance in his culture. While each starts from the same basis of self-pride and self-determination, the methods used to achieve the desired results differ and contain, in varying degrees of intensity, elements of violence: first, black separation aided by reparation for past evils; second, the destruction of society so that, like the phoenix, a new and better society may arise from its ashes; and last, selective retaliation or the establishment of transactional relations along the line of the "eye for an eye" principle. Freeman and Shawcross are likened to the myth of Prometheus. They obtain knowledge and skill from the white power structure to wage revolution against the oppressive system. Each believes that his is the only way to attain the good life, as he sees it, for blacks.

The other three characters analyzed in this section—Walter Lee Younger, Merle Kinbona, and Russell Parker—are symbolic representations of blacks in conflict with themselves. Primarily, each portrait focuses on a human problem or issue instead of a racial one, although no portrait neglects the psychological or other consequences of blacks living in white society. Each character, in his own way, is a unique product of that experience. Brother Younger represents the black man who overcomes personal problems and achieves responsible maturity. Merle Kinbona's problem is proper relatedness with other people, a problem that she is in process of overcoming at the end of the novel. Mr. Russell Parker is a failure as man, husband, father. He maintains, through ritual, a self-concept that is based on illusion and doomed to be shattered.

Notes

1. J. P. Kennedy, *Swallow Barn or a Sojourn in the Old Dominion,* Rev. ed. (New York, 1852), p. 466.
2. *Ibid.,* p. 479.
3. *Ibid.,* p. 453.
4. John William DeForest, *Miss Ravenel's Conversion from Secession to Loyalty* (New York, 1955), p. 241.
5. *Ibid.,* p. 246.
6. *Ibid.*
7. *Ibid.,* pp. 290ff.
8. *Ibid.,* p. 292.
9. Mark Twain, *The Adventures of Huckleberry Finn* (Boston, 1958), p. 67.
10. *Ibid.*
11. *Ibid.,* p. 68.
12. *Ibid.,* pp. 131ff.
13. *Ibid.,* p. 73.
14. *Ibid.,* pp. 73ff.
15. Stephen Vincent Benét, "Freedom's a Hard Bought Thing," *Selected Works of Stephen Vincent Benét,* vol. II (New York, 1942), p. 59. Reprinted by permission of Brandt & Brandt.
16. Stephen Vincent Benét, *John Brown's Body* (New York, 1928), p. 327. Reprinted by permission of Brandt & Brandt.
17. Paul Lawrence Dunbar, "The Scapegoat," *The Best Short Stories*

by Negro Writers, Langston Hughes, ed. (Boston, 1967), p. 18.
18. Gertrude Stein, "Melanctha," *Three Lives* (New York, 1909), p. 96.
19. *Ibid.,* p. 124.
20. *Ibid.,* p. 123.
21. Sutton E. Griggs, *Imperium in Imperio* (New York, 1969), p. 261. Originally published in 1899.

CHAPTER

5

CONCLUSIONS AND IMPLICATIONS

The investigation began with two assumptions: if cultural attitudes are changing, fictional symbols of black Americans may also be shifting from stereotyped to more individualized portraits; second, that if a trend toward individualization exists, it can be documented in popular fiction of the past century and a half. To find answers, aesthetic symbols of culture and personality were identified. Analytical data revealed three major kinds of stock characters, five basic archetypal patterns, and two general classifications of individuals. In all categories, cultural influences were noted. Within each category, shifts in portraiture significantly paralleled changes in cultural belief and attitude; the most dramatic changes are in the attitudes of blacks toward themselves and the autonomous emergence of black consciousness, pride, and assertion among twentieth-century individuals, as defined. Both assumptions were affirmed and substantiated.

In retrospect, the major cultural conflict has been observed as the inability of blacks and whites to relate transactionally in a culture dominated by the myth of black inferiority and white superiority, a specter that still haunts contemporary movement toward the international coexistence of all people in free and open societies. For the most part, attitudes and behavior of characters have reflected the myth in their relationships with others who were different. This pattern of social interaction is described as achievement of unity with others through dominance or submission.[1] We have seen that a character, if he were white, assumed power over blacks and achieved perverse unity by making blacks part, albeit in his estimation the inferior part, of himself. If the character were black, he acquired equally perverse unity with whites by experiencing his identity in inferior extension of theirs. This pattern has been documented many times over, among stock and archetypal figures delineated almost entirely by white writers.

Stock blacks, examined in three configurational patterns, have reflected images of blacks and patterns of relatedness that whites could accept, reject, or ignore without qualm of conscience or depth of emotional response. In all patterns black characters were devalued in ways that helped whites overvalue themselves. For example, in portraits of accommodationists, authors emphasized ignorant speech patterns, gullibility, cowardice, and animal-like physical descriptions in contrast with white figures whose portraits contain few, if any, of these characteristics. In the image running counter to this pattern, authors overidealized the accommodative blacks, revealing opposition to prevailing white attitudes at an early stage of black portraiture in American literary history. In the second stock pattern, the brute, authors vilified as prurient beasts those blacks who, because they defied prescribed rituals of race relations, deserved their punishment of torture and mutilation. Such portraits could be accepted with feelings of righteous indignation. The third stock pattern contains ludicrous inferiors, the buffoons or clowns, whom authors have made, for the most part, shallow, vain, trivial, inept, and irresponsible. By all of these stock patterns, audience response was channeled toward disdainful toleration, derision, sentimental adulation, or virulent hatred of a particular character. Whatever the response—laughter, tears, hisses—the characters' portraits were designed to corroborate and justify white supremacy. Persistence of such stock figures well into the twentieth century indicates the deep-rooted tenacity with which the culture has clung to this self-concept.

Among archetypal patterns, the myth functions also but elicits deeper and more conscientious responses than those elicited by the stock characters. The oldest archetypal pattern depicts the tragic mulatto, an image that created fear and pity in predominantly white reading or viewing audiences: fear because it was possible that any white, under certain adverse circumstances, might find himself in a situation similar to that of an octoroon slave; and pity because no one as white as a mulatto should have to suffer the indignities meted out to a coal black inferior. Probably, at a deeper level, were also elicited uneasy feelings of shame and guilt because the existence of the mulatto was proof of broken taboo, of culturally designated bestiality. The sacrifice symbol or victim of environmental and cultural determinism, probably the most revealing symbol of conscientious feeling against slavery and caste, elicited something approaching a numenous response to the lamb led to slaughter for the redemption of sinful man who misused another human being for the purpose of maintaining a way of life based on a hubristic concept of supremacy. The paradoxical "despot and slave," the black mammy, is a complex symbol, eliciting ambivalent responses. Sometimes she was romanticized as nurturer and sustainer of whites. In other works, she seemed more like the she-wolf that suckled Romulus and Remus. In still others, her symbolism is manipulated, in response to cultural demands, to argue against Northern accusations of inhuman treatment of blacks or to explain Southern mores to ignorant outsiders. The archetypal primitives—whether noble savage, animal, siren, harlot—was, and may still be, obvious symbol of the uncontrollable libido, enviable and, in line with the myth, justifiable in black exteriors. In depictions of the alter-ego symbol, the myth was attacked more openly and forthrightly than in any of the other patterns. Substituted for it were concepts of black-white interdependence and brotherhood. Only among mammies, mulattoes, and primitives are recorded shifts away from earlier archetypal manifestations. No change at all was discernible among alter-ego or sacrifice symbols.

At the same time that stock and archetypal figures were depicted in non-reciprocal social relationships, a trend away from these patterns became evident in the few early portraits of blacks who demonstrate self-knowledge, independent responsibility, and proper relatedness with other people. The trend toward individualistic treatment starts out as a minor undertone. Its inception in nineteenth-century literature records only a slight shift in cultural belief, indicating that although blacks were still considered inferior, they were entitled, as human beings, to some small allowance of social justice. Also at about this time appeared the concept of brotherhood that included blacks, noted among archetypes, in opposition to the dominant concept of inferiority. Some fictional examples reflecting this part of the trend have been documented in all three analytical categories, especially among individuals in transition from submissiveness to self-assertion. In twentieth-century literature, the minor variant increases in incidence, becoming significant, giving substance to changes in interpersonal relations that are reflected and have been documented in the analytical chapters.

In the late 1950's and early 1960's, when integration still seemed a possible and desirable consequence of the non-violent social revolution that appeared to be taking place, portraits of token blacks, those few partially integrated into American society, were delineated largely by white authors. Although these characters accept the rewards of tokenism, they are not blind to social discrepancies between themselves and the majority of blacks. More important, they possess some sense of black pride and are not entirely willing to lose their identity through assimilation into white society. They tend, however, in relationships with whites to be accommodative to the extent of believing that the best chance of advancement for the race will come gradually by working non-violently but definitely for change within the established social system. Their portraits are generally hopeful symbolic projections of the long anticipated alignment of traditional ideals with everyday behavior in race relations. That decade in fiction, from the mid-1950's through the mid-1960's, was an observable time of high hopes when young blacks and whites challenged the constitutionality of discriminatory practices and enactments, when organizations like NAACP were considered radical, and when the Supreme Court decision on school desegregation held out promise for social integration and unity.

It proved to be a time of lost opportunity. By the end of the 1960's, black self-assertive forces had taken over, negating the gradualism and integration of the earlier decade and resulting in portraits of black avengers and revolutionists who are committed to nothing less than transactionalism in interpersonal relations. Delineated mostly by black writers from in-group strength, these portraits have effectively put the black American experience into exciting symbolic form, with the writers' contact and rage the sources of their strength. Such authors are forcing American blacks to examine their lives and values by helping them recognize that existence or being for blacks must be black, not white as some blacks in the past have futilely tried to become. In these ways ethnic writers have succeeded in moving blacks from colored shame to black pride. Contrasting dramatically with stock and archetypal portraits, those of black avengers reflect the rediscovery of truth, goodness, and beauty in blackness and in celebration of one's self; they reflect also the contemporary high level of black aspiration and its corollary low level of frustration and tolerance of existing conditions; hence the explosiveness of situations or plots in which their portraits are depicted, all of which are frightening metaphors of contemporary American society. If at times a black author's work appears absurd, its absurdity reflects the quality of black life in white society and is a work from which, if proper relatedness is achieved, will emerge special meaning, value, and order for black people. As the ideals of 1776 resulted from theretofore revolutionary aspirations regarding human interrelationships, just so do black revolutionists aspire idealistically toward reforms in black-white relationships.

What of the future? It might be good to know. Mankind should know, by now, that any plan or "grand design" for the future will not succeed if it fails to take into consideration the conditions and aspirations of people who will live in the future, or if it underestimates the gravity and international dimensions of problems connected with interrelationships between darker and lighter-skinned human beings. Among blacks, the reemergence of black consciousness has been the most hopeful sign since the Marcus Garvey movement and the Black Renaissance of the 1920's; for until a man respects and loves himself, as he is, how can he ever enter into transactional relationships with other people? Stated differently, how can a people who consistently undervalue themselves ever really become the equals of other people? Obversely, how can a people who consistently overvalue themselves ever become the equals of other people? Therein lies one of the major deterrents to global transactional relationships—ethnocentrism. When a person has lived through one and remembers what he has learned about two major world conflicts, he begins to realize that neither excessive nationalism nor ethnocentrism offers a viable solution to problems facing diverse peoples on this planet. Moreover, one realizes that some solution other than ethnocentrism is imperative to insure survival of the human species, if it is to survive.

Insofar as black ethnocentrism is concerned, it has had to emerge full force if blacks are ever to free themselves from culturally indoctrinated inferiority. At the same time, hopefully, it will not degenerate into a mere ritual of self-aggrandizement, as observable in portraits of whites in early American fiction, or into a concept of black superiority and white inferiority, in line with the all too customary behavioral extreme of a pendulum swing. Nor, hopefully, in its recovery of African heritage will it deny the existence of a non-African cultural inheritance in the manner that many blacks formerly tried to deny their African heritage. On the positive side, it is also to be hoped that a new kind of ethnocentrism will emerge in which may be creatively reconciled all facets of cultural pluralism that are the heritage of all people on this planet. Is it too late in the history of mankind to remember that the one thing that binds men together is membership in the human species, the least common denominator of beings, all of whom are born different from each other in matters more important than skin color? If such memory be feasible, then it is finally hoped that blacks and whites can, on a massive scale, be desensitized to outmoded symbolic skin color values and that one day, people throughout the world will be born and develop according to their potentialities, and live coexistentially in humanness without the handicaps of either inferiority or superiority attributable to racial or ethnic differences. The danger point will have passed when man can break out of his either-or straitjacket and can say that it is possible for any symbolic skin color— not exclusively black, or white, or yellow, or red, or brown— to be beautiful under certain circumstances pertaining to proper concepts of self in relation to others of the human species. Perhaps then the age of racism will have passed and the task confronting all mankind will be universal improvement of the quality of life.

Note

1. See Erich Fromm, "Values, Psychology and Human Experience," *New Knowledge in Human Values*, Abraham Maslow, ed. (New York, 1959), p. 152.

Bibliography

Non-Fiction

ADORNO, T. W., E. FRANKEL-BRUNSWICK, and D. J. LEVINSON. *The Authoritarian Personality.* New York: Harper and Brothers, 1950. xxxii + 990 pp.

ALLPORT, GORDON W. *Becoming: Basic Considerations for a Psychology of Personality.* New Haven: Yale University Press, 1955. ix + 106 pp.

————. *The Nature of Prejudice* (Abridged). Garden City, N.Y.: Doubleday Anchor Books, 1958. xxii + 496 pp.

BODKIN, MAUD. *Archetypal Patterns of Poetry. Psychological Studies of Imagination.* London: Oxford University Press, 1934. xiv + 340 pp.

BONE, ROBERT A. *The Negro Novel in America.* Yale Publications in American Studies. Volume III. New Haven: Yale University Press, 1958. x + 268 pp.

BREITMAN, GEORGE, ed. *Malcolm X Speaks.* New York: Grove Press, 1965. viii + 226 pp.

BUTCHER, PHILIP. *George W. Cable.* New York: Columbia University Press, 1959. xiii + 286 pp.

CLARK, KENNETH B., and MAMIE P. CLARK. "Racial Identification and Preference in Negro Children" in *Readings in Social Psychology.* 3rd edition. Eleanor E. Macoby, Theodore M. Newcomb, Eugene L. Hartley, eds. New York: Henry Holt and Company, 1958. xi + 674 pp.

CLEAVER, ELDRIDGE. *Soul on Ice.* New York: Dell Publishing Co., 1968. xvi + 210 pages.

CLODD, EDWARD. *Magic in Names and in Other Things.* London: Chapman and Hall, 1920. 238 pp.

DEEGAN, DOROTHY YOST. *The Stereotype of the Single Woman in American Novels: A Social Study with Implications for the Education of Women.* New York: King's Crown Press, Columbia University, 1951. xiv + 252 pp.

DEWEY, JOHN. *Art as Experience.* New York: Minton, Balch and Company, 1934. vii + 355 pp.

DEWEY, JOHN, and ARTHUR F. BENTLEY. *Knowing and the Known.* Boston: The Beacon Press, 1949. xiii + 334 pp.

DOYLE, BERTRAM W. *The Etiquette of Race Relations.* Chicago: University of Chicago Press, 1937. xxv + 249 pp.

DU BOIS, W. E. BURGHARDT. *The Souls of Black Folk: Essays and Sketches.* New York: Fawcett World Library, 1961. 191 pp.

DUNBAR, ERNEST. *The Black Expatriates.* New York: E. P. Dutton and Co., 1968. x + 251 pp.

DUNN, L. C., and TH. DOBZHANSKY. *Heredity, Race and Society.* Revised and enlarged edition. New York: The New American Library of World Literature, 1956. 143 pp.

FRAZIER, E. FRANKLIN. *The Negro Family in the United States.* Chicago: University of Chicago Press, 1939. xxxii + 686 pp.

FROMM, ERICH. "Values, Psychology, and Human Experience," in *New Knowledge in Human Values.* Abraham Maslow, ed. New York: Harper and Brothers, 1959. xiv + 268 pp.

FURNAS, J. C. *Goodbye to Uncle Tom.* New York: William Sloane Associates, 1956. 435 pp.

GLOSTER, HUGH M. *Negro Voices in American Fiction.* Chapel Hill, N.C.: The University of North Carolina Press, 1948. xiv + 295 pp.

GORDON, ELIZABETH HOPE. "The Naming of Characters in the Works of Charles Dickens," in *University of Nebraska Studies in Language, Literature and Criticism.* Volume I. Lincoln, Neb.: University of Nebraska Press, 1917. 35 pp.

GRIER, WILLIAM H., and PRICE M. COBBS. *Black Rage.* New York: Basic Books, 1968. viii + 213 pp.

HENDIN, HERBERT. *Black Suicide.* New York: Basic Books, 1969. x + 176 pp.

HERSKOVITS, MELVILLE J. *The Myth of the Negro Past.* Boston: Beacon Press, 1958 (Originally published by Harper and Brothers, 1941.) xix + 368 pp.

HYMAN, STANLEY EDGAR. *The Armed Vision: A Study in the Methods of Modern Literary Criticism.* New York: Alfred A. Knopf, 1948. xv + 417 pp.

JUNG, CARL GUSTAV. Preface, in *Psyche and Symbol: A Selection from the Writings of C. G. Jung.* Violet S. de Laszlo,

ed. Garden City, N.Y.: Doubleday and Company, 1958.
xxxiv + 363 pp.

————. "Psychology and Literature," from *Modern Man in
Search of a Soul,* translated by W. S. Doll and Cary E.
Baynes, in *A Modern Book of Esthetics.* 3rd edition.
Melvin Rader, ed. New York: Holt, Rinehart and Win-
ston, 1960. xxxii + 540 pp.

KARDINER, ABRAM, and LIONEL OVESEY. *The Mark of Oppression: A Psychosocial Study of the American Negro.*
New York: W. W. Norton and Company, 1951. xvii + 396
pp.

KARON, BERTRAM P. *The Negro Personality: A Rigorous Investigation of the Effects of Culture.* New York: Springer
Publishing Company, 1958. vii + 184 pp.

KATZ, DANIEL, and KENNETH W. BRALY. "Verbal Stereotypes
and Racial Prejudice," in *Readings in Social Psychology.*
3rd edition. Eleanor E. Macoby, Theodore M. Newcomb,
Eugene L. Hartley, eds. New York: Henry Holt and Company, 1958. xi + 674 pp.

KIELL, NORMAN. *The Adolescent Through Fiction: A Psychological Approach.* New York: International Universities
Press, 1959. 345 pp.

KLUCKHOHN, CLYDE. *Mirror for Man: The Relation of Anthropology to Modern Life.* New York and Toronto: Whittle-
sey House (A Division of the McGraw-Hill Book Company), 1949. xi + 313 pp.

KROEBER, A. L. *Configurations of Culture Growth.* Berkeley
and Los Angeles: University of California Press, 1944.
x + 882 pp.

LANGER, SUSANNE K. *Feeling and Form: A Theory of Art
Developed from "Philosophy in a New Key."* New York:
Charles Scribner's Sons, 1953. xvi + 431 pp.

LEVIN, HARRY. *The Power of Blackness.* New York: Alfred A.
Knopf, 1958. xii + 263 + ix pp.

LEWIS, R. W. B. "Contemporary American Literature," in
Contemporary Literature Scholarship: A Critical Review.
Lewis Leary, ed. New York: Appleton-Century-Crofts,
1958. x + 474 pp.

LINTON, RALPH. *The Cultural Background of Personality.*
New York and London: D. Appleton-Century Co., 1945.
xix + 157 pp.

✓MALCOLM X. *The Autobiography of Malcolm X* with Alex Haley. New York: Grove Press, 1964. xvii + 460 pp.

MASLOW, ABRAHAM H., ed., *New Knowledge in Human Values.* New York: Harper and Brothers, 1959. xiv + 268 pp.

MENCKEN, H(ENRY) L(OUIS). *The American Language: An Inquiry into the Development of English in the United States.* 4th edition. New York: Alfred A. Knopf, 1936. xi + 769 + xxix pp.

MONTAGU, ASHLEY. *Statement on Race: An Extended Discussion in Plain Language of the UNESCO Statement by Experts on Race Problems.* 2nd edition. New York: Henry Schuman, 1952. xii + 182 pp.

PERCY, WILLIAM ALEXANDER. *Lanterns on the Levee: Recollections of a Planter's Son.* New York: Alfred A. Knopf, 1941. 348 pp.

PODHORETZ, NORMAN. "My Negro Problem—And Ours," in *Doings and Undoings.* New York: Farrar, Straus and Giroux, 1963.

RADER, MELVIN, ed. *A Modern Book of Esthetics: An Anthology.* 3rd edition. New York: Holt, Rinehart and Winston, 1960.

Report of the National Advisory Commission on Civil Disorders. New York: Bantam Books, 1968. 608 + pp.

ROURKE, CONSTANCE. *American Humor: A Study of the National Character.* New York: Harcourt, Brace and Company, 1931, x + 324 pp.

ROWLEY, BRIAN A. "Psychology and Literary Criticism," in *Psychoanalysis and the Social Sciences.* Volume V. Warner Muensterberger and Sidney Axelrod, eds. New York: International Universities Press, 1958, 297 pp.

SCHOMBURG, ARTHUR A. *"The Negro Digs Up His Past,"* in *The New Negro, An Interpretation.* Alain Locke, ed. New York: Albert and Charles Boni, 1925. xviii + 446 pp.

SEWALL, SAMUEL. "The Selling of Joseph," *Early American Reprints, 1639–1800,* Clifford K. Shipton, ed. No. 951.

SHOEMAKER, FRANCIS. *Aesthetic Experience and the Humanities: Modern Ideas of Aesthetic Experience in the Reading of World Literature.* New York: Columbia University Press, 1943. xviii + 339 pp.

SMITH, ED. *Where To, Black Man?* Chicago: Quadrangle Books, 1967. 221 pp.

SMITH, LILLIAN. *Killers of the Dream.* New York: W. W. Norton and Company, 1949. 256 pp.

TATE, ALLEN. *The Forlorn Demon: Didactic and Critical Essays.* Chicago: Henry Regnery, 1953. xii + 180 pp.

WHITE, WALTER. "The Paradox of Color," in *The New Negro, An Interpretation.* Alain Locke, ed. New York: Albert and Charles Boni, 1925. xviii + 446 pp.

WRIGHT, RICHARD. *Black Power: A Record of Reactions in a Land of Pathos.* New York: Harper and Brothers, 1954. xv + 358 pp.

Unpublished Material

LASH, JOHN S. "The Academic Status of the Literature of the American Negro: A Description and an Analysis of Curriculum Inclusions and Teaching Practice in Selected American Colleges and Universities." Unpublished doctor's dissertation, The University of Michigan, Ann Arbor, 1946. 499 pp.

Periodicals

ABRAHAMS, PETER. "The Blacks," *Holiday,* xxv (April, 1959): 122.

ALSPACH, E. N. "On the Psychological Response to Unknown Proper Names," *American Journal of Psychology,* XXVIII, 2 (July, 1917): 436–443.

ATTWOOD, WILLIAM. "Malcolm X: A Very Personal Recollection," *Look* (January 7, 1969), n.p.

BAYTON, JAMES A. "The Racial Stereotypes of Negro College Students," *Journal of Abnormal and Social Psychology,* XXXVI (January, 1941): 97–102.

BROWN, STERLING A. "Negro Characters as Seen by White Authors," *The Journal of Negro Education,* I (January, 1933): 180–201.

CARLSON, EARL R. "Attitude Change Through Modification of

Attitude Structure," *Journal of Abnormal and Social Psychology,* LII (March, 1956): 256–261.

DAYKIN, WALTER L. "Negro Types in American White Fiction," *Sociology and Research,* XXII (September–October, 1937): 45–52.

ERIKSON, ERIK H. "Identity and the Life Cycle: Selected Papers," *Psychological Issues,* I (1959): v + 171.

FEY, WILLIAM F. "Correlates of Certain Subjective Attitudes Towards Self and Others," *Journal of Clinical Psychology,* XIII (January, 1957): 44–49.

FLATLEY, GUY. "Senegal Is Senegal, Not Harlem," *The New York Times.* Section II, November 2, 1969. P. 17.

FOX, BYRON. "American Social Problems in a World Setting," *Social Problems,* VI, 2 (Fall, 1958): 99–106.

HAYAKAWA, S. I. "The Semantics of Being a Negro," *Etc.,* X, 3 (Spring, 1953): 163–175.

ISAACS, HAROLD R. "The American Negro and Africa: Some Notes," *Phylon,* XX, 3 (Third Quarter, 1959): 219–233.

KATZ, DANIEL, CHARLES McCLINTOCK, and IRVING SARNOFF. "The Measurement of Ego-Defense as Related to Attitude Change," *Journal of Personality,* XXV (June, 1957): 465–474.

NICHOLS, CHARLES. "The Origins of Uncle Tom's Cabin," *Phylon,* XIX, 3 (Third Quarter, 1958): 328–334.

OVERSTREET, H. A. "Images and the Negro: Do Our Writers Really Know and Understand This American?" *Saturday Review of Literature,* XXVII (August 24, 1944): 5–6.

SECORD, PAUL F. "Stereotyping and Favorableness in the Perception of Negro Faces," *Journal of Abnormal and Social Psychology,* LIX (November, 1959): 309–314.

WILSON, ROBERT N. "Aesthetic Symbolism," *The American Imago,* XII, 3 (Fall, 1955): 275–292.

Novels, Drama, Poetry

ANDERSON, SHERWOOD. *Dark Laughter.* New York: Boni and Liveright, 1925. 319 pp.

BALDWIN, JAMES. *Another Country.* New York: The Dial Press, 1962. ii + 436 pp.

————. *Go Tell It on the Mountain*. New York: Alfred A. Knopf, 1953. 303 pp.

————. *Tell Me How Long the Train's Been Gone*. The Dial Press, 1968. 370 pp.

BASSO, HAMILTON. *The Light Infantry Ball*. Garden City, N.Y.: Doubleday and Company, 1959. 476 pp.

BENÉT, STEPHEN VINCENT. *John Brown's Body*. New York: Rinehart & Company, 1928. xv + 336 pp.

————. *Selected Works of Stephen Vincent Benét*. Volume II. New York: Farrar and Rinehart, 1942. 483 pp.

BOUCICAULT, DION. *The Octoroons: or Life in Louisiana. A Play in Four Acts*. London: Thomas Hailes Lacy (1859). N.p.

BROWN, WILLIAM WELLS. *Clotel; or, The President's Daughter*. 1853. New York: Arno Press and the New York Times, 1969. xix + 245 pp.

BULLINS, ED. "Clara's Ole Man," in *Five Plays by Ed. Bullins*. Indianapolis and New York: The Bobbs Merrill Company, 1968. Pp. 249–282.

————. "The Electronic Nigger," in *Five Plays by Ed. Bullins*. Indianapolis and New York: The Bobbs Merrill Company, 1968. Pp. 216–247.

CABLE, GEORGE W. *Creoles and Cajuns*. Garden City, N.Y.: Doubleday and Company, 1959. 432 pp.

————. *The Grandissimes*. 1880. New York: Sagamore Press, 1957. xi + 339 pp.

CARUTHERS, WILLIAM ALEXANDER. *The Cavaliers of Virginia, or The Recluse of Jamestown, An Historical Romance of the Old Dominion*. 2 volumes. New York: Harper and Brothers. Volume I, 1834, 228 pp. Volume II, 1835, 246 pp.

CHESNUTT, CHARLES W(ADDELL). *The House Behind the Cedars*. Boston and New York: Houghton Mifflin and Company, 1900. 294 pp.

————. *The Wife of His Youth and Other Stories of the Color Line*. Boston and New York: Houghton Mifflin and Company, 1899.

CHOPIN, KATE. *Bayou Folk*. Boston and New York: Houghton Mifflin and Company, 1894. 313 pp.

COOPER, JAMES FENIMORE. *Satanstoe; or The Littlepage*

Manuscripts: A Tale of the Colony. Volume X. Leather-Stocking Edition. New York: G. P. Putnam's Sons, n.d. (1845). 490 pp.

———. *The Spy, A Tale of the Neutral Ground.* 1821. New York: Charles Scribner's Sons, 1931. xlvii + 508 pp.

CORLEY, EDWIN. *Siege.* New York: Avon Books, 1969. 349 pp.

COZZENS, JAMES GOULD. *By Love Possessed.* New York: Harcourt, Brace and Company, 1957. 570 pp.

CRANE, STEPHEN. *The Red Badge of Courage.* New York: Dell Publishing Co., 1960. 351 pp.

CULLEN, COUNTEE. *One Way to Heaven.* New York and London: Harper and Brothers, 1932. 250 pp.

DAVIS, OSSIE. *Purlie Victorious.* New York: Samuel French, 1961. 82 pp.

DE FOREST, JOHN WILLIAM. *Miss Ravenel's Conversion from Secession to Loyalty.* 1867. New York and Toronto: Rinehart and Co., 1955. xxii + 485 pp.

DIXON, THOMAS. *The Clansman: An Historical Romance of the Ku Klux Klan.* New York: Doubleday, Page and Company, 1902. 374 pp.

———. *The Leopard's Spots: A Romance of the White Man's Burden, 1865–1900.* New York: Doubleday, Page and Company, 1902. 465 pp.

DRURY, ALLEN. *A Shade of Difference.* Garden City, N.Y.: Doubleday and Company, 1962. 603 pp.

DUNBAR, PAUL LAWRENCE. "The Scapegoat," in *The Best Short Stories of Negro Writers.* Langston Hughes, ed. Boston: Little Brown and Company, 1967. xiii + 508 pp.

D'USSEAU, ARMAND, and JAMES GOW. *Deep Are the Roots.* New York: Charles Scribner's Sons, 1946. xxvi + 205 pp.

EASTMAN, MRS. MARY H. *Aunt Phillis's Cabin; or, Southern Life As It Is.* Philadelphia: Lippincott, Grambo and Company, 1852. 280 pp.

ELDER, LONNE, III. *Ceremonies in Dark Old Men.* New York: Farrar, Straus and Giroux, 1965. 180 pp.

ELLIOTT, SARAH BARNWELL. *An Incident and Other Happenings.* New York and London: Harper and Brothers, 1899. 273 pp.

ELLISON, RALPH. *Invisible Man.* New York: The New American Library of World Literature, 1953. 503 pp.

FAIRBAIRN, ANN. *Five Smooth Stones*. New York: Bantam Books, 1966. 933 pp.

FAULKNER, WILLIAM. "The Bear," in *Six Great Modern Short Novels*. New York: Dell Publishing Company, 1954. 120 pp.

———. "The Fire and the Hearth," in *Go Down, Moses*. New York: Random House, 1955. 98 pp.

———. *Intruder in the Dust*. New York: The New American Library of World Literature, 1948. 188 pp.

———. *The Portable Faulkner*. New York: The Viking Press, 1946. 756 pp.

———. *The Sound and the Fury* and *As I Lay Dying*. New York: Random House, 1929. 532 pp.

FRIEDMAN, BRUCE JAY. *Scuba Duba*. New York: Pocket Books, 1968. 158 pp.

GLASGOW, ELLEN. *In This Our Life*. New York: Harcourt, Brace and Company, 1941. 467 pp.

GOVER, ROBERT. *J. C. Saves*. New York: Pocket Books, 1968. 175 pp.

———. *one hundred dollar misunderstanding*. New York: Ballantine Books, 1961. 158 pp.

GREEN, PAUL. *Lonesome Road: Six Plays for the Negro Theatre*. New York: Robert M. McBride and Company, 1926. xviii + 217 pp.

GREENLEE, SAM. *The Spook Who Sat by the Door*. New York: Bantam Books, 1969. 248 pp.

GRIGGS, SUTTON E. *Imperium in Imperio*. 1899. New York: Arno Press and the New York Times, 1969. vi + 265 pp.

HANSBERRY, LORRAINE. *A Raisin in the Sun*. New York: Random House, 1959. 142 pp.

———. *A Raisin in the Sun* and *The Sign in Sidney Brustein's Window*. New York: New American Library, 1966. 318 pp.

HARRIS, JOEL CHANDLER. *Balaam and His Master and Other Sketches and Stories*. Boston and New York: Houghton Mifflin and Company, 1891. 293 pp.

———. "Free Joe and the Rest of the World," in *American Short Stories 1820 to the Present*. Eugene Current-Garcia and Walter R. Patrick, eds. New York: Scott, Foresman and Company, 1952. lii + 633 pp.

————. *Uncle Remus, His Songs and His Sayings*. New and revised edition. New York and London: D. Appleton and Company, 1929. xvii + 265 pp.

HENRY, O. *Strictly Business: More Stories of the Four Million*. New York: Doubleday, Page and Company, 1910. 310 pp.

HEYWARD, DU BOSE. *Porgy*. New York: Bantam Books, 1957. 147 pp.

HILDRETH, RICHARD. *The Slave: or Memoirs of Archy Moore*. 1836. London: Scott, Walter, Ltd., n.d. 355 pp.

HIMES, CHESTER. *The Heat's On*. New York: Dell Publishing Company, 1967. 192 pp.

————. *Hot Day, Hot Night*. New York: Dell Publishing Company, 1970. 238 pp.

————. *A Rage in Harlem*. New York: Avon Books, 1965. 192 pp.

HOWELLS, WILLIAM DEAN. *An Imperative Duty*. New York: Harper and Brothers, 1893. 150 pp.

HUGHES, LANGSTON. *Not Without Laughter*. New York: Alfred A. Knopf, 1963. 324 pp.

————. *Tambourines to Glory*. New York: The John Day Company, 1958. 188 pp.

HURSTON, ZORA NEALE. *Their Eyes Were Watching God*. Philadelphia and London: J. B. Lippincott Company, 1937. 286 pp.

JEWETT, SARAH ORNE. "The Mistress of Sydenham Plantation," in *Strangers and Wayfarers*. Boston and New York: Houghton Mifflin and Company, 1891. 279 pp.

JOHNSON, JAMES WELDON. *The Autobiography of an Ex-Coloured Man*. New York and London: Alfred A. Knopf, 1937. xii + 211 pp.

JONES, LE ROI. *Dutchman and the Slave*. New York: William Morrow and Company, 1964. 88 pp.

KELLEY, WILLIAM MELVIN. *dem*. New York: The Macmillan Company, 1969. xii + 141 pp.

————. *A Different Drummer*. Garden City, N.Y.: Doubleday and Company, 1967. 223 pp.

————. *A Drop of Patience*. Garden City, N.Y.: Doubleday and Company, 1965. 237 pp.

KENNEDY, J(OHN) P(ENDLETON). *Swallow Barn or A Sojourn*

in the Old Dominion. Revised edition. New York: George
P. Putnam, 1852. 506 pp.

LINDSAY, VACHEL. "The Congo: A Study of the Negro Race,"
in *The Oxford Anthology of American Literature.* Volume
II. William Rose Benét and Norman Holmes Pearson, eds.
New York: Oxford University Press, 1939. xxiv + 753–
1658 pp.

LITTLE, SOPHIA L. (MRS.). *Thrice Through the Furnace: A
Tale of the Times of the Iron Hoof.* Pawtucket, R.I.:
A. W. Pearce, Printer, 1852. 190 pp.

MARSHALL, PAULE. *The Chosen Place, The Timeless People.*
New York: Harcourt, Brace and World, 1969. 472 pp.

McCULLERS, CARSON. *The Member of the Wedding.* New
York: Bantam Books, 1950. 153 pp.

McKAY, CLAUDE. *Home to Harlem.* New York and London:
Harper and Brothers, 1928. 340 pp.

MEANS, E(LDRED) K(URTZ). *E. K. Means.* New York and
London: G. P. Putnam's Sons, 1918. vii + 385 pp.

MELVILLE, HERMAN. *Moby Dick, or, the Whale.* 1851. New
York: The Modern Library, 1950. xxxi + 565 pp.

————. *Selected Tales and Poems.* Richard Chase, ed. New
York and Toronto: Rinehart and Co., 1950. xix + 417 pp.

MOON, BUCKLIN. *Without Magnolias.* London: Secker & War-
burg, 1950. 274 pp.

O'NEILL, EUGENE G. *The Emperor Jones, Plays by Eugene
O'Neill.* New York: Boni and Liveright, 1921. 285 pp.

————. *The Iceman Cometh.* New York: Random House,
1946. viii + 260 pp.

PAGE, THOMAS NELSON. *In Ole Virginia or Marse Chan and
Other Stories.* New York: Charles Scribner's Sons, 1887
and 1915. 281 pp.

————. *Red Rock, a Chronicle of Reconstruction.* 1898. New
York: Charles Scribner's Sons, 1945. ix + 586 pp.

PETERKIN, JULIA. *Green Thursday.* New York: Alfred A.
Knopf, 1924. 188 pp.

————. *Scarlet Sister Mary.* New York: Grosset and Dunlap,
1928. 345 pp.

PETERSON, LOUIS. *Take a Giant Step,* in *The Best Plays of
1953–1954.* Louis Kronenberger, ed. New York: Dodd,
Mead and Company, 1954. 433 pp.

PETRY, ANN. *The Street*. Boston: Houghton Mifflin Company, 1946. 435 pp.

POE, EDGAR ALLAN. *The Viking Portable Library*. Philip Van Doren Stern, ed. New York: The Viking Press, 1957. xxxviii + 664 pp.

PORTER, KATHERINE ANNE. *The Leaning Tower and Other Stories*. New York: Harcourt, Brace and Company, 1934. 246 pp.

SACKLER, HOWARD. *The Great White Hope*. New York, Toronto, and London: Bantam Books, 1969. 239 pp.

SIMMS, WILLIAM GILMORE. *The Forayers, or the Raid of the Dog Days*. 1855. New York: W. J. Middleton, 1864. 560 pp.

————. *The Yemassee, A Romance of Carolina*. 1835. New and revised edition. New York: A. G. Armstrong and Son, 1882. 454 pp.

SMITH, LILLIAN. *Strange Fruit*. New York: Reynal and Hitchcock, 1944. 371 pp.

STEIN, GERTRUDE. *Three Lives*. New York: Random House, 1936. 279 pp.

STEINBECK, JOHN. *Of Mice and Men*. New York: Bantam Books, 1958. 118 pp.

STOCKTON, FRANK R. "The Cloverfields Carriage," in *The Novels and Stories of Frank R. Stockton*. Stories II. Volume XVI. New York; Charles Scribner's Sons, 1900. 342 pp.

STOWE, HARRIET BEECHER. *Uncle Tom's Cabin*. 1852. Boston: Houghton, Mifflin and Company, 1897. lxvii + 529 pp.

STRIBLING, T(HOMAS) S(IGISMUND). *Birthright*. New York: The Century Company, 1922. 309 pp.

————. *The Forge*. Garden City, N.Y.: Doubleday, Doran and Company, 1931. 525 pp.

————. *The Store*. Garden City, N.Y.: Doubleday, Doran and Company, 1932. 571 pp.

————. *Unfinished Cathedral*. New York: The Literary Guild (Country Life Press, Garden City, N.Y.), 1934. 383 pp.

STYRON, WILLIAM. *The Confessions of Nat Turner*. New York: Random House, 1966. 429 pp.

TOOMER, JEAN. "Blood-Burning Moon," in *Cane*. New York: University Place Press, 1967. Pp. 51–67.

TOURGÉE, ALBION W. *A Royal Gentleman and 'Zouri's Christ-*

mas. New York: Fords, Howard and Rulbert, 1874. xii + 529 pp.

TROWBRIDGE, J(OHN) T(OWNSEND). *Cudjo's Cave.* Boston: Lee and Shepard, 1895. 504 pp.

———. *Neighbor Jackwood: A Domestic Drama in Five Acts.* New York: Samuel French, 1885. 414 pp.

TUCKER, (NATHANIEL) BEVERLY. *The Partisan Leader: A Key to the Disunion Conspiracy.* 2 vols. (Note: Secretly Printed in Washington in the year 1836 by Duff Green, for Circulation in the Southern States. But afterwards suppressed.) New York: Reprinted by Radd and Carleton, 1941. xiii + 392 pp.

TURPIN, WATERS E. *O Canaan!* New York: Doubleday, Doran and Company, 1939. 311 pp.

———. *The Rootless.* New York: Vantage Press, 1957. 340 pp.

———. *These Low Grounds.* New York and London: Harper and Brothers, 1937. 344 pp.

TWAIN, MARK. *Adventures of Huckleberry Finn.* 1885. Boston: Houghton Mifflin Company, 1958. 273 pp.

VAN DYKE, HENRY. *Blood of Strawberries.* New York: Farrar, Straus and Giroux, 1968. 278 pp.

———. *Ladies of the Rachmaninoff Eyes.* New York: Pocket Books, 1966. 174 pp.

VAN VECHTEN, CARL. *Nigger Heaven.* New York and London: Alfred A. Knopf, 1926. iii + 286 pp.

WALLACE, IRVING. *The Man.* New York: Fawcett World Library, 1969. 769 pp.

WILLIAMS, JOHN A. *The Man Who Cried I Am.* New York: The New American Library, 1967. 334 pp.

———. *Sons of Darkness, Sons of Light.* Boston and Toronto: Little, Brown and Company, 1969. 279 pp.

WOLFE, THOMAS. *Look Homeward, Angel: A Story of the Buried Life.* New York: Grosset and Dunlap, 1929. 626 pp.

WRIGHT, RICHARD. *Native Son.* New York: The Modern Library, 1940. xi + 394 pp.

———. *The Outsider.* New York: Harper and Brothers, 1953. 405 pp.

Fiction in Periodicals

ALLAN, GLENN. "Boysi's Yaller Cha'iot," *Saturday Evening Post*, CXCIV (December 27, 1941): 12–13, 46–48.

CHESNUTT, CHARLES W. "The Goophered Grapevine," *The Atlantic Monthly*, LX (August, 1887): 254–260.

COBB, IRVIN S(HREWSBURY). "J. Poindexter, Colored," *Saturday Evening Post*, CXCIV (June 10, 1922): 12–33, 122–129.

———. "J. Poindexter, Colored," *Saturday Evening Post*, CXCIV (June 17, 1922): 24–28, 73–80.

———. "J. Poindexter, Colored," *Saturday Evening Post*, CXCIV (June 24, 1922): 18–19, 50–58.

———. "J. Poindexter, Colored," *Saturday Evening Post*, CXCV (July 1, 1922): 20–21, 48–54.

COHEN, OCTAVUS ROY. "Horse-and-Buggy Daze," *Saturday Evening Post*, CCXV (August 29, 1942): 29, 42–46.

SPENCER, ELIZABETH. "First Dark," *The New Yorker*, XXXV, 18 (June 20, 1959): 30–39.

Index